SOLVING LOCAL
GOVERNMENT PROBLEMS

Solving Local Government Problems

*Practical Applications of
Operations Research
in Cities and Regions*

CHARLES E. PINKUS
ANNE DIXSON

London
GEORGE ALLEN & UNWIN
Boston   Sydney

First published in 1981

GEORGE ALLEN & UNWIN LTD
40 Museum Street, London WC1A 1LU

© Charles E. Pinkus and Anne Dixson, 1981

British Library Cataloguing in Publication Data

Pinkus, Charles E.
  Solving local government problems.
  1. Local government – Great Britain
  2. Operations research
  I. Title   II. Dixson, Anne
  352.041   JS3111

  ISBN 0-04-658232-0
  ISBN 0-04-658233-9 Pbk

Typeset in 10 on 11 point Times by Alan Sutton Ltd,
Gloucester, and printed in Great Britain
by Mackays of Chatham Limited.

Contents

Preface

Operations research, sometimes known as systems analysis, policy analysis, cost-effectiveness or management science, has been widely used since the 1940s to help examine and solve business or military problems. In recent years there have been many successful applications of operations research in the public sector. However, there are still many elected officials and administrators at all levels of government who are unaware of the value of operations research, but who are dealing with problems that could benefit from the techniques concerned.

Many public officials believe they do not have the mathematical training to understand these new techniques; they are uncertain how operations research can help; and they find that the information available to them about operations research is generally too technical for them. This book is intended for these public officials. It will also be of value to students of public administration, urban and regional studies and operations research. Our purpose is to show some of the many ways in which operations research and other quantitative methods can be successfully applied to public sector problems. We hope to demonstrate that the basic concepts of operations research can be understood by readers without special technical knowledge or skills.

This book is organized around the reports of twelve studies carried out over a period of fifteen years for city or county governments or regional bodies. These reports were originally written for elected officials and public administrators. As such they concentrate on giving a clear description of the problem and of the results of the study, without recourse to lengthy or detailed technical explanations. Additionally, we have edited and condensed the reports to suit a more general audience.

One of the questions most often asked by administrators is whether or not the results of the study were actually used. To help answer this question each of the studies presented in the book is prefaced by an analysis of the events following the submission of the original report. This analysis is based on personal interviews and investigations conducted by ourselves up to the date of publication. We have deliberately included some failures along with success stories. We believe that the analysis of why the results of a particular study were not used, or not used in full, is of equal value to that of a study where the recommendations were fully implemented.

The twelve studies included in the book represent problems found in many functional areas and at several levels of government. We have grouped them into three broad categories: health and social services; transportation and environmental problems; and planning and administrative services. These categories form the three main parts of the book. Each part begins with a brief introduction to the studies that follow and concludes with a chapter (Chapters 6, 11 and 16) which discusses the problems and methods of solution for those readers who are interested. Studies in other parts of the book that might be of particular interest are identified and references for further information provided.

A full list of references is given in the bibliography at the end of the book, which also includes the original study reports. We should point out that these reports were not, even in their original form, particularly technical, and anyone primarily looking for detailed descriptions of methodology would probably be better advised to consult a more conventional operations research text.

Chapter 1 outlines the main steps in a typical operations research study. The concluding chapter, Chapter 17, draws on all the studies in the book to illustrate this process more fully. Instructors using this book as a student text or for supplemental reading might like to consider asking their students to follow reading Chapter 1 with Chapter 17, which thus provides a useful guide to what to look for in each study. Administrators might choose to read the book in the order the studies are presented, or selectively choose parts of the book or individual studies that are of greatest interest to them.

Eleven of the twelve studies included were undertaken by the Local Government Operational Research Unit (LGORU) of Reading, England. The Unit was established in 1965 by the Royal Institute of Public Administration (RIPA). It is a nonprofit research association set up to assist United Kingdom local governments. The twelfth study, on planning emergency ambulance services, was carried out by the National Health Service Operational Research Group (NHSORG), formed by the RIPA in 1974 to concentrate on applications for health authorities. Although the studies take place in the United Kingdom they cover problems which arise in many countries. The only significant variation from country to country might be the level of responsible government (city, county, regional or state) at which the problems are tackled.

We are indebted to many present and former staff of LGORU and NHSORG for their help and advice. This book is based on the results of their efforts to assist local governments and health authorities in their policy and management decisions. The variety of studies presented in this book and the success of many of them attest to the skill and accomplishments of the staff of these two organizations. We should like to thank LGORU, NHSORG, the RIPA and the British Library for allowing us to reproduce these studies. Special thanks are due to Brian Whitworth, director of LGORU, Peter Thursfield, head of LGORU Northern Group, and John Green, deputy director of LGORU, for their encouragement, advice and support.

A number of people have helped in a variety of ways, from providing information to preparing the manuscript for publication. We especially want to thank Clemens Bartollas, Harry J. Berman, Margaret Crisfield, Rick J. Espitia, Robert J. Healey, Christine Howarth, Charles Kirchner, Mary Jane MacDonald, Leo J. Pinkus, Philip Proctor, Shiori Sakamoto and Ivor Shelley. We also want to thank our spouses and families for their encouragement and support during the project. Although many people have contributed to this book, we accept full responsibility for any errors or omissions.

Finally, many councillors and staff of local authorities in the United Kingdom have contributed to the studies we describe, either at the time the study was performed or during our follow-up studies to learn how the results were used. The successful implementation of the results of many of these studies is due in no small measure to these dedicated public officials. Although there are too many to name here, we want to thank them for their efforts and dedicate this book to them.

Charles E. Pinkus
Claremont, California

Anne Dixson
Lytham St Annes, Lancashire

1

Introduction

Local government today is big business. In the United States in the early 1980s combined local, county and state governments employ around 12 million people and provide goods and services to a total value of over $350 billion a year. In comparison, General Motors Corporation, the largest industrial employer in the United States in 1980, employed about 800,000 people and had sales of approximately $66 billion a year. Moreover, local government is getting bigger as population expands and demand for public services grows. Between 1960 and 1980 local government expenditures in the United States increased in real terms by nearly 300 percent and the number of people employed doubled.

Thus it is not surprising to find that local government practitioners are increasingly using the same techniques for management that big business has been using for some time. The traditional skills required in local government – wide local knowledge, sound political judgment and concern for the welfare of people – are still essential. But to be most effective these skills now have to be allied with a battery of new techniques once more closely associated with industry or commerce. Terms such as cost-benefit analysis, discounted cash flow and cost-effectiveness have become common currency at council meetings, at legislative sessions and in departments at all levels of government.

The trouble is that it has all happened so quickly. Local government administrators and decision-makers – especially elected members, many of whom work on a voluntary part-time basis – have had little opportunity to keep up with the new developments, let alone acquire a good understanding of the new techniques. This book aims to help government practitioners at all levels, and students of government, to appreciate the value and wide variety of uses of one branch of the new technology particularly relevant to their problems: operations research. The book presents studies of twelve real-life applications of operations research methods to public sector problems. All the studies were undertaken over a period of about fifteen years for city and county administrations or regional bodies in the United Kingdom, but the problems they tackle in fields as varied as health and transportation, planning and social services are common to local governments around the world. We hope the book will serve to demystify operations research and help to encourage policy-makers to investigate further the use of some of these methods to help solve problems in their own organizations.

Before discussing the layout of the book, it will be helpful to examine briefly what is meant by operations research. Many definitions of the term have been suggested, and some of the better-known will be found in the specialized textbooks listed in the bibliography. A particularly apt definition for the purposes of this book is provided in *An Administrator's Handbook on the Application of Operations Research to the Management of Mental Health Systems*, published by the Department of Health, Education and Welfare (Halpert, Horvath and Young, 1970):

> Operations research is the name given to a group of techniques that can be used to help solve problems encountered in human organizations and systems. It is a pragmatic and eclectic discipline developed out of the need during World War II for assistance in making decisions about those military operations which involved the coordination of a large number of complicated organizational and operational elements.

We would add to this definition that operations research is particularly applicable to problems of decision-making where many interacting considerations are involved, and where more than one solution is feasible. In these cases the analytical processes that constitute the operations research method can help find a best course of action where intuitive methods might not.

Looked at in this way, it can be seen that operations research is ideally suited to the kind of complex problems encountered daily by government. Yet in our experience relatively few of the people concerned with solving these problems are familiar with the techniques involved or recognize the uses to which they can be put. Consequently operations research is not used in many cases where it could be of real benefit. Government administrators are understandably reluctant to abandon old ways of doing things in favor of unknown or at best partially understood methods; and their reluctance is often reinforced by the tales of those who claim to have used operations research and found it not to work. We would not suggest for one moment that operations research is a universal panacea. Not all problems lend themselves to the operations research approach. Indeed in any setting there are usually many possible ways of looking at a problem – and of solving it. Nor does it necessarily follow that a method that has been found to work in one organization will work in another similar organization. What we would claim is that operations research, wisely used, can help make better decisions. Local politicians and administrators will still need to exercise all their experience and judgment, but the quality of the basic information on which they have to base their decisions, and their understanding of the scope and limitations of this information, can be vastly improved by the use of operations research methods.

A full discussion of the principles and processes of operations research is given in Chapter 17 and we hope that readers who are stimulated by the applications described in the intervening chapters will want to read this. For the main purpose of the book, however, such a detailed description is not essential. All that is necessary is to know that a typical study would include the following seven stages (based on Ackoff, 1956). These stages are discussed in greater detail in Chapter 17 of which the following section is a summary and simplification.

(1) *Recognize that a problem exists.* Problems are identified in many ways. In the public sector some of the most common are through a routine evaluation, often at year's end, which determines that goals are not being met; by complaints from the public about the delivery of a particular service; or by a need to economize, which usually means making more efficient use of the resources available to provide a parcticular service.

(2) *Define the problem.* The next step is to make a formal definition of the problem. Such a definition would include some or all of the following elements: problem statement – the question or questions to be answered by solutions to the problem; objectives – the criterion or criteria for selecting one of a number of potential solutions to the problem; measure of effectiveness – the yardstick for judging alternative solutions in light of the objective(s); alternative solutions – the alternative courses of action being considered; constraints – limitations or restrictions that help determine the courses of action that are feasible and the value of a particular solution, or that establish the time and money available to derive a solution; decision-makers – who they are and what special information they possess; larger system – interactions between this problem and other parts or activities of the organization, or system, within which the problem exists.

(3) *Construct a model of the system.* Once the problem has been defined, a model is built to represent the system within which it exists. This consists of mathematical (or economic or statistical) relationships based on the elements of the problem definition. It expresses the effectiveness of the system in terms of a set of variables, at least one of which is subject to control. The controllable, or decision, variables are those variables of the model that, when manipulated, provide answers to the problem statement.

(4) *Derive a solution from the model.* Deriving a solution requires successive manipulations of the decision variables of the model in order to produce alternative values. This step is often carried out by computer, which allows many alternatives to be derived in a short time. The best solutions are those values of the decision variables that best satisfy the criterion or criteria established by the defined objective, subject to the constraints that have been placed on the problem.

(5) *Test the solution.* Having derived a solution, tests can be made to determine how sensitive this is to changes in the basic information. Would changes of a particular magnitude, for example, invalidate the solution? If it were possible, a pilot scheme of the solution might be carried out and the results observed.

(6) *Make a decision and implement it.* Several equally good courses of action are often derived from a model. In this case the decision-makers must weigh the alternatives against their experience and common sense in order to select the best solution for implementation. Putting the solution into practice might involve changing administrative procedures, hiring or firing staff, committing capital expenditures, or convincing staff, colleagues or the public that the course of action proposed is the right one. The difficulties of implementing a solution can be enormous and should not be underestimated.

(7) *Evaluate the results.* When implemented, the solution to a problem is expected to achieve some specific results – to accomplish some goal. A method of determining whether the result or goal has been accomplished should be developed and implemented at the time the solution is implemented in order to enable a future assessment of the solution in terms of the problem it is supposed to solve.

In practice, the process of identifying and solving problems is never-ending. Implementation of the solution to a problem creates a new situation and the potential for a new set of problems. Thus most implemented solutions require monitoring and evaluation that may in turn lead to the identification of new problems requiring solution. Because of this circular aspect of problem-solving it is useful to view the seven stages of an operations research study as shown in Figure 1.1. It is important to recognize that the steps presented in Figure 1.1 are *typical* steps. Although they serve as a general guide when

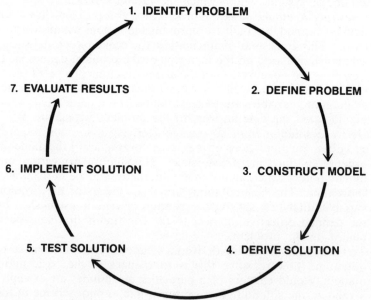

Figure 1.1   *Phases of a typical operations research study*

conducting an operations research study, each problem is unique and each study differs. There are many occasions when it is necessary to backtrack or even to restart the process. Occasionally a step is omitted, and sometimes steps are taken out of order. The value of the approach is that it provides a framework for tackling complex decision problems systematically.

Most books on operations research are written for operations research analysts and consequently concentrate on stages 3 and 4 of the process described in Figure 1.1, the mathematical stages. They give only cursory attention to stages 1 and 2 and 5 through 7. We would argue that a detailed knowledge of the mathematical techniques employed in operations research is not essential to the appreciation of its uses by the administrators and elected officials who have to make the decisions. If they are convinced of the value of the approach they will hire operations research analysts to develop the necessary models. Conversely, however, we believe that a good understanding of the context of the mathematical model – that is, the reasons behind the problem, the constraints on its solution and the problems of implementation – is vitally important to the good construction of the model and solution derived from it. We aim in this book to fill the gap in the current literature and in doing so hope to build bridges between the policy-makers on one side and the operations research analysts on the other. We believe that both policy-makers and practitioners of operations research will find the book useful in helping them to work together to solve problems in the future.

The book is divided into three parts covering the main services provided by various levels of local government: health and social services (Chapters 2–6), transportation and environmental problems (Chapters 7–11), and planning and administrative services (Chapters 12–16). Over 200 studies were reviewed in determining the ones that would be included. Those finally selected represent a variety of applications, methodologies and points of interest that we believe will help the reader better understand how operations research can be used to solve government problems. To illustrate, three studies, one from each part, tackle the following problems.

How many emergency ambulances are needed to serve a regional health authority and where should they be located? The solution to these problems (Chapter 2) is governed by the need to ensure a predetermined level of service to patients in terms of ambulance response times, which should not exceed a specified number of minutes. An integral part of the study was exhaustive testing of the solution to identify changes that might be needed to meet a practical rather than a theoretical set of circumstances. The results of these tests had an important bearing on the final recommendations and almost certainly eased their acceptance and implementation. We also learned that the study yielded many side benefits that management considered to be just as important as the original recommendations.

How can the current level of bus service in a community be maintained at minimum subsidy? This is a problem faced by many municipal bus systems and in this study (Chapter 8) of a network of bus routes changes were recommended that cut costs while maintaining or improving the level of service. This study is a good example of how an organization's objectives and the constraints placed on the organization are often interchangeable. For example: should the objective be to maximize the level of service provided to the community, given a limitation on the amount of money available to accomplish this, or should the objective be to minimize the cost of providing the service, subject to a restriction on the level of service that is to be provided? Both options were explored and their implications spelled out in the final report.

Will the proposed plan for a new workshop to repair and maintain a fleet of city-owned vehicles be able efficiently to handle both the present and future fleet? In this study (Chapter 14) a computer model was used to simulate arrivals to, repairs in and departures from the workshop over many weeks in order to evaluate proposals for the new workshop and to study alternative workshop designs. In the event the results of the study had little direct impact on the design of the new workshop, although this does not mean they were of no practical value. At the time the study began the organization's objectives – that is, the ground rules for repairing and maintaining vehicles – were only provisionally defined. The study demonstrated in practical terms the need for more rigidly specified rules and indirectly helped bring these about, with consequent improvements in efficiency of the repair and maintenance facility.

The introduction to each part of the book contains a brief description of the studies included and their context. The applications themselves are presented in the form of the original reports submitted at the completion of the studies, shortened where necessary. At the start of each chapter there is an assessment of the results of the study several years later. The final chapter in each part summarizes the main themes to have emerged.

It will be seen that most studies included in the book are accredited to two or more authors, and it would seem appropriate at this stage to describe briefly the organization of an operations research study. The study is invariably a team effort, often involving a large number of people under the guidance of a project leader. Often the members of the team will be from different disciplines to ensure that a range of experience is available to bring to bear on the different facets of a problem. Throughout the study the team works in close cooperation with the officers of the administration concerned. Indeed without fully incorporating the experience and judgment of the administrators no study could expect to reach a successful – or a practicable – outcome. All the studies described here were carried out by operations research analysts acting as consultants to the commissioning organization. It is quite possible, however, for in-house teams to be set up, provided the necessary skills are available from among existing staff.

Clearly not all the applications of operations research described in this book will be of interest to all readers. In many cases a reader will be able to relate an application directly to a problem in his or her organization. But simply because a particular application seems to have no direct relevance to the problems faced by a particular administration does not mean that no value can be derived from it. In these cases an understanding of how one problem was solved may suggest ways of using the same approach to solve a completely different type of problem. Most problems in local government fall into a small number of main categories. For example, one of the largest groups includes those studies where the advantages of implementing a particular course of action have to be weighed against the costs involved. The analyses of the best bypass route for a small town (Chapter 7) and the best form of flood relief for an inland town (Chapter 9) are both of this basic type. Thus an organization with this type of problem could find these studies useful even if the subject matter was quite different. A second group includes studies to find the best number and location of particular facilities; for example, kitchens to provide welfare meals for the elderly (Chapter 3) and refuse plants (Chapter 10). Yet another group is concerned with providing a given level of service at the least cost. The studies of an emergency ambulance system (Chapter 2) and a local bus system (Chapter 8) are of this type.

We hope that readers will make transfers of their own – not just between studies in this book but between these and problems in their own organizations. In all cases we have tried to present as much detail as necessary to give public sector policy-makers, or students of public administration, enough information to appreciate fully the rich variety of applications of operations research.

Part One

Health and Social Services

INTRODUCTION

The provision of social services, including health, education, housing, welfare and leisure services, accounts for a large and growing proportion of total government expenditure in many countries. In the United States, for example, these services amounted to just under 40 percent of combined federal, state and local government expenditures in 1950. By 1980 this total had climbed to about 60 percent, and the indications are that this trend will continue throughout the 1980s. A similar pattern can be seen in many other industrial countries.

One reason for this increase is the comparatively recent growth of social welfare programs such as those for housing and urban renewal. Another is the continuing shifts in the age distribution of the population. The number of people in the United States who are 65 or over increased from approximately 3 million (4 percent of the population) in 1900 to 23 million (11 percent) in 1977, and it is estimated that this figure will continue to rise (US Department of Commerce, 1977). In parallel with this increase in the number of people surviving to old age there is a decrease in the number of people in the older age groups who remain economically active. In 1950, 60 percent of men aged 65–9 in the United States were still working. By 1970 this figure had dropped to just over 40 percent (Sheppard, 1976). The net effect of these trends is steadily to increase the demand for government-provided services ranging from health care to leisure programs.

However, although an ever-increasing proportion of public funds is allocated to social services, many governments have not been able to keep pace with demand. Furthermore, taxpayer revolts of the kind successfully mounted against government expenditure in the United States in the late 1970s show every sign of continuing. Thus it has become more important than ever for all levels of government to seek ways of using scarce resources more efficiently. The four studies in this part all address themselves to the problem of determining the best way to allocate scarce resources in the fields of health and social services although each one operates at a different level of government, depending on the service in question.

Chapter 2, 'Planning Emergency Ambulance Services' recommends the best sites for a regional health authority's ambulance stations so that national standards of response time (the time between receipt of an emergency call and arrival of an ambulance) will be achieved. Chapter 3, 'Locating Facilities for Meals on Wheels', examines how to achieve a planned expansion of a service providing subsidized meals to the elderly and handicapped in their own homes at minimum cost. Chapter 4, 'Ranking Applicants for Local Government Housing', offers a systematic method for determining the priority of applicants for limited numbers and types of housing based on a measure of housing need. And Chapter 5, 'Routing Inter-Library Loans', presents a study of the feasibility of establishing a national transportation system for inter-library lending, which was prompted by the rising cost of sending books by post and the urgent need to find a more economic long-term solution.

The final chapter of this part discusses the implications of these studies and shows how they illustrate some of the common themes of operations research problems and methods of solution. References to other applications in health and social services are provided for further reading.

2

Planning Emergency Ambulance Services

Prior to reorganization of the national health service (NHS), responsibility for ambulance services in the West Glamorgan area rested with Glamorgan County Council and Swansea City Council. The NHS Reorganization Act of 1973 transferred this responsibility to the new West Glamorgan Area Health Authority, which was faced with the problem of forming a single efficient service. In the past, ambulance arrangements had been determined empirically by experienced and skilled ambulance officers reacting to slowly changing conditions. Reorganization provided an excellent opportunity to assess the consequences, in terms of service to patients, of different levels of ambulance provision.

Such a study was conducted in 1975 by Kenneth N. Groom, Keith E. Holloway and W. Roger Mann. The study team found that the area health authority could amalgamate two ambulance stations into a new station and discontinue emergency services from a third station. They showed that a system under which emergency services were located at seven stations around the area would provide excellent ambulance coverage and would more than achieve the response time standards recommended by the Department of Health and Social Security. The report of this study, *Planning Emergency Ambulance Cover in West Glamorgan*, was submitted to the area health authority in March 1975.

We met with the area chief ambulance officer, Mr William McCallum, to learn how the recommendations of the study had been used. We found that most of the recommendations had been implemented, with the result that there are now 40 percent fewer ambulances operated on the day shift and 20 percent fewer on evenings and nights than there were in 1974. An obvious contributory factor had been the care taken by the operations research analysts in arriving at and presenting the recommendations. We further found that several additional benefits of the study had accrued.

Before the 1975 study the area health authority operated twelve ambulances out of eight stations. At a purely theoretical level the study could have finished with the derivation of the minimum number of ambulances needed to provide the specified response-time standards: six during the daytime and five at night, all operating out of six stations. However before making their final recommendations the study team tested this solution for its practical effects and made several modifications as a result. Clearly trials of the proposed scheme could not be made using the area's ambulances, as this might have placed lives at risk. Instead a series of tests was made on paper, using the mathematical model developed in the course of the study. The results showed that although the theoretical minimum number of ambulances was the best for the area health authority as a whole, it did not necessarily serve the needs of the separate communities making up the area. This is because the average expected response-time standards were being achieved by balancing long response times in rural areas against short response times in urban areas. Therefore the study team recommended using eight ambulances sited at seven stations during both day and night periods in order to provide a better service in rural areas and a better balance of service between the two health districts that comprise the area health authority. A further consideration in increasing the number of ambulances needed was to allow time for a new integrated ambulance radio-control system to become fully operational.

Presenting these more conservative conclusions based on thorough testing of the study results was instrumental in ensuring the successful implementation of the recommendations. Anything less would almost certainly have been too drastic a change for acceptance by ambulance personnel and by the public. As it was, the value of the scientific approach was amply demonstrated and a gradual transition from the existing to the new scheme made possible. In fact by the time of our visit in 1978 the new radio-control system was operating smoothly. And as the ambulance controllers have gained experience with the new arrangements the ambulance service has found itself able to move beyond the report's conservative recommendations. Currently six ambulances are in use during the day and eight at night, all operating out of six stations. There is some evidence however that the current assignment of ambulances during the day shift falls slightly below the recommended response-time requirements and it has been suggested that the original recommendations should be reconsidered with a view to bringing the coverage up to standard (Mathie, 1978). In particular, the decision not to replace an existing ambulance station (at Gorseinon) with a new station (at Crofty) could usefully be reviewed.

Apart from leading to specific recommendations for action, the study resulted in a number of side benefits, considered by Mr McCallum and his staff to be equally important. We were told that the study motivated the ambulance service to consider changes in working methods that would enable the study results to be implemented more efficiently and to think about solutions to other problems that had only an indirect bearing on the allocation of ambulances.

A major change was to centralize control of ambulance operations. Before centralization West Glamorgan had two control centers, remnants of the two former health authorities. As Mr McCallum recalled:

Each controller did his own thing. He planned his work; he deployed his vehicles. It was all done the night before, and there was no marriage between the demand and the resources available next day. We realized our operation was not compatible with the recommendations of the study. It was clear that we needed a coordinated control center to deploy our resources in line with the operations research study and the standards established by the Orcon report (Orcon Services, 1974). We also created a planning section, and we looked at a simple fact – division of labor. Now the operations research report didn't say anything about this, but its findings encouraged us to think along these lines.

In any event centralizing the control function has meant considerable savings in manpower. Where formerly twenty-one staff members had been employed in control now only fifteen are needed, and this saving is directly credited to the operations research study.
Other spin-offs of the study include:

- standardized documentation, enabling the collection and collation of data that will be used to reevaluate the ambulance coverage in future years;
- a system of 'dynamic' coverage, which shifts the locations of standby and suitably equipped ambulances used for the non-emergency outpatient service to ensure the best service to the area when an emergency ambulance is on call;
- a radio procedure whereby the location of ambulances is monitored at all times;
- ambulance liaison offices at the hospitals to coordinate requests for non-emergency services;
- a more flexible procedure for the requisition of non-emergency ambulances for use for emergency services.

Finally, on the strength of this study operations research has also been applied to other aspects of ambulance administration, notably vehicle maintenance, where annual cost savings in the order of 25 percent have been achieved.
Planning Emergency Ambulance Cover in West Glamorgan is in fact an excellent example of the type of benefits a go-ahead management can gain from an operations research study. By approaching these new methods with an open mind, the West Glamorgan Ambulance Service officials allowed themselves to grow professionally and to appreciate new ways of thinking about old problems. Mr McCallum regards the study as 'one of the greatest things that ever happened to us in an ambulance service'.
The report of the study follows. In Section 1 the authors outline the background to the problem faced in West Glamorgan and describe the measures used for assessing standards of emergency ambulance coverage. Section 2 describes the general approach to the problem and Section 3 presents the findings of the study.

Planning Emergency Cover in West Glamorgan

KENNETH N. GROOM, KEITH E. HOLLOWAY and W. ROGER MANN

1 INTRODUCTION

Reorganization of the national health service has posed a challenge and opportunity for the new West Glamorgan Area Health Authority to determine the best emergency ambulance arrangements for the area. There have been few opportunities in the past for forming a completely new service. As well as posing the problem of building a new service from the old, reorganization has given the authority the chance to take an overall objective view of the service.

The area and its ambulance service

West Glamorgan consists of an urban core comprising Swansea, Neath and Port Talbot, surrounded mainly by the rural areas of the Gower, Lliw Valley and parts north and east of Neath and Port Talbot. The total population of the area is 366,000 spread over 200,000 acres, but with about three-quarters living in the urban core. Speeds that emergency ambulances can make on the road network are variable, with good roads along the coast between Swansea and Port Talbot and elsewhere. But much of the road network, especially in the urban areas, the Gower and along the Neath and Swansea valleys, requires slower speeds. As with all major towns Swansea and Neath experience major traffic holdups, particularly at peak periods. And additionally the influx of tourists during the summer months increases the traffic density, especially in the area of the Gower. These factors are essential to a consideration of an emergency ambulance service.

At the outset of our study the ambulance service deployed fifty-four vehicles from eight stations. Of these about twenty-five were suitably equipped and crewed for emergency duty; the remainder were equipped for non-emergency service and could provide useful additional support. The number of vehicles operating on a typical weekday depends on how many are withdrawn for repairs and maintenance, and on manpower availability.

To fulfil its duties an ambulance service can organize itself on one or two tiers. In a single-tier service, such as is operated in West Glamorgan, some dual-purpose vehicles, that is, vehicles suitably equipped to deal with emergencies as well as non-emergency services, stand by at predetermined locations while the others perform general service duties such as carrying outpatients to and from their clinics. When an emergency arises the nearest available standby vehicle is directed by a radio controller to attend the incident and its place is taken by the first vehicle to come available. This could be either a vehicle completing a non-emergency job or a vehicle completing an emergency job.

The double-tier service earmarks some vehicles exclusively to deal with emergencies, and general service duties are performed by a separate fleet. Details differ between services but in general the two fleets keep to their appointed tasks, with specially equipped vehicles standing by at set locations, in the manner of fire engines, ready to respond immediately to any emergency call, while the non-emergency vehicles continually pick up, deliver and set down patients on what is known in the service as 'the milk round'. An extension of this system is the three-tier service in which the most routine of outpatient journeys are allocated to a hospital car service, thus releasing trained ambulance personnel for more demanding work. No such car service exists in West Glamorgan.

Yardstick for measuring emergency coverage
Whatever system is adopted the new authority needs to establish a measure for determining the ambulance coverage it should have. The Department of Health and Social Security has recommended the following standards for ambulance services in England and Wales:

- *Activation time*, the interval between notification of an incident and dispatch of a fully equipped and crewed vehicle, should be three minutes or less for 95 percent of all calls;
- *Response time*, the interval between notification of an incident and arrival at the scene, should be eight minutes or less for 50 percent of all calls and twenty minutes or less for 95 percent of all calls.

It has been pointed out by professional ambulance officers that these standards based only on times, although necessary, are not of themselves sufficient indicators of satisfactory service. We agree with this view. However since the other components of good service – skill, courtesy, and so on – are controllable only in the long term through in-service training and recruitment policies, we believe that these time standards provide a useful yardstick for planning the provision of emergency services.

2   GENERAL APPROACH

We have developed a computer model to make predictions of service that would be given by different levels and arrangements of ambulances. The main features of the method are described below. In order to use the model we need to know the conditions under which the service operates. Data have been collected for us by the West Glamorgan Ambulance Service. In this section we describe this information and how we have used the model to predict the service that will be provided under different conditions.

Method of calculation
We have developed a method of calculating the emergency coverage given by different numbers and locations of ambulances operating

under conditions described by several different parameters. Coverage is calculated as a distribution of response time. The 50 and 95 percentage points of this distribution give measures of performance in the same form as those required by the recommended monitoring system. By varying the condition parameters (time of day, single-tier or double-tier and so on) we can see how the performance would change if the service were operated in different ways. We can also change the number and locations of vehicles so that we are able to examine the consequences of virtually any plausible way of running the service.

We have in essence a method that translates ambulance control procedures into models programmed for evaluation by a computer. Since procedures vary between day and night we have developed different versions of the model to reflect the different circumstances. For example:

- *Daytime*. During the day we can assume that a number of ambulances will be reserved for emergency service. In general they will not be the same ambulances throughout the day. The ambulances will be located at points that are thought to give the best overall coverage to the area. When any ambulance is dispatched the others will provide back-up support by moving to new locations in order to restore coverage to the area normally covered by the now busy ambulance. Full coverage will be replenished as soon as possible by allocating the first suitable ambulance from non-emergency duty to come available.
- *Night time*. At night there will be no non-emergency ambulances to call on for replenishment. It would be unreasonable to ask men to stand by in their vehicles so we only include as sites ambulance stations and other locations with facilities for night-time standby. Thus for night time we have assumed standby in a restricted set of locations, without replenishment but with back-up support.

In fact day and night is an oversimple classification. More basic considerations in choosing a regime under which to operate the model are:

- Can coverage be replenished from ambulances on non-emergency work?
- Is it reasonable to assume back-up support?
- Are crews standing by in vehicle or in station?

Our computer program can be recast to calculate the emergency coverage given by different numbers and locations of ambulances under different regimes. The regimes can be chosen to reflect conditions relating to, say, summer/winter, weekday, weekend/holiday, and day/night. One regime we commonly use – no replenishment, back-up support, standby in vehicle – reflects the conditions of the emergency tier in a segregated two-tier service.

Information required

The first step in gathering the information was to break the geographical area into manageable proportions. We chose local government communities for rural areas and political wards for urban areas. These are convenient because maps with such areas marked are readily obtainable as are data from the national census. Using maps we selected a point or points to represent the centers of population in each community or ward. To these points we added important road junctions, the locations of ambulance stations and some of the area's hospitals. In all we identified ninety-four points, or nodes, which were joined together by a road network. Figure 2.1 shows only those nodes that are used as potential sites for ambulances in this report.

We then estimated, with the help of ambulance officers, typical ambulance travel times on the network between each node and its immediate neighbors, for non-peak daytime travel by a fully equipped emergency ambulance. From this we calculated the complete matrix of shortest travel times for each node to every other node in the area. Table 2.1 illustrates the form of this matrix that actually contains, for all ninety-four nodes, 4,371 internodal times. To form actual response times for an ambulance at one node and an emergency at another, we add to these travels times a time to represent the activation and search times. In conducting the analyses that lead to the results shown in Section 3, we vary these times up or down to reflect the situation appropriate to, for example, peak periods or night time.

Table 2.1   *Travel times between selected nodes under normal travel conditions (in minutes)*

	Reynoldston	Crofty	Gorseinon	Mumbles	Tonna	Port Talbot	Glynneath	Singleton Hospital	Swansea	Pontardawe	Morriston Hospital	Neath
Reynoldston	—											
Crofty	18	—										
Gorseinon	26	9	—									
Mumbles	25	20	20	—								
Tonna	55	39	32	36	—							
Port Talbot	50	35	33	31	25	—						
Glynneath	72	56	49	53	19	42	—					
Singleton Hospital	27	16	15	5	31	26	48	—				
Swansea	31	14	13	16	25	23	42	11	—			
Pontardawe	52	35	27	34	21	27	34	29	21	—		
Morriston Hospital	38	21	13	24	23	24	40	19	10	17	—	
Neath	50	35	29	31	9	16	26	26	22	18	20	—

We also need to know the frequency of calls and where they can be expected to occur. These were obtained by examining all emergency and urgent cases dealt with by the West Glamorgan Ambulance Service between June 30 and July 22, 1974, to identify the number of

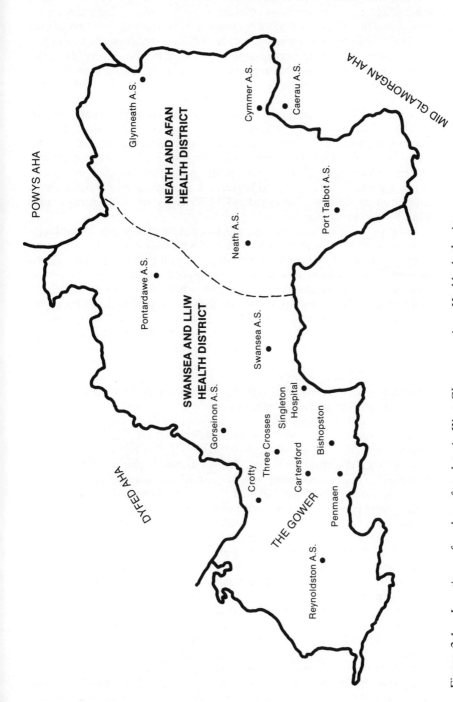

Figure 2.1   Locations of nodes referred to in West Glamorgan Area Health Authority

calls in each zone. The model does not distinguish between urgent and emergency calls, so we have combined the two and called them emergencies. This assumes that the situation is worse than an ambulance control officer would see it because he would not necessarily dispatch a fully equipped vehicle immediately to an urgent case. However at the end of our calculations, having made conservative assumptions, we can be confident that in practice the service will be somewhat better than we have calculated.

It is clear that the majority of emergencies – over 60 percent – occur in the urban areas of Swansea, Neath and Aberavon/Port Talbot, leaving the rural areas with a much lower accident density (see Figure 2.2). We found that the number of emergency calls to each node was closely related to the population at the node; and because our emergency statistics were recorded for only a short period of time we have estimated the number of accidents likely to occur at each node in a year by reference to the node population.

Finally, a list of nodes to be used as potential ambulance locations was assembled. These include nodes at which are located the present ambulance stations, hospitals, and other sites that might be considered as useful for locating emergency ambulances in the future. In all our analyses the locations refer to places where ambulances stand by, waiting to respond to emergency incidents; they should not be regarded as sites for ambulance locations. Of course ambulances can stand by at stations, but station locations should be determined by consideration of convenient garaging and staffing.

Application of the method
In order to test the effect of different numbers of vehicles and different locations on the overall emergency coverage provided we carried out a number of experiments using our computer models. We did not try all possible combinations and not all of those that we tried are reported here.

The first experiment was to establish a scheme for offpeak daytime coverage. This basic scheme was later used as a starting point for considering other conditions. To find the basic scheme we used the daytime model described above, with replenishment of emergency vehicles from those on non-emergency work. We measured the 'performance' of each potential site on its own; that is, the proportions of emergency calls that it could cover within eight and twenty minutes. No single ambulance, no matter where it be located, could cover the whole area adequately. Therefore a second vehicle was added to assess the coverage given by various pairs of sites. We found that it was always better to locate the second vehicle at a different site from the first. We proceeded to add vehicles from the non-emergency fleet until, with a particular combination of sites, we were able to satisfy the recommended standards of responding to 50 percent of the calls within eight minutes and 95 percent within twenty minutes.

Having established a basic satisfactory service for offpeak daytime conditions we continued to experiment in order to see how this service

The density of shading is proportional to the relative frequency of incidents.

Figure 2.2   *Relative accident densities*

changed as we made changes in conditions to reflect other circumstances under which the ambulance service has to operate. The results
of the most important of these experiments are reported in the next
section.

3 RESULTS

Using the models is quite straightforward once the data have been
assembled. In the course of the study we carried out several dozen
different evaluations. After conducting an initial set of evaluations, we
discussed the results with the chief ambulance officer to obtain suggestions for additional evaluations. Based upon his comments, a second
series of evaluations were conducted. In this report we give only the
most significant results, which are arranged under topic headings.

Daytime operations
During the daytime periods the service can operate on a one- or two-
tier arrangement.

Single tier operation. With a single tier the best procedure is to ear-
mark some of the twenty-five suitable vehicles for emergency standby.
When an emergency occurs the nearest vehicle is deployed and the
others will be assigned to new positions to cover the deficiency. The
deployed vehicle will be replaced as soon as possible by the first suitable vehicle from the non-emergency fleet to come available.
  We have found that the recommended standards can be met for the
whole West Glamorgan area by six standby vehicles located at:

> Swansea Ambulance Station
> Singleton Hospital
> Port Talbot Ambulance Station
> Neath Ambulance Station
> Pontardawe Ambulance Station
> Glynneath Ambulance Station.

These basic six vehicles give the performance shown in Table 2.2.

Table 2.2 *Daytime service given by six vehicles in a single-tier regime*

	activation = 3 minutes; travel times = normal; regime = 1-tier, day	
	Total service	
	Percentage of calls reached within	
	8 minutes	*20 minutes*
Performance of basic six sites	55	97
Recommended standard	50	95

Double-tier operation. When a separate tier is reserved for
emergencies no advantage can be taken of the opportunity to replace a
vehicle when it is dispatched to an emergency. To reach the recommended standards for service with a double-tier operation, West

Glamorgan would need two additional vehicles on standby. We do not believe that the simplification of control arrangements that results from the strict separation of duties in a double-tier service is worth the cost of the additional provision.

Night-time operations
At night there will be no non-emergency vehicles available so when an emergency vehicle is despatched its service area will not be covered until that vehicle returns, on average seventy-five minutes later. In this situation back-up support is desirable. At night the frequency of emergencies is about half that of the daytime periods and the vehicles can travel somewhat faster because of the clearer roads. It would be just possible to meet the recommended standards at night with five vehicles located at:

> Swansea Ambulance Station
> Singleton Hospital
> Pontardawe Ambulance Station
> Port Talbot Ambulance Station
> Glynneath Ambulance Station.

The performance of these five sites is shown in Table 2.3

Table 2.3   *Night-time service with five vehicles*

activation = 3 minutes; travel times = 0.8 of normal; regime = night

	Service percentage	
	8 minutes	*20 minutes*
Performance of five sites	51	95
Recommended standard	50	95

Weekends and holidays
During weekends and holidays the non-emergency vehicles will not be available for replenishment. The situation is similar to that for night-time operations except that the emergency frequency and vehicle speeds have daytime values. The recommended standards can be met with six vehicles located as for daytime coverage, but because of the special problems caused by holiday population increases in the Gower there is a good reason to locate a seventh vehicle there, ideally at Catersford but acceptably at Crofty.

Peaks in demand
For the periods considered above we have taken steady average values for the emergency frequency. However over all periods there are peaks and troughs. The peaks can be as high as twice the average value. We have tested the sensitivity of our results to a doubling of emergency frequency and have found in each case that there is sufficient spare capacity in the arrangements proposed to meet the peaks.

Sensitivity of locations

The model assumes static vehicles at fixed locations. We can however examine the consequences of movement by altering the locations to see how critical the coverage is to the locations we have found best. How far each vehicle can be moved before service falls below the recommended standards has been determined by finding the allowed movement from each location in turn, assuming the other five ambulances keep to their best location. Our results are perhaps surprising as they suggest that for some sites the range of movement within the area is very wide.

For daytime periods we find that:

(1) the ambulance at Swansea Ambulance Station may move within an arc through North Swansea from the ambulance station to Fforestfach;

(2) the ambulance at Singleton Hospital may not move at all (except, of course, to an emergency);

(3) the ambulance at Port Talbot Ambulance Station may move within the area of Margam West and Aberavon;

(4) the ambulance at Neath Ambulance Station can move within an area bounded by Crofty and Nicholaston in the west; Bishopston, Fforestfach, Morriston, Aberavon and Cymmer in the south; Tonna, Crynant and Ystalyfera in the west; and Pontardulais, Clydash, Brynamman and Pontardawe in the north;

(5) the ambulance at Pontardawe can move within the area bounded by Brynamman in the north, Clydash in the south, Rhos and Ystalyfera to the east and north-east;

(6) The ambulance based at Glynneath can move down the Neath Valley as far as Tonna and round as far as Dylias Higher.

This freedom for movement gives scope for controllers to operate a system of dynamic coverage whereby standby vehicles can be sent toward non-emergency jobs, being relieved by different vehicles coming available at different positions within the area.

Since the selection of possible locations is restricted for night and holiday periods to places where it would be convenient for crews to stand by we did not look at the sensitivity of position for these periods.

Coverage in isolated areas

For each period we have found a set of locations from which the recommended standards for the whole area can be met. However, we felt it necessary to look at the consequences of the overall solutions on isolated areas, as they will make up the 5 percent having the worst response time, that is, response times greater than 20 minutes.

The Gower. The basic arrangement offers only the vehicles at Singleton hospital and Swansea ambulance station to serve the Gower and the service is poor (see top line of Table 2.4). To improve the service we considered moving the Neath vehicle to each of several

potential sites in the Gower. We found little to choose between possible locations on a line roughly joining Bishopston and Crofty. Table
2.4 shows the results of our analyses.

Table 2.4 *Service with various Gower sites replacing Neath*

activation = 3 minutes; travel times = normal; regime = 1-tier, day

	Whole area		Gower only	
	Service percentage			
	8 mins	20 mins	8 mins	20 mins
Basic six sites	55	97	8	84
Gower vehicle at:				
Gorseinon	55	96	0	87
Crofty	52	97	40	89
Three Crosses	56	95	39	89
Bishopston	51	97	44	88
Penmaen	50	97	20	94
Reynoldston	49	97	4	98

Although Bishopston looks best on the basis of the percentage of
responses within eight minutes, a vehicle there would only be in use
about half as much as a vehicle at Crofty or Three Crosses. We understand that the ambulance service has a potential site for a new station
in Crofty. When this station is built we recommend that it be used as a
location for an emergency ambulance.

Cymmer. The Cymmer ambulance station services a small rural area.
An emergency ambulance located at Cymmer would serve 2.8 percent
of all calls, making the contribution to total service and local service
shown in Table 2.5.

Table 2.5 *Service given to Cymmer*

activation = 3 minutes; travel times = normal; regime = 1-tier, day

	Whole area		Cymmer catchment	
	Service percentage			
	8 mins	20 mins	8 mins	20 mins
Basic six sites	55	97	0	58
Basic + Cymmer	57	98	62	93

To make the improvement that a vehicle at Cymmer offers would
require the twenty-four-hour manning of the station up to the levels
required for a double-manned vehicle. The relative utilization for a
Cymmer vehicle would only be 2.8 percent (compared, for example,
with 7.2 percent for Crofty in the Gower). Therefore we do not believe
that the location of an emergency vehicle at Cymmer offers sufficient
return for the resources that would be committed. An alternative way
of enhancing the coverage in the Cymmer catchment area would be by
arranging for service to be provided from the Mid Glamorgan Area
Health Authority ambulance station at Caerau. This would bring the
Cymmer service figures to 42 percent and 93 percent for the eight- and
twenty-minute levels. There may be other possibilities for reaching a

reciprocal agreement with Mid Glamorgan for cross-border service in this area and these should be investigated.

Balance of service between health districts

The West Glamorgan Area Health Authority is made up of two health districts defined by the administrative areas: Swansea and Lliw Valley; and Neath and Afan. It is of interest to see separately the service that any arrangement gives to each district since it is likely that the authority will wish to give an equal level of service to each one. Table 2.6 shows the results broken down between the districts for the basic arrangement and the alternative arrangement of moving the Neath vehicle to Crofty.

Table 2.6 *Balance of service between districts by day with six vehicles*

activation = 3 minutes; travel times = normal; regime = 1-tier, day

	Service percentage					
	Whole area		Swansea district		Neath district	
	8 mins	20 mins	8 mins	20 mins	8 mins	20 mins
Basic six sites	55	97	57	97	50	96
Crofty for Neath	53	96	62	97	34	92

It is clear that the movement of a vehicle from Neath greatly disturbs the balance between the districts. Therefore we suggest that the Crofty vehicle be regarded as *additional*. The resulting seven-vehicle arrangement with locations at the basic six sites plus Crofty satisfies the recommended standards for the whole area and for each district considered separately. The performance of this arrangement is shown in Table 2.7.

Table 2.7 *Balance of service between districts by day with seven vehicles*

activation = 3 minutes; travel times = normal; regime = 1-tier, day

	Service percentage					
	Whole area		Swansea district		Neath district	
	8 mins	20 mins	8 mins	20 mins	8 mins	20 mins
Performance of seven sites	58	97	61	98	50	97

At night we found that five vehicles at the basic six sites minus Neath and Crofty could meet the standards for the whole area, but to preserve balance between the districts a vehicle at Neath should be included. Performance figures are shown in Table 2.8.

Table 2.8   *Balance of service between districts by night with five and six vehicles*

activation = 3 minutes; travel times = 0.8 of normal; regime = night time

	Whole area		Service percentage Swansea district		Neath district	
	8 mins	20 mins	8 mins	20 mins	8 mins	20 mins
Five sites	51	95	63	98	31	88
Five + Neath	59	96	63	98	52	92

Activation time

Throughout our analyses we have taken three minutes as the activation time of all vehicles. If activation time can be lowered the benefits in terms of increased service are great as every minute saved in activation gives an extra minute for travel. As an example, Table 2.9 shows the change in performance of the daytime seven-ambulance arrangement for different activation times.

Table 2.9   *Daytime service with various activation times*

travel times = normal; regime = 1-tier, day

	Service percentage	
	8 minutes	20 minutes
1 minute	71	98
2 minutes	64	97
3 minutes	58	97
4 minutes	35	96
5 minutes	18	95

Summary of recommendations

In presenting the findings of this study we have followed several threads which are now drawn together. We have found generally that the key to providing a good emergency service is preplanning backed by an efficient radio control. A new integrated radio-control system is about to be introduced in West Glamorgan. Inevitably it will need some time to settle down. Therefore it would be prudent to leave the number of vehicles deployed in Swansea at three for the time being, two at the Swansea Ambulance Station and one at Singleton Hospital.

Daytime operations. The service should operate as a single tier with eight vehicles on standby for emergencies. These vehicles will provide sufficient capacity to respond to normal peaks in accident frequency if they are located at the following positions:

> Swansea Ambulance Station (two)
> Singleton Hospital
> Port Talbot Ambulance Station
> Neath Ambulance Station
> Pontardawe Ambulance Station
> Glynneath Ambulance Station
> Crofty.

This arrangement includes the minimum six vehicles needed to achieve the recommended response-time standards (see Table 2.2); an additional vehicle at Crofty to serve the isolated areas of the Gower and to enable a balance of coverage between the two health districts which comprise the area; and another vehicle assigned to the Swansea Ambulance Station while the new integrated radio-control system is being implemented.

When a vehicle is dispatched to an emergency its service area will be covered by the first suitably equipped non-emergency vehicle to come available. On completing the emergency the first vehicle will take up non-emergency work if its standby position has been filled. We would expect the standby vehicles and the non-emergency vehicles to change roles from time to time. Since many non-emergency vehicles go to Singleton hospital all a controller need do is make sure that at least one suitable vehicle is there. Thus, subject to work breaks, any crew that has arrived can be considered as the standby crew at Singleton.

Controllers have some freedom to operate a system of dynamic coverage whereby a standby vehicle can be dispatched towards a non-emergency job. The vehicle will not pick up a non-emergency patient until the controller has found another vehicle to restore the coverage. As a general guide to the freedom for dynamic coverage, we have prepared the map shown in Figure 2.3.

Weekend and holiday operations. Eight standby vehicles are required at the same locations as for daytime operations. A back-up support system should be used to preserve coverage in the event that one of the busy standby vehicles is called out. The simplest procedure would be as follows. When the Swansea or Singleton vehicle is dispatched, the Crofty vehicle should move to cover its area; and when the Port Talbot or Neath vehicle is dispatched, the Glynneath vehicle should move to cover its area. If several vehicles are away from their sites at the same time the remaining vehicles should be moved so that the critical locations of Swansea, Singleton, Port Talbot and Neath are covered as far as possible.

Night-time operations. At night the frequency of emergencies is generally lower but rather more variable with higher peaks and lower troughs. The operating conditions are essentially the same as for weekends and holidays, so we recommend that the same deployment of eight vehicles be adopted. Back-up support is important at night and the procedure should be the same as that described for weekends and holidays.

Changes to present arrangements. The changes in deployment from the present arrangements would be:

(1) amalgamation of Reynoldston and Gorseinon into a new station at Crofty at which one emergency vehicle would be located;
(2) discontinuation of Cymmer as a site for an emergency vehicle but enhancement of rural service in this region to be affected through a

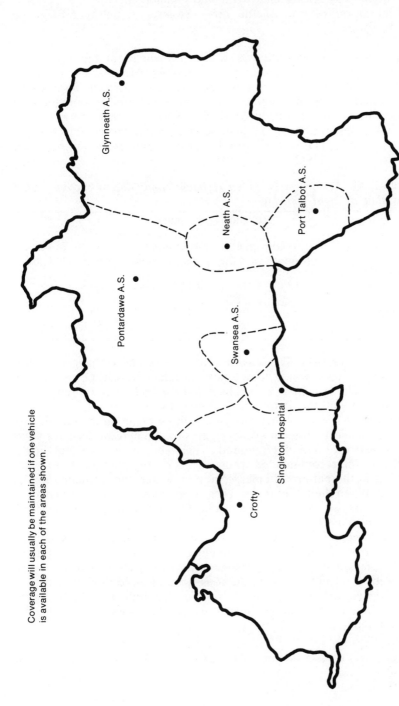

Coverage will usually be maintained if one vehicle is available in each of the areas shown.

Figure 2.3   *Freedom for dynamic coverage*

mutual aid arrangement with Mid Glamorgan;
(3) relocation of one of the three Swansea vehicles to Singleton Hospital.

Our calculations indicate that when the benefits of the new radio-control system are realized the second Swansea vehicle could be dropped. We therefore recommend that the service in Swansea be reexamined after the radio-control system has been in operation for one year. However, with two vehicles at Swansea and one at each of the six other locations, excellent service should be maintained under all conditions. The service given by these recommended arrangements is shown in Table 2.10.

Table 2.10 *Service given under different conditions by recommended provision of eight vehicles*

	activation = 3 minutes					
	Service percentage					
	Whole area		*Swansea district*		*Neath district*	
	8 mins	*20 mins*	*8 mins*	*20 mins*	*8 mins*	*20 mins*
Single-tier						
daytime	58	97	61	98	50	97
Weekends and						
holidays	55	96	58	97	50	95
Night time	62	98	66	99	55	95

Reliability of results. The sensitivity of these results to changes in information has been tested to see how confident we can be in our predictions. The system is very robust and the findings are insensitive to all but one of the data sets. Altering the balance of emergencies between town and country has no significant effect on the service provided. Increasing the emergency figures by 100 percent does not affect the number of vehicles required. Thus we can be confident in the ability of the recommended arrangements to cope with any foreseeable change in the pattern of emergencies. However, the calculated service *is* sensitive to the travel times. These were conservatively estimated, so over a year we can be confident that the monitored performance will be as calculated.

If the regimes are altered the results would change. For example, a change from single-tier to double-tier operations would necessitate an additional vehicle. If major changes are contemplated the model would have to be rerun to evaluate the consequences on service. Now that we have developed the basic information for this study, if in the future the health authority requires further evaluations these can be readily performed.

3

Locating Facilities for Meals on Wheels

Meals on wheels form a large and growing segment of those welfare services whose aim is to help the elderly or the handicapped live independent lives in their own homes. In the county of Worcestershire funding for this service comes from the county council and local district councils. However, much of the work is provided by local volunteers from the Women's Royal Voluntary Service (WRVS) who help to prepare the meals and make the deliveries.

This chapter describes the results of a study carried out in 1972 by Keith Roberts and David Gwynne for Worcestershire Social Services Department. (It should be noted that since then, the county of Worcestershire has been amalgamated with the former county of Herefordshire to form the new county of Hereford and Worcester. For ease of comparison, we continue to refer to the county of Worcestershire and confine ourselves to discussion of developments within the old county boundaries.) By 1980 the department planned to expand the meals-on-wheels service to cover the whole of the county area, to ensure that each recipient got five meals a week from this or other sources and to provide meals for all those who needed them. The purpose of this study was to help the department meet these goals in the most efficient manner by determining the best number of kitchens, their size and location and which areas they should serve. In order to meet the department's goals for the program at minimum cost the study recommended that seven of the existing twenty kitchens be phased out and ten new kitchens opened.

Six years after the study was completed we visited Worcestershire to find out whether the recommendations had been implemented. We learned that the recommendations had in fact been only partly achieved, although they had been well received by both the officers of the social services department and the volunteers of the WRVS. The reasons behind the failure to implement completely the study recommendations reveal both the strengths and weaknesses of the study as it was originally conceived and executed.

The bare facts are that although more than twice the number of meals are now being served than at the time of the 1972 study this still falls short of the original target. Although the meals-on-wheels service is now reaching the whole county area some kitchens are providing only four meals a week, while others are still serving only two or three. Since 1978 services operating in Worcester have started making deliveries five days a week – the target originally set by the study for 1975. The WRVS hopes to increase deliveries to seven a week as soon as availability of staff will permit.

One reason for the shortfall in service is that it proved difficult in practice to open and close kitchens according to plan. Understandably, volunteers in a particular community get attached to a particular kitchen and resist any change, even though the new locations would make it easier to deliver a larger number of meals. Thus although five new kitchens were opened between 1972 and 1978 (against seven proposed in the report) these are not generally at the locations recommended. Three new kitchens are replacements for smaller ones that have been closed. Another kitchen has been built on a site that was not intended to come on stream until later. In addition, one other kitchen in the 'wrong' place has been kept open for sentimental reasons despite several attempts by the WRVS to close it. Because the social services department is dependent on volunteer help for providing the meals service, it can only recommend, not insist on changes.

But the location of kitchens only partly explains the failure to meet the target figures. The main reason, and one that is virtually intractable, is the difficulty of finding sufficient volunteers to cook and deliver meals. With benefit of hindsight, this would seem to have been the major weakness of the study: the failure at the outset (that is, at the stage of problem definition) to take full account of the constraint on the number of volunteers who could be expected to come forward as the program expanded, although the WRVS did point out the possible difficulties. Had this information been used as a constraint on solving the problem we believe that the recommendations of the study would have been different. It would have become clear at an early stage that the twin goals of serving more people more meals a week could probably not be met by the means proposed. Instead, alternative solutions would have been sought.

Several possibilities might have been considered. An obvious solution would seem to be to pay for the preparation and delivery of meals; but in practice this would prove far too costly for the social services department to entertain. A cheaper alternative would be to set up communal facilities (for example, a day center), where elderly people could be brought for meals. In fact in Worcestershire this has by necessity been the course of action largely adopted. However the cost of transporting people to meals is greater than the cost of transporting meals to people and consequently a smaller number of recipients can be served. A third alternative would be to introduce a modified scheme under which a smaller number of people in greatest need would be served seven meals a week in their own homes. The WRVS is already considering this possibility. However they recognize the difficulties they would face in discontinuing service to existing, but less needy, recipients unless an alternative service – possibly transport to a day center – could be offered.

Despite the difficulties encountered in implementing the final recommendations, the value of the study as it was originally conceived has been to focus attention on these much more specific questions. It could be argued that without the study recommendations to act as a catalyst, no radical reassessment of the goals of the meals-on-wheels program would have been undertaken. Moreover, before the study neither the social services department nor the WRVS had adequate information on which to base their decisions. The results of the study demonstrably led to important changes in the short-term provision of meals on wheels. Perhaps even more important, the study also provided a valuable framework for long-term planning.

Meals on Wheels in Worcestershire, the final report of the study by Roberts and Gwynne, follows. It includes a plan suggesting the best locations for the new kitchens and the best times to open them and close existing ones. The first section provides the background to the study and presents the approach used to solve the department's problem. The results of the analysis for achieving the immediate goals of the department for the period 1973–5 are given in Section 2, and Section 3 presents plans for further expansion of the program through 1979. All costs have been expressed in dollars at 1972 prices. The average exchange rate in 1972 was 0.3999 pounds sterling per dollar.

Meals on Wheels in Worcestershire

KEITH ROBERTS and DAVID GWYNNE

1 SETTING THE SCENE

In 1970, 106,000 meals on wheels were served in Worcestershire, an increase of nearly 12 percent over the 1969 total. About 1,200 elderly people received, on average, two or three meals each week.

Although the service is financed by the county council and the borough and district councils, the organization and day-to-day work is done by the Women's Royal Voluntary Service (WRVS). Volunteers help in the preparation and cooking of the meals and make the deliveries, either using their own cars or small vans belonging to the service. There are twenty kitchens currently preparing meals. Nine of these operate primarily for another purpose – schools meals, hospitals, and so on – while the rest are either linked to luncheon clubs or run exclusively for the meals-on-wheels service.

The social services department aims to expand the service in three ways.

(1) To cover the whole of the county's area. In 1971 some areas of the county, mainly rural districts, were not able to receive the meals service. Even if the number of people in these areas is small, the service should be available to all who need it.

(2)   To ensure that each recipient has at least five meals each week.
(3)   To provide meals for all people in need. The council suspects that there may be a significant demand for meals on wheels that so far has not been expressed to the social services department. The department intends to identify this need by all available means, and plans must be made for the subsequent increased demand for meals service.

From the point of view of planning the provision of meals, the second and third aims are largely interchangeable. However it is still necessary to investigate the timing of the expansion necessary to realize these aims. To achieve the desired expansion more vans, drivers and helpers will be needed, new kitchens may have to be built or existing ones extended. This means acquiring more land, buildings and equipment. It also raises the problem of deciding which kitchens should be extended and where the new kitchens should be sited to make most economical use of the available resources.

The best use of resources depends on finding the minimum distance to be traveled from each kitchen to its delivery area. If the distance is too long, time will be wasted traveling and there will be less time to serve meals. This will eventually mean that more vans and drivers are needed. The choice between building an extra kitchen or making vans travel longer distances can be very difficult, especially when there are several possible sites for the new kitchen. However, a wrong decision could be costly in terms of finance, administrative efficiency and volunteers' time.

For a county as large as Worcestershire (700 square miles), the alternative arrangements just for maintaining the present level of service are numerous and complicated. Even when the more unlikely possibilities are rejected the problem is still too great to approach by manual methods. Accordingly we have constructed a mathematical model that can be used to find the most economic arrangement. The model is also used to examine future possibilities. Target dates can be set for the expansion of the service in the three ways described above and the best arrangement of kitchens found for each of these stages. The results can be used in making plans to develop the service.

The following sections discuss the assumptions used in formulating the model, the information needed and the method of analysis.

Assumptions
The most important assumption is that the present methods of preparation and delivery of meals are not likely to be changed within the next five to eight years. In particular we assume the following.

• That the existing methods of preparing and cooking meals will continue to be used. The only major alternative at present is to use frozen foods which require less labor and equipment for preparation. However the food itself costs more and is generally used only in kitchens producing large numbers of meals for delivery to densely populated areas. This is not the case in Worcestershire, where the recipients are spread over great areas and the volume of food prepared in any one area does not justify the use of frozen foods.

- That meals will continue to be delivered only at midday.

- That vans used for meals on wheels will be single-purpose vehicles. If other uses could be found the cost could be spread.

- That any new kitchens needed by the service will be built primarily for meals on wheels.

- That the capacity of new and existing kitchens will be restricted to 250 meals a day.

- That the time between cooking and delivery should be kept to a minimum.

- That the ratio of recipients to the elderly population as a whole will increase uniformly over the county once a county-wide service has been attained.

- That the present division of service between meals on wheels and lunch clubs or day centers will continue. Most of the urban centers have a lunch club or day center and, as a result, the number of meals-on-wheels recipients in the surrounding area is lower than areas where these facilities do not exist. Some kitchens produce meals for both types of service so their capacity for expansion for meals on wheels is limited.

Information
Three kinds of information were needed for the study: numbers and distribution of recipients; meal delivery times; and various costs. In order to obtain detailed information on the first of these we based the study on the smallest unit of local government, in the UK the parish. In the analysis it was sometimes necessary to amalgamate parishes in order to obtain average values. In doing this we retained the distinction between rural and urban areas.

The main items and sources of data used in the study are listed below:

- General population and elderly population estimates for 1971 and future years were compiled by the social services department using the census data

- An important set of data was collected for us by the WRVS, who conducted a survey of every delivery round in the county area. On one day for each round information was recorded on the time and distance from kitchen to first recipient, the number of recipients, the time taken to deliver each meal and the time and distance between one recipient and the next. From this we were able to find average meal delivery times for each region, average traveling times per mile between kitchen and first recipient and between one recipient and the next

- The costs of building and equipping kitchens, and of staff to cook, prepare and deliver the meals were provided by the social services and treasurer's departments

- The running and overhead costs of small vans to deliver meals were obtained from data gathered during previous studies of vehicles and transport in a number of authorities and from published data.

Analysis

The aim of the mathematical model constructed for this study was to find the most economic number, sizes and locations of kitchens, given:

- the number of recipients in each parish,
- the average number of meals each recipient gets per week,
- the location and capacity of present kitchens,
- a number of possible sites for new kitchens,
- the cost data referred to above.

The model also takes account of three other important factors: geographical barriers that restrict the routes that delivery vans may take, such as rivers and limited access highways; fast through routes on which speeds may be expected to be higher than on ordinary roads; and traffic density. These geographical features are shown in Figure 3.1. The shaded parts are urban areas of high traffic density.

The model was computerized to facilitate its use in deriving solutions and was first used to find the most economic arrangement of kitchens for the present situation. This is considered in detail in Section 2. We then considered three target situations:

- to give each present recipient four meals a week,
- to give a four-meals-a-week service throughout the county,
- to raise this to five meals a week.

To make these targets more concrete we assumed they would be achieved in 1973, 1974 and 1975 respectively. The results of running the computer program for these three situations and the changes necessary to arrive at each successive target are also given in Section 2.

Finally, we examined what happens when the third way of developing the service – providing meals for all needy people in the county – is introduced. We took the average figures for the number of recipients per 1,000 population and gradually increased them. The ratios for each parish were increased by the same percentage in each run of the program. The runs considered (with target dates in parentheses) were:

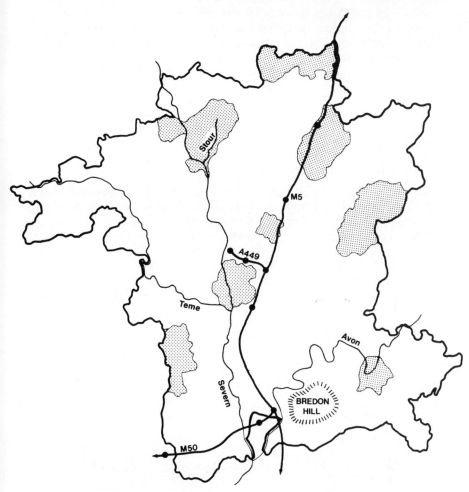

Figure 3.1   *Geographical features*

(a)   county-wide service of five meals per week but with the recipient
ratios increased to 20 percent (target date 1976);
(b)   as *(a)* with recipient ratios up a further 20 percent (1977);
(c)   as *(b)* with recipient ratios up a further 20 percent (1978);
(d)   as *(c)* with recipient ratios up a further 20 percent (1979).

The results of these runs are discussed in Section 3.

As the level of service is raised over the years, the cost to
Worcestershire will increase. In order to compare the cost of the future
service with the present one we have chosen to present all future costs
as if the level of service they represent was being given in 1972. Before
valid comparisons of costs for the future can be made, however, one
other factor must be considered. The present service relies heavily on

volunteer help from the WRVS and it would be almost impossible to forecast the number of volunteers that will be available in the future. So, to avoid any possible misunderstanding and to show the true cost of providing the meal services, we have made our calculations as if all drivers, helpers, cooks and vans were paid for in full.

Nevertheless we trust that the WRVS will continue to support the service as well as they have done in the past. Any help received will of course reduce the total cost of the service to the county. As long as this help is fully and properly utilized, the kitchen arrangements identified by the mathematical model as the most economic will remain the best.

2   MEETING IMMEDIATE GOALS

The present system of kitchens and deliveries in Worcestershire has resulted from a steady growth over the years as needs were identified. The end product is twenty kitchens serving from twelve to 180 meals a day. Some kitchens are not producing at full capacity and at others there is room for expansion. The first task was to find the most economic way of providing the present level of service.

The present kitchens together with the areas served are given in Figure 3.2. Figure 3.3 shows the solution to the problem of finding the

Figure 3.2   *Present kitchens (deliveries in unshaded areas only) 1972*

Figure 3.3   *Best system for 1972*

most economic arrangement for providing the present level of service. The main changes are the closures of existing kitchens at Astwood Bank and Childswickham. The meals served by these kitchens are of course taken over by neighboring kitchens. The closure of these two kitchens is suggested on the assumption that volunteers would transfer to another kitchen. If this is not possible they could be kept open for strictly local use.

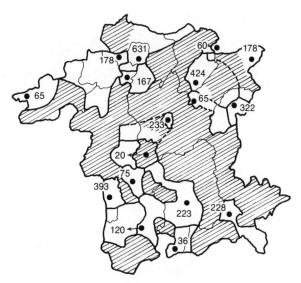

Figure 3.4   *Four meals a week: 1973*

The cost of the new scheme is $70,832 per year, $3,159 less than at present. This scheme formed the basis for examining the three target situations discussed below.

- *Four meals a week in 1973.* The first target situation is to raise the average number of meals given to each recipient to four a week in 1973. Figure 3.4 shows the best way to do this. In fact no new kitchens are needed as the kitchens used in the best arrangement for the present level of service have sufficient spare capacity to cope with the increase. Under the new system, however, more meals will have to be produced per cooking and in addition many kitchens will have to be used for more days each week than at present. The main changes to arrive at this target are in the geographical areas served by each kitchen. As the service is raised some kitchens realize their capacity and are not able to provide four meals a week to each recipient within their present delivery area. This happens at Rubery, Redditch, Malvern, Upton and Powick. Rather than build new kitchens in those areas it is cheaper to deliver meals from kitchens farther away. The kitchens expanding their service areas in this way are Wythall, Bromsgrove, Stoke Works and Pershore.

- *A county-wide service in 1974.* The next step is to extend the service to cover the whole county. In this case we assume that the number of recipients in areas previously not served will be on par with the average for similar parts of the county already covered. We also assume that the service will give four meals a week to each recipient. The results for this situation are given in Figure 3.5 and show that again the spare capacity in the existing kitchens is enough to allow

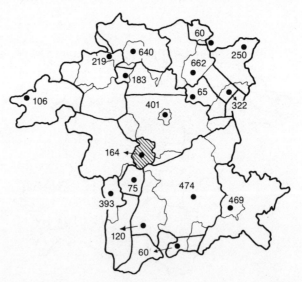

Figure 3.5   *County-wide services: 1974*

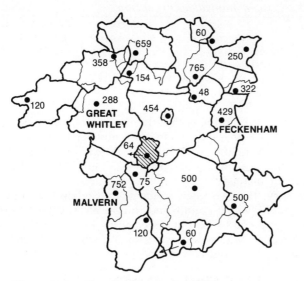

Figure 3.6   *Five meals a week: 1975*

for this expansion. Obviously most kitchens are now producing meals every weekday and have enlarged their delivery areas. However, the increased traveling costs for delivery of meals to places far from the kitchens is still not enough to warrant the building of a new kitchen in any locality.

• *Five meals a week county-wide by 1975*. To have a five-meals-a-week service available throughout its area must be a prime aim of any local meals-on-wheels service. In Worcestershire this was thought to be a suitable target for 1975. The best arrangement of kitchens to meet this target is given in Figure 3.6. The increase from four to five meals a week to all recipients brings many kitchens to full capacity. In fact the existing kitchens cannot cope with the total demand and new facilities are required at Malvern, Feckenham, and Great Witley.

The costs of each of these target situations together with the cost of the most economic arrangement for the present service is given in Table 3.1. Costs are given subject to the assumptions listed in Section 1. Cost per meal includes food preparation and delivery. Preparation costs include cooking and the overhead cost of the building and equipment. Delivery costs include depreciation and running costs for small vans plus costs of driver and helpers. Preparation costs decrease rapidly as the overheads are spread over larger numbers of meals while delivery costs increase, especially in 1974 when the service becomes county-wide, as distances from the kitchen to the recipients increase.

Table 3.1 *Cost of immediate expansion*

Target year	Target description	Meals per year	Cost per meal $	Annual cost $
1972	Present service	108,141	0.655	70,832
1973	4 meals/week	178,319	0.595	106,100
1974	4 meals/week, county-wide	243,176	0.603	146,635
1975	5 meals/week, county-wide	311,847	0.591	184,302

One point worth noting is that the number of meals increases faster than the costs of providing them. The number of meals served each year increases from 108,141 in 1972 to 311,847 in 1975 (that is, by 188 percent), while costs increase from $70,832 in 1972 to 184,302 in 1975, a 160 percent increase.

In summary, the two main forms of expanding the present service are to cover the whole county and to give each recipient five meals a week. This goal can be best achieved using the present kitchens every weekday together with new purpose-built kitchens at Great Witley and Feckenham and a large new replacement kitchen in Malvern.

3. PLANNING FOR FURTHER EXPANSION

After a five-meals-a-week, county-wide service has been attained, the main form of expansion will be through identifying previously unknown demand. The identification may be through greater publicity or house-to-house surveys and we shall assume that new recipients will be found at the same rate throughout the county. We discuss below four stages in expansion of this kind, each involving an increase in recipients of 20 per cent above the previous stage. We begin by assuming that in 1976 there will be a five-meals-a-week county-wide service to 20 percent more recipients than in 1975, the last target situation discussed in the previous section.

• *1976.* If a 20 percent expansion over 1975 is to be achieved arrangements must be made for three new purpose-built kitchens. These should be sited at North Bromsgrove, North Redditch and East Evesham. The East Evesham kitchen will ease the situation at Pershore and at Evesham. The North Redditch kitchen will replace the ones at Wythall and Redditch and the North Bromsgrove kitchen will replace the one at Rubery Hospital. A number of boundary changes will be necessary as a result of these arrangements.
• *1977.* The second stage considered is an expansion of the 1976 service by 20 percent and again, to meet the expansion, new purpose-built kitchen capacity is required. This time one new kitchen must be built at Welland. This relieves the pressure at Upton. No kitchens are closed but there are a number of boundary changes.
• *1978.* A further 20 percent expansion requires the erection of no new kitchens as the extra meals can be provided from the spare capacity in the new kitchens. A few minor boundary changes are needed.
• *1979.* The final stage of expansion requires three new kitchens: a larger purpose-built replacement at Droitwich and two new sites at

Figure 3.7   *Best system for 1979*

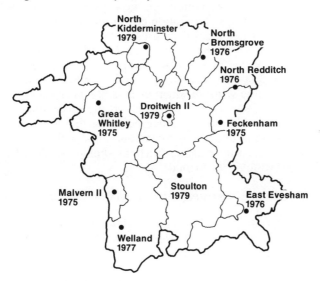

Figure 3.8   *Kitchens open at start of year shown*

Stoulton and North Kidderminster to plug gaps that might otherwise
emerge in these areas. There are a number of boundary changes
associated with these changes.

The solution for 1979 is shown in Figure 3.7 and Figure 3.8 shows
the locations and opening dates of new kitchens between 1975 and
1979.

In Table 3.2 we summarize the estimated long-term costs of providing the meals-on-wheels service to the standards described above. Present costs and costs in 1975 are also given for comparison. All costs are in 1972 prices.

Table 3.2   *Cost of long-term expansion*

Target year	Target description	Meals per year	Cost/meal (1972 $)			Annual cost (1972 $)
			Prepa-ration	Delivery	Total	
1972	present situation	108,141	0.460	0.195	0.655	70,832
1975	5 meals/week, county-wide service	311,847	0.378	0.213	0.591	184,302
1976	as 1975 plus 20 per-cent more recipients	384,234	0.378	0.195	0.573	220,166
1977	as 1976 plus 20 per-cent more recipients	461,031	0.373	0.185	0.558	257,255
1978	as 1977 plus 20 per-cent more recipients	543,053	0.365	0.183	0.548	297,593
1979	as 1978 plus 20 per-cent more recipients	645,909	0.365	0.173	0.538	347,499

In 1976 and 1977 a number of new purpose-built kitchens are needed. As a result the preparation cost of meals stablizes, but in 1978 and 1979 the cost per meal decreases as the kitchens expand to their full capacity. Delivery costs in 1976, 1977 and 1979 decrease sharply because the locations of the new kitchens reduce travel.

The overall cost per meal falls steadily, reflecting the continuing advantages of large-scale production and organization. In fact if the intended level of service for 1979 were being given today, about six times as many meals would be delivered at less than five times the cost.

Table 3.3 summarizes the recommendations of this study. It shows the dates when certain existing kitchens should be closed and when new kitchens should be opened.

Table 3.3   *Closure of existing kitchens and opening of new kitchens by year*

Year	Kitchens to be closed	Kitchens to be opened
1972	Astwood Bank Childswickham	
1975	Malvern	Feckenham Great Witley Malvern II
1976	Redditch Rubery Wythall	East Evesham North Bromsgrove North Redditch
1977		Welland
1979	Droitwich	Droitwich II North Kidderminster Stoulton

4

Ranking Applicants for Local Government Housing

The city of Manchester owns over 100,000 housing units ranging from single bedroom apartments to six-bedroom houses. Although these constitute almost 50 percent of the city's housing stock, people wanting to rent local government housing usually cannot be satisfied immediately and must join a waiting list maintained by the Manchester Housing Department. This list can contain as many as 35,000 applicants at any one time although usually about half of the applicants on the list are requesting a transfer from one rental property to another.

Like other British local governments, Manchester endeavors to house people according to their degree of need. Many housing departments use a classification, or points, scheme which enables housing officials to assign priorities (points) to competing applicants in accordance with a set of predefined rules. In 1975 the Manchester Housing Department was using a points scheme which had been developed prior to World War II. Although a number of important modifications had been made since then, the city council was concerned that the waiting list did not accurately reflect housing need.

This conclusion was supported by a survey conducted in 1975 to examine ranking on the waiting list as a measure of housing need. The survey found that some applicants high on the list were not in urgent need, while others in desperate need were not even on the list. To remedy this situation, the city council authorized a two-year research and development program.

First, the council commissioned a study, conducted by Jasper Renold and Robin Wilson, to devise a new points scheme. This study involved working with the housing department to develop a new set of definitions of housing need, and to convert these definitions into a draft points scheme for consideration by the city council. The aim of this study was to construct a scheme that would give highest priority to applicants considered to be in greatest need.

Secondly, the council approved the purchase of computer terminals for the department's sixteen area offices and the development of an information system. The new computer information system was intended to enable the department to give tenants a service at least as good as that which a buyer or renter of private property would receive from a real estate agent.

Our major interest in this chapter is to present *Developing a Housing Points Scheme*, the report of the study conducted by Renold and Wilson. The study found that there was broad agreement among housing department officials on the factors that were important in assessing need. However, there was less agreement on the relative importance of these factors. For example, should an applicant with a medical problem be given more points than one living in overcrowded conditions? And if so, how much more? To overcome this difficulty Renold and Wilson devised an experiment in which housing officials compared two applicants at a time from a sample of applicants on the waiting list. The results of this exercise showed that housing officials were often in complete agreement when deciding which of the two applicants should be offered a vacant dwelling. By using this 'paired comparisons' approach to rank a large sample of applicants Renold and Wilson determined that a high degree of consistency existed among housing officials, even though their reasons varied. The data from this exercise were used as input to an operations research model called linear programming. The model was used, in turn, to derive a set of weights (points) for the various need factors and these weights were thought to reproduce accurately decisions that would be made by housing department officials.

Developing a Housing Points Scheme was submitted to the city council in 1976, and the council gave the housing department approval to begin implementing the new system. Implementation involved reassessing the needs of all the applicants on the housing waiting list at the time in terms of the new needs factors, as well as determining the needs of all new applicants. A temporary staff was hired to assist the department in interviewing over 28,000 applicants.

While this process was taking place a new computer information system was also being developed which would be used to calculate an applicant's points based upon the interview and the new points scheme. The system would also provide a range of other information. It would automatically update an applicant's points from time to time; would select a short list of applicants on the waiting list to whom an offer would be made when a property became vacant; and would provide reports which would show applicants how many points were needed to qualify for a given house at a given location. In addition the new information system would enable the housing department and the city council to analyze and summarize the data stored by the system for the purpose of making management decisions. For example, data on applicants' needs and preferences would assist in making decisions regarding the types and locations of new housing construction.

Results of the research and development program begun in 1975 were presented by the housing department to the city council in September 1977. Interviews of applicants on the waiting list necessary to determine the information required to assign them points under the new needs factors were nearing completion; the new points scheme based upon these needs factors had been developed; and much of the work on the computer information system was finished. The department outlined its plan for implementing the new system and received approval to move ahead.

In 1978 we met Malcom Clarke and Michael Wall, from the housing department's research section, to discuss the outcome of this decision. By then the new system had been fully implemented and had already proved highly successful. A great deal of attention is paid to communicating the new system to the public. After being interviewed each applicant is sent a letter giving his or her total points under the new scheme and a breakdown of the number of points received for each needs factor. Included with this notification is a form requesting the applicant to provide new information if circumstances change. In addition each applicant is given a booklet which clearly explains the needs factors and the number of points that could be awarded for each factor. Another booklet, which is periodically brought up to date, provides a catalog of the 1,400 different types and locations of properties that the council owns and shows the number of points needed by an applicant to qualify for each type of property. Figure 4.1 is the instruction page from this booklet and gives an example of the type of tables it includes for each of the eighty sub-areas into which the city has been divided.

We were told that the consistency of the paired comparisons exercise (which showed that housing officials generally agreed with each other about the relative needs of two applicants even though they might not agree on the exact weights to be assigned to a particular needs factor) was instrumental in getting the new points scheme (based on this exercise) accepted by the housing department and the city council. The new scheme cannot however be viewed in isolation from the new computer information system, which was introduced at the same time and which made the entire system accessible to the public through sixteen area offices. The public is served more quickly and applicants no longer must travel long distances or wait for several hours at the main housing department office to apply for housing or pay rent. The staff, who were at first apprehensive, find the new system easier to use. and the politicians – the members of the city council – are now routinely provided with the detailed analysis of housing problems that can be obtained from the system and are able to make better informed decisions as a result.

The main requirements of the new points scheme were that it should be based on need, that it should be fair and seen to be fair by the public, that it should be based on decisions that would be made by housing officials and that it should be more understandable than the existing system. The new scheme appears to satisfy these objectives. One measure of its success is that fewer complaints are reaching the city council. Applicants know how their points are calculated and know that there is no way to increase their total number of points, and hence their rank on the waiting list, without increasing their need. There were some complaints from the public when the new method of needs assessment was introduced. The major complaint was that the amount of time an applicant had been on the waiting list prior to the reassessment was not fully considered. This had been anticipated and transitional points were granted when the new system was implemen-

How to use this booklet

In this booklet an attempt is made to answer the question "Will I receive an offer of a new home?" For each area of the city the points required for an offer of each type of accommodation available are set out. For example, an applicant in Group B who has 40 points and wishes to move to one-bedroomed accommodation in Clayton would first look up this area on the map

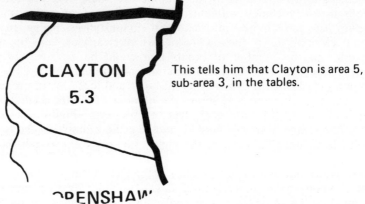

This tells him that Clayton is area 5, sub-area 3, in the tables.

Area 05		Sub-Area 3 – Clayton			
	Bed-sitter	1 bedroom	2 bedrooms	3 bedrooms	4+ bedrooms
*Bungalow		240			
House General			228	223	237
House Pre War Unmodernised				88	
Cottage flat – Ground	16	75	80		
Cottage flat – 1st	14	40	60		
Maisonette – 1st and 2nd				62	75

This indicates that he would be eligible for an offer of a 1st floor cottage flat, provided there are enough vacancies to satisfy demand.

The tables represent the best information available at the time of going to print. They will be corrected from time to time and a copy of the up-to-date figures can be obtained from your local area housing office.

Households including children under the age of 16 years are not normally considered for accommodation marked*

From *Renting a Home*, February, 1980.
Reprinted by permission of the Manchester Housing Department.

Figure 4.1   *Example listing of the points needed to qualify for various types of dwellings in Manchester*

ted, based upon the amount of time an applicant had been on the former waiting list. However not all applicants believed themselves satisfactorily treated.

Implementation of the new points scheme and computer information system have resulted in a number of benefits for the housing department. The major ones are as follows:

(1) *Calculation of points.* Computer calculation and processing of the points for applicants has minimized inconsistencies and enabled the waiting list and an applicant's points to be updated from the area offices, as well as providing quick identification of applicants who are eligible for a vacant dwelling.
(2) *Ease of operation.* Housing department staff have found the new system easier to operate. Fewer mistakes are made and mistakes are easier to identify.
(3) *Monitoring and decision-making.* It is now possible to monitor the housing system continuously. Each month reports are generated on how many applicants have joined the waiting list, how many have been rehoused, and so on. Special problems can be readily investigated and corrective action taken. For example, the new system has enabled the department to keep track of how quickly families with children living in unsuitable high-rise buildings were being relocated. The system was used to study to what extent different temporary changes in the points scheme were successful in moving these families up the waiting list and hence out of these buildings.
(4) *Management and control.* The information system is being used for many management and control functions. For example, it is used to generate routine maintenance schedules for all the properties managed by the department. When it is necessary to renovate a group of houses there is now much better information on the opportunities for moving the occupants to other housing.
(5) *Research.* The department's research staff have used the new information system to provide data for a number of studies, including assessing the demand for different types and locations of dwellings, studying how different categories of applicants have fared under the new system and assessing the number of applicants who are likely to become homeless.

The entire project – devising the new points scheme and developing the information system – proved to be a great success. We believe that the report of the study will be of special interest to many readers because it illustrates particularly well a practical way of formalizing difficult decisions. The same approach can be applied to other local government problems which call for a ranking of people or things. As just one example, we learned that the research staff of the Manchester Housing Department have recently revised the department's rent structure using similar methods to those employed by Renold and Wilson in developing the housing points scheme.

The report, *Developing a Housing Points Scheme*, which follows, is in three sections. The background to the problem faced by the housing department is introduced in Section 1. In the next section the method used to devise the new points scheme is described and Section 3 presents the proposed new scheme.

Developing a Housing Points Scheme

JASPER RENOLD and ROBIN WILSON

1   INTRODUCTION

Not everybody wanting and eligible for local government housing can be housed immediately. They may have to join a housing waiting list, which can sometimes include several thousands of applicants. Whenever a vacancy occurs the housing department has to decide which applicant should be housed first. This decision can be made either on the basis of 'first come first served', or on the basis of need.

Most local governments aim to house people according to their degree of need: those in greatest need receive highest priority, although for various special reasons this does not necessarily mean they are housed first. The difficulty in operating such a system equitably is that there is no generally accepted definition of need. There are many indicators of need – lack of basic amenities, overcrowding, medical condition, and so on – but the final decision on the degree of need of a particular applicant inevitably has to contain an element of subjective judgment, which can vary from local government to local government. The means of translating the administration's judgment of what constitutes need into housing action also vary. One method commonly used is a classification, or points, system, which enables housing officials to assign priorities (points) to competing applicants in accordance with a set of predefined rules.

It is in theory possible to devise a points scheme that will closely reproduce the judgments of need made by the officials and council members concerned. In practice the points system has usually been developed bit by bit over a period of years and very often does not now accurately reflect current opinion on the definition of need.

This was the situation faced by Manchester City Housing Department. Manchester's priority scheme was developed before World War II, and although a number of important modifications have been made since then, the department believed strongly that the existing system was deficient. Evidence for this view was provided by a special survey undertaken by the department of the housing circumstances of a sample of waiting list applicants. A comparison was made between the priority assigned to an applicant under the existing points scheme and the applicant's housing need as measured by factors such as overcrowding or lack of standard amenities. Briefly, the results of this analysis showed that 40 percent of applicants qualified under the present system for priority treatment. Of the remaining 60 percent who did not qualify, however, a fifth were living in overcrowded conditions by the standards set by the housing department, a fifth lacked at least one of the standard amenities (stove, bath/shower, toilet, sink), and a further two-fifths shared one or more amenities.

This study was undertaken to help the Manchester Housing Department devise a new points scheme. The main objective of the new scheme was that when it was applied by the housing officials it should give highest priority to those applicants who in their judgment would have been considered to be in greatest need. The scheme had also to be:

- *consistent* – sufficient agreement had to be reached beforehand between all the officials concerned on the measurement of housing need, so that once it was devised the scheme could confidently be applied to all applicants and obtain the required results;
- *comprehensive* – Manchester currently operates several different classification schemes for different groups of applicants, for example households containing elderly people; apart from a few specified exceptions, the new scheme was intended to apply to all housing applicants:
- *comprehensible* – the means of assessing relative housing need should be clearly understandable to applicants and to taxpayers, and should offer the minimum opportunity for providing misleading information to the department.

The approach taken to develop the new points scheme is described in detail in the next section.

2   METHOD OF DEVISING A HOUSING POINTS SCHEME

The test of any scheme for determining the relative needs for rehousing of applicants on the housing waiting list is whether it can predict the decisions that those responsible for assessing housing need would take if they had full knowledge of all the housing circumstances of the applicants. At its simplest this means that if two applicants are to be considered for a vacancy suitable for both then the applicant to whom the points scheme gives priority should also be the one whom the person or persons responsible for assessing need consider should have priority.

We have developed a mathematical technique to devise a scheme that will reproduce with a high degree of accuracy the judgments made by the housing department. The method is described in detail below. Before applying the method, however, an essential first step is to check that the housing officials whose views the scheme is intended to reflect are consistent in their assessments of housing need. Checks

are needed to confirm (1) that judgments made by one official of
different cases are consistent with each other and (2) that judgments
made by different officials of the same case are also consistent.

In Manchester we used a method of 'paired comparisons' to perform
these checks. A sample of twenty-four applicants – chosen so as to
have broadly similar housing requirements, but in various degrees of
need – was drawn from the special waiting list survey referred to
above. Thirteen officials from the housing department were each given
a sequence of pairs selected from these twenty-four cases and also a
summary of the main housing circumstances of the two households.
Each official was then asked to decide which household of each pair
was, in his judgment, in most urgent need of rehousing.

By giving each judge about thirty-five comparisons, we ensured that
all possible pairs among the twenty-four cases were covered by at least
one judge, and some by two or three. From these assessments a rank
order of applicants could be built up, based on the average judgment
of the officials – what we have called a 'consensus' ranking. The consistency of any one judge's decisions could then be checked by comparing
his individual judgments with the consensus order. In statistical terms
the results of this comparison showed good agreement between all officials and all cases. In subsequent stages of the study it was therefore
considered simplest to rely on the judgment of one official only – in
this case the assistant director (management).

The method of finding the housing points scheme that best reproduced the official's judgments was in four steps:

First, an initial list was drawn up of those factors considered to have
greatest bearing on housing need – we have called them 'needs
factors'. Ten main items were selected in discussion with the housing
department, ranging from the degree of overcrowding of the household to the time the household had been in need. The means of
measuring the various factors had also to be agreed. For example, in
Manchester need in relation to 'use of amenities' was measured by the
number of people sharing a particular amenity. A more detailed discussion of the measures is given in Section 3 of this report.

When the needs factors and their measures had been agreed, estimates were made of the likely weights to be attached to the different
items. The housing department suggested a reasonable set of weights
on a scale of 0 – 100, where 0 represented no need and 100 greatest
need. The various measures of overcrowding were used as a baseline
against which to judge the degree of need to be associated with
different levels of the other factors.

The initial list of needs factors used in Manchester, the method of
measuring them, and the estimated weights attached to each one are
given in Table 4.1.

Table 4.1 *Initial list of housing needs factors*

	Needs factors	Estimated weights
1	Overcrowding	
	living room shortage (per living room)	4
	bedroom shortage (per bedroom)	8
	bedspace shortage (per bedspace)	4
	overcrowding bonus	10
2	Separated households (per month separated)	1
3	Medical priority	
	priority A	50
	priority B	40
	priority C	2
4	Insecurity of tenure	
	priority A	50
	priority B	10
	priority C	5
	priority D	2
	priority E	2
5	Use of amenities	
	sharing a stove with 3 people or less	1
	sharing a bath with 3 people or less	1
	sharing a toilet with 3 people or less	1
	sharing a sink with 3 people or less	1
	sharing a stove with 4 people or more	2
	sharing a bath with 4 people or more	2
	sharing a toilet with 4 people or more	2
	sharing a sink with 4 people or more	2
	lack of a bath	2
	lack of hot water	2
6	Condition of dwelling	
	priority A	5
	priority B	3
	priority C	1
7	Environmental problems	
	priority A	5
	priority B	2
8	Traveling problems	
	priority A	5
	priority B	2
9	Children living at a height	
	2nd floor and above (per child)	8
10	Time in housing need (per year)	1

Secondly, a sample was drawn and a paired comparisons exercise carried out. There are several means of selecting this sample provided that each characteristic of housing need is well represented, even though it may be comparatively rare in the full list. One example of a characteristic in this category is medical condition, which would normally appear in only one or two cases. In Manchester 152 applicants were selected from the original waiting list survey.

Because it would be impossible to rank so many households by eye, they were first put into estimated priority order using the estimated weights from step (1) above. This enabled attention to be concentrated on the difficult – that is, closely matched – comparisons. If these could be reproduced accurately it was safe to assume that the method would be reliable for other, easier comparisons as well. Paired comparisons were then carried out between each applicant and the applicants next to him and next but one and with the applicant about ten positions away from him. For each pair the official concerned assessed the relative needs of the applicants. A total of 500 comparisons were made, taking about a day to complete.

Thirdly, a points scheme was found that reproduced as closely as possible the results of the paired comparisons exercise. This step was performed by a computer program specially written for this study which makes use of the technique of linear programming.

Finally, the new points scheme was examined to see whether further improvements could be made. There were two main sources of improvement. First, the points scheme arrived at by the linear program contained fractions which it would be impractical to retain in the final system. A second computer program was used to adjust the scheme to whole numbers while still keeping it as close as possible to the original results. Secondly, in the course of the evaluation process the officials of the housing department gained valuable insight into the relative importance of different needs factors and wished to introduce changes to bring the system closer in line with this thinking.

Two kinds of adjustment were made and tested using the same computer programs. Most obvious, measures included in the initial list were deleted and new ones added. For example, 'time in need' was deleted and points for lacking a stove, sink and toilet were added. A special bonus item was also introduced to measure special needs associated with children under 16 or elderly people in a household. At the same time the rules for measuring the needs factors were modified. Two measures of 'children living at a height' – at first and second floor, and third floor and above – were substituted for the initial single measure, the number of children at or above second floor.

A final list of needs factors and their measures is given in Table 4.2 which also includes the points to be awarded for each factor. A more detailed description of the scheme and how it will be applied is given in Section 3.

Table 4.2 *Final list of housing needs factors*

Needs factors	Housing points
1 Overcrowding	
living room shortage (per living room)	2
bedroom shortage (per bedroom)	8
bedspace shortage (per bedspace)	8
overcrowding bonus	5
2 Separated households (per month separated)	1
3 Medical priority	
priority A	45
priority B	25
priority C	2
4 Insecurity of tenure	
priority A	25
priority B	12
priority C	8
priority D	1
5 Use of amenities	
sharing a stove with 3 people or less	1
sharing a bath with 3 people or less	1
sharing a toilet with 3 people or less	1
sharing a sink with 3 people or less	2
sharing a stove with 4 people or more	2
sharing a bath with 4 people or more	2
sharing a toilet with 4 people or more	2
sharing a sink with 4 people or more	3
lack of a stove	2
lack of a bath	2
lack of a sink	5
lack of a toilet	2
6 Condition of dwelling	
priority A	9
priority B	3
7 Environmental problems	
priority A	5
priority B	2
8 Traveling problems	
priority A	10
priority B	2
9 Children living at height	
1st and 2nd floor (per child per year)	1
3rd floor and above (per child per year)	2
10 Bonus for households in need	
households with children aged under 16	8
households with persons aged over 60	4

3 DESCRIPTION OF THE PROPOSED HOUSING POINTS SCHEME

As stated earlier, Manchester has at present several housing lists, all of which will be replaced by the new points scheme. Certain types of household, however, representing the two extreme ends of the housing list, will continue to be treated separately. First are applicants who according to certain defined criteria qualify for special priority over applicants included in the scheme – for example, applicants living in property scheduled for clearance, or wishing to transfer to property less in demand than their present accommodation. Second are applicants not in housing need as defined in the scheme, but who would receive consideration in order of date of application after applicants who are included. Examples of households in this group are those owning residential property who would make a capital gain in excess of $3,250 (£1,800) if they sold to move into council accommodation.

In this section we describe more fully the needs factors included in the proposed scheme and listed briefly in Table 4.2. We explain how the various factors are measured and how the points awarded for each one are calculated.

Ten needs factors were finally selected.

1 *Overcrowding*
Unless otherwise stated, an applicant's household includes not only those who are to be rehoused with him, but all other persons who share any of his living rooms or bedrooms. In addition, babies expected to be born within three months count as an extra person. Four aspects of overcrowding are considered:

(a) Lack of living rooms: the following rules determine the living room requirements of different-sized households:

- single person households are allocated one living room;
- households of three people or less are allocated one living room;
- households of four or more people are allocated two living rooms unless one or two people from one household are moving (except where the two people are a single parent and child).

If the number of living rooms in the house is inadequate, then their number is made up from double bedrooms. If there are not enough double bedrooms then single bedrooms are considered to be suitable. In effect, therefore, a living room shortage would arise only in cases where there are four or more people living in one room. *(2 points are awarded for every living room lacking.)*

(b) Lack of bedrooms: separate bedrooms are required for:

- couples living together as man and wife;
- the parent of a single parent family;
- each other adult aged 18 or over except those who could share with siblings of their own sex;
- children over 10 of a different sex from other children in the household, whether or not they are siblings.

The number of bedrooms lacking is calculated as the difference between the requirements of the household and the number actually available, taking into account any bedrooms already allocated as living rooms in the previous calculation. *(8 points are awarded for every bedroom lacking.)*

(c) Lack of bedspace: each person in the household is held to require one bedspace. Single bedrooms provide one bedspace. Double bedrooms are considered to provide two bedspaces except in cases where one person has been allocated to a double bedroom in the previous allocation. *(8 points are awarded for each bedspace lacking.)*

(d) Overcrowding bonus: if an applicant scores points for overcrowding on any of these three measures, extra points are automatically awarded irrespective of the size of household or its accommodation. This device was adopted in Manchester to ensure that the total points awarded for overcrowding, which was considered to be of fundamental importance in determining housing need, bear the right priority in relation to other needs factors. *(5 additional points are rewarded to applicants who are overcrowded.)*

2 Separate households

Where the separation of one or more members of the applicant's household is considered to be a direct result of his housing problem extra points are awarded. *(1 point is awarded for every month of separation.)* In cases where the household would receive overcrowding bonus points if they were all living in the applicant's present accommodation, the applicant will be given *either* the separated household points, *or* the overcrowding bonus, whichever is the greater. The objective of the rule is to remove the incentive for a household to separate in order to gain additional housing points.

3 Medical priority

An applicant's medical condition qualifies him for priority only where it is considered by a suitably qualified person that a change of accommodation would be likely to relieve the effect of the condition. Three priorities, each carrying a different number of points, are recognized:

- priority A – where the condition is likely to be aggravated should the applicant remain in the present accommodation *(45 points)*;
- priority B – where the condition makes normal life difficult at the present house and where more suitable accommodation exists that would relieve its effect *(25 points)*;
- priority C – where the effect or the condition is unlikely to be influenced by the present accommodation or by any move to alternative accommodation *(2 points)*.

Such classification of medically related housing need clearly requires a great deal of judgment. It is Manchester's intention to build up over time a set of case law to aid future decisions.

4 Insecurity of tenure

This factor is designed to take account of those situations where an applicant can be evicted through no particular fault of his own.

However where the lack of security is of his own making, as with non-payment of rent, then his housing needs would probably be considered by the Homeless Families Unit. The following priorities are distinguished:

- priority A – where an eviction warrant has been served *(25 points)*;
- priority B – where an applicant has a court order for possession standing against him/her *(12 points)*;
- priority C – where an applicant has an effective notice to quit standing against him/her *(8 points)*;
- priority D – where an applicant has no formal tenancy because of living with friends or relatives *(1 point)*.

The award of these points is made at the discretion of the housing letting official, who may use his own judgment to vary the precise number of points in certain cases.

5   Use of amenities

This factor relates to an applicant's and his household's access to standard amenities. Points are awarded, first, for each amenity lacking and, secondly, where the amenity has to be shared with people in the applicant's present household who will not be rehoused with him and any other persons not belonging to his household. In this case points are awarded according to whether each amenity is shared *either* with three other people or less, *or* four or more people. The rules for calculating the points are as follows:

- lack of a sink *(5 points)*
- lack of a stove *(2 points)*
- lack of a bath *(2 points)*
- lack of a toilet *(2 points)*
- share sink with three or less people *(2 points)*
- share stove with three or less people *(1 point)*
- share bath/shower with three or less people *(1 point)*
- share toilet with three or less people *(1 point)*
- share sink with four or more people *(3 points)*
- share stove with four or more people *(2 points)*
- share bath/shower with four or more people *(2 points)*
- share toilet with four or more people *(2 points)*.

Manchester Housing Department consider that where an applicant only scores points on the lack or sharing of amenities the appropriate action to relieve housing need may be to encourage or enforce housing improvement. This view also applied to the next needs factor.

6   Condition of dwelling

Applicants whose property is required for clearance are considered in a special priority category. This factor relates to all other ways in which the state of repair of the dwelling may affect the habitability of the dwelling and the health of the occupants. The main circumstances are likely to be the presence of damp and infestation. Two priority categories are distinguished:

- priority A – property in a bad state of repair where the health of persons in the household may be impaired *(9 points)*;
- priority B – property in a poor state of repair that may make normal life difficult *(3 points)*.

As with the medical priority above, a set of case law will need to be developed over a period of time to help decide which states of repair qualify for which priority. Where an applicant has been awarded points for medical priority he may also qualify for points under this needs factor.

7 Environmental problems

This factor is intended to take account of those situations where there is a significant risk that the local environment of the dwelling will have detrimental effects on the applicant or his household. Under this heading are included social effects, such as disputes with neighbors, and physical effects, such as inadequate environment for bringing up children. For example, the household may be living next to a busy main road. Two categories are distinguished:

- priority A – where there is a risk to the health and safety of the applicant's household *(5 points)*;
- priority B — where it is difficult to lead a normal life *(2 points)*.

These points are to be awarded at the discretion of the lettings official.

8 Traveling problems

An applicant may be awarded points where the location of his accommodation with respect to shops, work, school, clinics, hospitals, relatives, and so on, makes essential journeys to these places, or by other people to his household, difficult or impossible. Again these points will be awarded at the discretion of the lettings official who after a period will be able to refer to case law to decide which of two priority categories, if any, is appropriate:

- priority A – where essential journeys are impossible or can only be undertaken at risk to applicant's health *(10 points);*
- priority B – where essential journeys are difficult to make *(2 points)*.

9 Children living at a height

This factor takes account of the special problems that applicants with children of 15 years or less face in bringing them up in accommodation where the front door is above the ground floor. For dwellings that are not self-contained the relevant floor is that of the lowest room used by the applicant. Basement rooms count as being on the second floor. Points are awarded for each child in the applicant's household according to the floor level and how long the applicant has been living there. All children are counted whether or not they were born at the time the applicant moved to his present address. In addition, extra years' residence may be taken into account where the applicant lived at a height in his previous accommodation. The points awarded are:

- first or second floor and basement *(1 point per child per year's residence);*
- third floor and above *(2 points per child per year's residence).*

10   *Children and elderly person's bonus*

This factor gives preference to applicants who have already scored points on previous needs factors and whose household contains children aged 15 or under or persons aged 60 or over. The housing department believes that not only are such households less well able to cope with conditions of housing need, but that the choice of alternative accommodation open to them may be more limited. The points awarded are:

- household containing children aged 15 or under *(8 points)*
- household containing any persons aged 60 or over *(4 points).*

The points system described above accurately reflects the assessment of officials in Manchester's housing department of the degree of need of housing applicants. This scheme – with the minor modifications referred to in Section 2 – should remain stable for at least the next few years. However, just as Manchester's original points scheme gradually became outdated until it had to be redesigned in this study, so this new points scheme will in time also become less responsive. The methodology described in this report can be used to monitor the points scheme and to ensure that it continues to reflect current judgments on the degree of need. In the future completely new needs factors may emerge and the present factors become less important.

5

Routing Inter-Library Loans

In 1975 inter-library lending in the United Kingdom was running at more than 2.5 million books and other items per year and nearly all loans and returns traveled by mail. For two years, however, one of the nine regional library systems had been using vans to deliver inter-library loans. In the wake of the success of this scheme and of the steadily rising cost of postage there was growing interest within the other library regions in establishing their own transportation scheme. The British Library, which supplies about three-quarters of the total loans, was concerned that regional and local libraries might develop transportation networks that were uncoordinated and inefficient. In addition it would be very difficult for the Lending Division of the British Library, which sells prepaid request forms to cover the handling and postage of items, to work with a number of different regional schemes without lowering its standard of service. There was also concern about the effect that different regional transportation schemes, each using different methods of pricing, might have on inter-lending between regions.

Therefore in 1975 the British Library commissioned a study of the feasibility of establishing a national transportation system for inter-library loans. The study was conducted by Anthony G. Houghton and Mark Nixon who identified and examined four options for organizing such a system. The options varied in terms of the number of libraries served, the arrangements for running the system, the cost of the service and the fees to participating libraries. These options ranged from one which would be limited to about 160 of the biggest users, including forty local governments, to one which would include all borrowers except those in geographically remote areas. The final report of the feasibility study, *A National Transport System for Inter-Library Loans*, was completed early in 1976. It concluded that a national transportation system was not only feasible but also economic and could possibly yield substantial savings of the order of two-thirds of a million dollars a year to the library sector without any appreciable lowering in the level of service. Houghton and Nixon recommended a two-tier system in which items would be sent by rail from the British Library Lending Division (BLLD), located in Yorkshire, to points in the regions from where they would be transferred to vans for delivery to local libraries. The researchers found, however, that there were insufficient data on which to build a specific set of recommendations with regard to the pricing and implementation of such a system. They therefore recommended that the British Library establish a pilot inter-library loan transportation system in one or more of the regional areas served by the library. By doing this the British Library would gain sufficient information about the problems of running an inter-library loan transportation system to be able to select the best national system.

The board of the British Library agreed with this recommendation, and in March 1976 authorized its research and development department to fund two pilot schemes. The first took place in the North West Library Region and began in October of the same year. The second was set up to deliver inter-library loans in the Greater London area and began in March 1977. The two pilot schemes were monitored by Houghton and Nixon for a study group consisting of representatives from the British Library and many of the library regions it serves.

In order to gain as much experience as possible about operating an inter-library loan transportation scheme, it was decided that the pilot scheme in the North West Region should attempt to serve the maximum number of libraries. Therefore all BLLD user libraries in the region were offered free membership in the system, with payment for services made by purchasing the BLLD request form already in use. The North Western Regional Library System agreed to organize the pilot scheme on behalf of the British Library and proceeded to plan the details of the system. It was initially decided to limit the items carried to the loan and return of books and periodicals from the BLLD to participants, the delivery of photocopies from the BLLD to users and the loan and return of items between scheme users. It was also decided that the scheme would attempt to provide a level of service at least equal in speed to that of the delivery of a first-class letter. Having made these decisions, it was possible to calculate the number of vans needed, the areas they would serve and the pricing scheme. Rather than buy or rent vans and hire a staff to make the deliveries, a private firm was employed to run the required number of vans needed to make daily deliveries to the participating libraries. These vans were operated exclusively for the scheme. A contract was also made with British Rail to provide the trunk link from BLLD, located at Boston Spa in Yorkshire, to Preston, where the loans would be transferred to the vans for delivery in the region, or transferred from the vans to the train for delivery back to BLLD.

Most of the large BLLD user libraries in the North West Region (over 240) participated in the pilot transportation scheme, which began making deliveries on October 4, 1976. The pilot scheme was closely monitored by Houghton and Nixon during its first nine months of operation. In addition to determining the various costs of operating the scheme, a record was kept of the number of deliveries and collections at each participating library on each day of this period. From this data an assessment was made of the performance of the pilot scheme, which generally delivered between 3,200 and 3,400 items a week. The level of service proved to be excellent, with most items being delivered the day after they were sent, and with approximately 8 percent of the loans between libraries in the region being delivered on the same day they were collected by the van. Although income from the prepaid request forms failed to cover the cost of operating the system the user libraries no longer had to pay the return postage on loans. The scheme was a financial success and produced a net saving to the British Library and the participating libraries in the North West Region of $17,600 for the first nine months it was in operation.

In their report Houghton and Nixon (1977, p. 35) conclude:

As a result of the pilot scheme, we can now see that the organization of library transport resolves into three main issues: the technical details of book delivery, the determination of the pricing mechanism and the methods of management and overall control. Before the pilot scheme began, the first of these issues was seen as the major problem and a considerable amount of time was spent on planning this aspect of the scheme. In practice, we found very few problems with this part of the system. The pricing mechanism, initially considered a side-issue to the main problems, was eventually recognized as an important part of the system. Although there were problems with the way in which this operated in the North West, we feel that the experience of the pilot scheme has shown how these could be put right in future schemes. The third issue was given hardly any thought at all before the pilot scheme began, but we feel has now become the most pressing problem of all.

The pilot scheme for delivering inter-library loans in the Greater London area began in March 1977. This pilot benefited in a number of ways from the experiences in the North West. For example, the North West scheme showed that there was much to be gained from contracting out the delivery operation, rather than having the participating libraries establish their own fleet. Also, based upon the experience of operating the first pilot scheme, the scheme in London opted for a simplified management structure. The level of service established for the London scheme was similar to the one for the North West, with items collected one day to be delivered on the next working day. The major difference between the two schemes was in the way the income was raised to finance the transportation services. Rather than using the BLLD request forms, a system of vouchers was used to cover the delivery of items between libraries in London and a system of direct charging was used for BLLD items.

Like the North West pilot, the performance of the London scheme was closely monitored during its first nine months of operation. The results were reported to the British Library and to the London and South East Library Region (Houghton, 1978), who were formally responsible for the management of the pilot scheme. The main results were as follows.

- The traffic carried was well below expectations as fewer libraries in the area participated than had been expected.

- The standard of service was very good. It was found that over 95 percent of items were delivered on either the same day or the day after collection.
- The scheme operated at a financial loss of approximately $10,000 for the nine months it was monitored. When the pricing policy was established, it was anticipated that the scheme would make a profit. However, the lower than expected level of traffic was one of the main factors causing this loss.
- The libraries participating in the scheme paid considerably less for inter-library loan services than they would have done if items had been sent by mail. The total user savings amounted to over $120,000 during the nine-month trial.

There were a number of objectives for testing an inter-library loan transportation scheme in the Greater London area and Houghton assessed the pilot in terms of these objectives. The study group wanted to know what special difficulties would arise from operating such a scheme in a heavily built-up area and Houghton found that no special problems were encountered. By selecting a voucher system for the payment of services, this scheme was able to test a pricing system that had been rejected in the North West as being unnecessarily complicated. The pricing system adopted in the North West proved to be administratively complex, whereas the voucher system used in London turned out to be simpler to operate. It was also found that the overall administrative effort to operate the London scheme was less than originally envisioned. Most important, the London pilot also showed that a two-tier inter-library loan transportation system was feasible and economic and could be operated at a very high standard of service.

The study group established by the board of the British Library used the results of the two pilot schemes and the original feasibility study as a basis for a set of recommendations. The group considered that the pilot schemes clearly demonstrated the practicality of a two-tier transportation system for different areas. It concluded that such systems could provide savings to the users and to the BLLD and offered a viable alternative to continued use of the postal service to deliver inter-library loans to all but the most remote areas of the country. The group recommended that any regional transportation scheme for inter-library loans should:

- provide a standard of service comparable to the delivery of first-class mail, operate five days a week and visit individual libraries daily if necessary;
- use a uniform price for each item provided by the BLLD;
- price the delivery of regional items to reflect local costs;
- serve all the libraries in the region, as far as economically possible.

The study group issued its recommendations in 1978. Since then the British Library has appointed a full-time officer to coordinate the various regional schemes. The two initial pilot schemes are now operating on a permanent basis, and all other regions have either set up their own systems or are in process of discussions with the BLLD on the best arrangements for their area.

It is interesting to note how the problems of setting up a national inter-library loan transportation system changed as a result of the pilot schemes. Initially it was felt that the technical details of book delivery, that is, determining the number of vans, routing the vans, coordinating with rail deliveries and sorting the items, would be the major problem associated with implementing a transportation system. But the technical details resulted in few problems (possibly because they were given a good deal of prior thought), while the pricing mechanism and methods of management and control became the major issues of concern. Thus the pilot schemes more clearly identified the problems that would result from implementing an inter-library loan transportation system on a national basis, and the information gained from these pilot schemes enabled a set of specific recommendations to be formulated.

The total effort, from feasibility study to final recommendations, illustrates one approach to the solution of a problem where there is insufficient data. Clearly not all such problems lend themselves to pilot schemes, for in many cases a pilot scheme would be too costly or too disruptive to mount. Alternative methods of testing solutions are illustrated by other studies contained in this book.

A National Transport System for Inter-Library Loans, the report of the feasibility study which prompted the pilot schemes and the results we have described, follows. The report is divided into five sections. The introduction presents the context for the study: the volume of loans involved and the alternative existing methods of transportation of loans. Section 2 sets out the various criteria determining the design of a transportation system and Section 3 describes four alternative options for meeting these criteria, which are evaluated in Section 4. The concluding section summarizes the results of the study and recommends setting up a pilot transportation system to gain additional information. All costs have been expressed in dollars at 1975 prices. The average exchange rate in 1975 was 0.4501 pounds sterling per dollar.

A National Transport System for Inter-Library Loans

ANTHONY G. HOUGHTON and MARK NIXON

1 INTRODUCTION

Volume of inter-library lending
Inter-library lending in the UK is currently running at more than 2.5 million items per year and the figure is increasing. An estimated three-

quarters of the total is dealt with by the British Library Lending Division (BLLD) at Boston Spa. About 13 percent of inter-lending takes place within or between the regional library systems and probably a similar amount as a result of requests between libraries.

BLLD lending. BLLD provides a loan and photocopying service for nearly 5,000 registered institutional users. These consist chiefly of public libraries, firms and academic establishments. Each working day an average of 7,320 items are despatched from BLLD at Boston Spa, while a further 780 or so are sent on behalf of BLLD from other libraries. Roughly 10 percent of the items sent out go to libraries overseas.

In order to assess various transportation schemes we needed to derive a distribution of BLLD lending by the number of items lent to each user. Unfortunately BLLD does not keep comprehensive records of the numbers of items received by individual libraries in the past and so we were unable to find the true distribution of loans and photocopies among users. From the information available to us we were able to make a reasonable estimate of the pattern of use.

We also needed to find out where the items were being sent to from Boston Spa. For this we used a list of the names and addresses of BLLD users. Each one had been assigned a geographical code by the BLLD, indicating whether it was in London, a particular English county, Wales, Scotland or Ireland. We went on to assume that each of these areas, and therefore any combination of them, contained a representative sample of BLLD users. This enabled us to calculate the number of items borrowed by the BLLD users in any particular area. In addition, by adjusting the scale of the user axis of the distribution of all BLLD borrowing to make it equal to the number of users in the area, we could obtain a distribution of borrowing for the libraries in that area.

These distributions of BLLD borrowing by area provided the basis for our subsequent calculations. Before they could be used in the evaluation of different schemes, however, it was necessary to increase the borrowing figures for each library to take account of other types of inter-library lending that would be included in the schemes. These adjustments are dealt with in the following sections.

Intra-regional lending. For the purpose of inter-library lending England is divided into seven regions, each with its own regional bureau, while Scotland and Wales each form a region in their own right. The members of each regional system consist of all local governments within the regional boundary and, in most regions, a number of industrial and academic libraries. Participating libraries make requests for books to their respective regional bureaus who try to satisfy the requests from the stocks of their other members. Table 5.1 lists the regions and the amount of lending carried out between members in each region together with the numbers of members and the numbers of BLLD users.

Table 5.1   *Intra-lending in the regions 1974/5*

Name	No. of members	Intra-lending (no. of items)	No. of BLLD users
London and South East Region	54	155,619	2,174
South West	72	27,052	470
East Midlands	38	8,500*	396
West Midlands	45	16,442	317
Yorkshire and Humberside	16	17,200	398
North West	54	24,464	377
North	58	14,625	142
Wales	50	3,547	141
Scotland	131	17,200*	345

*estimated.

Other lending. BLLD and regional transactions together probably account for some 90 percent of total inter-library lending. The remainder consists of loans in response to direct requests from one library to another. There seems to be no reason why these types of loan should be excluded from a transportation scheme but because of the uncertainty of the flows we could not take explicit account of them. Accordingly we evaluated the various schemes on the assumption that they would deliver and collect only BLLD and intra-regional loans. Ways in which these other types of lending could be incorporated are dealt with in Section 2.

Existing transportation arrangements
Nearly all inter-library loans and returns at present travel by mail. However, with regular increases in postal costs and evidence of a deteriorating level of service, there has been growing interest from a number of sources in inter-library transport schemes.

Postal services. All photocopies and nearly all books leaving the BLLD are mailed to users. The BLLD charges for this service by selling request forms to cover photocopying costs, a small contribution to processing costs and handling and postage. In addition users must also pay the postage for all returns. Most regions also use the postal service for all inter-lending. Each member library pays the postage on all outgoing books, both returning books that it has borrowed and sending out loans to other members.

Thus we can calculate the savings in postal costs to all parties of handling an item by a transportation system. At present (January 1976) prices, average savings of 91 cents per item could be achieved. These savings must be offset against the costs of introducing and running a transportation system. Incidentally the distribution of these savings between the BLLD and its users will be determined by the pricing policy of whatever transportation system is implemented.

Transportation schemes. Some regions are already running transportation schemes for their members while others are considering setting them up. In the Northern Region a proposal has been worked out by Cleveland County Research and Intelligence Unit for a daily van scheme linking all local governments and major academic libraries in the area. The North West Region has studied proposals for a transportation scheme put forward by Wirral District Council. This scheme is currently envisaged as serving only the local governments on a daily basis, although the possibility of including other libraries is being considered. The Yorkshire and Humberside Region already have a scheme in operation. This scheme originally linked the local governments to each other and to the BLLD and has recently been extended to include universities in the region. The West Midlands are using a trial transportation service serving all local governments. However, deliveries are only made weekly and this is considered by users to be an unsatisfactory level of service. The Welsh region is also conducting an experimental scheme which includes selected service points in all of the Welsh local governments.

In the time available we have only been able to contact a small number of local governments, but we believe that they all run van schemes to move books between their service points. This means that it would be possible, at least in theory, to serve all public libraries by collecting from and delivering to just one point in each local government area and leaving the transportation system run by the local administration to carry out the final distribution.

2   CRITERIA FOR SETTING UP A TRANSPORTATION SCHEME

Before we could plan the details of any transportation scheme we had to decide on the minimum acceptable speed of delivery that the scheme should provide. Five basic services could be provided: collection of loans from lending libraries; delivery of loans to borrowing libraries; return of books to lenders; transportation of requests; and other general deliveries between libraries in the scheme. We believe that these should each be considered separately as the delivery speeds are of varying degrees of urgency.

First, however, we had to look at the constraints imposed by the Post Office Acts of 1953 and 1969. The Post Office operates under the terms of a common carrier monopoly. We have made inquiries about the legal restrictions that this could impose on a library transportation system. It appears that the crucial distinction is between parcels, which can be carried privately, and communications, which cannot. It seems, then, that books and photocopies will be exempt from the monopoly, but that request forms may be included.

(1) *Borrowing*. The speed of delivery to the borrower is calculated from the moment that the book is collected from the lender. It was decided at the outset of our study that, to be acceptable, this delivery speed should be comparable to that of the postal service. We found that by the time a loan had traveled through the system and had been put on the van serving the borrower who had made the request, it was necessary to deliver it that same day if the postal delivery speeds

were to be matched. In other words, every day each van must visit all its customers for which it has a loan. In practice this arrangement would mean that large borrowers would be visited daily since they receive loans every day. All other libraries would only be visited if there was a loan for them.

(2) *Lending*. If an issuing library has set aside a book for loan and the van fails to call on that day, then a delay has been added to the system that is not present in the postal service. Obviously to compete with the mail this delay must be kept to a minimum. It would therefore be worthwhile making daily collections from specially chosen large lenders. Other libraries would have to arrange for the van to call to pick up their loans.

(3) *Returns*. The return of a loan to the issuing library is less urgent than the transportation of the original loan, except when the book is required by another reader. Unless the issuing library recalls the book there is no need to arrange for a special collection.

(4) *Requests*. While it would obviously be uneconomical to make special visits to collect requests for books, request forms could quite easily be sent by the van if it called for some other reason. An increasing number of libraries use telex for their requests and would be unlikely to change from this method, while others might prefer to pay the relatively small postage for request forms to ensure that their requests were delivered quickly.

As we state above, we believe that the transportation of requests falls within the Post Office common carrier monopoly, and we have therefore not evaluated savings from transportation of requests in the proposed scheme.

(5) *Other items*. Once a transportation scheme has been established it clearly becomes worth using it for the transportation of items of any kind between participating libraries. These items could include books traveling to repositories and boxes of new request forms. However the benefits are small and not easily quantifiable and we have not attempted to include them in our evaluations.

The transportation schemes that we designed to meet these purposes are based on a two-tier system with a trunking system moving books throughout the country and delivery vans visiting participating libraries. The delivery vans would be arranged in groups operating from a common point – a 'node' – and serving a defined area. This will enable books to move quickly within delivery areas, since a book collected on one day by one van can travel out on one of the other vans serving the same node on the next day. In some cases it may be desirable to introduce an intermediate tier into the distribution system. This would mean that a region would be served by one trunking link and a number of nodes. One or more linking vans would be needed to connect the trunking link with the nodes in the region. The following factors were taken into consideration.

(1) *Area distribution*. In the schemes that we have designed each delivery van would be allocated a list of participating libraries and

would carry out all deliveries to and collections from them. The maximum number of libraries that could be served by each van depends on several factors, for example, the length of the working day, the average journey speed and the density of libraries in the area. With such a large and complex problem as a national transportation system we were unable within the time available to calculate the number of libraries to be served by each delivery van or its average daily journey by plotting points on a map. Instead we have used a mathematical formula for these calculations.

The costs of operating each delivery van consist of two elements: the standing cost and the running cost. The standing cost comprises all the charges that must be met whether or not the van is actually being used. These include the wages of the driver, tax, insurance, rent and interest on capital. Running costs are the charges that are only incurred when the van is driven. These are bills for fuel, lubricants, tires, maintenance and an allowance for depreciation, and can be expressed in costs per mile. Total operating costs are found by first calculating the number of vehicles required; the standing costs of each vehicle are then added to the total running costs which are derived from the mileage run by each vehicle.

(2) *Nodal points.* Nodal points are the locations from which the groups of delivery vans operate. Each node will act as a depot for the vans based there and may also provide storage facilities for books in transit. As the area served by a particular node increases, so does the number of vans based there. This in turn results in some vans having to travel extra mileage at the beginning and end of each day, to and from users in distant locations. A point is eventually reached where it becomes worthwhile to establish a second node to serve the area; however, the savings resulting from greater accessibility must be set against the extra cost of linking the two nodes.

We have found that this trade-off results in there being an optimum-sized area for service by one node. The extent of this area will depend on the density of users in the area and the proportion to be visited daily. We have incorporated these extra costs of traveling to and from nodes and of linking nodes in our evaluation.

(3) *Trunking.* The purpose of the trunking system is to link BLLD at Boston Spa to the regions. Because the focus of the system is at Boston Spa, that will mean that some interregional lending can travel via Boston Spa and be transferred there. We considered two alternative methods of trunking: by rail and by road. These alternatives are illustrated in Figure 5.1.

British Rail would be prepared to collect books and photocopies from Boston Spa by road for distribution from their Leeds parcel depot to all major destinations. It would not be economical to implement a transportation scheme that delivered to all BLLD users: loans to users in inaccessible areas would continue to be sent by mail. Taking this into account we calculated the rail trunking charge for 90 percent of the total two-way flow to and from the BLLD. We estimate that the average daily cost would be $370.

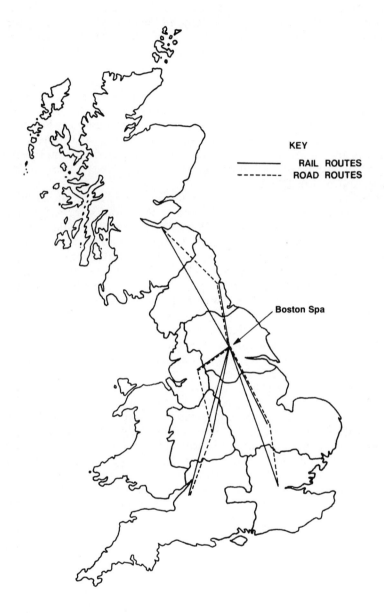

Figure 5.1   *The trunking option.*

We compared this figure with the cost of a road trunking scheme from BLLD. This would consist of three routes making good use of major trunk roads. The first route would deliver to nodes at Nottingham and London, the second would visit Manchester, Birmingham and Bristol and the third would deliver to Newcastle and Edinburgh. We calculated that to operate these routes would cost $460 per day.

Thus the rail trunking scheme is more economical. It becomes even more attractive for schemes that handle less than 90 percent of BLLD material. This is because the charge imposed by British Rail is on a tonnage basis and the cost depends on the volume carried, while total van costs do not alter significantly with the amount transported.

(4) *Sorting*. Sorting the books carried by the transportation scheme would be undertaken at three stages: on the delivery vans; at the nodes; and at the BLLD.

At the start of each day van drivers would be given all the items at their nodes which were to be delivered to the libraries for which they were responsible. The vans would be fitted with adjustable racking, with one pigeon hole for each library served by the van, and the items would be sorted into these. The pigeon holes would be arranged in the order giving the shortest round tour of all the libraries. Visiting all libraries with something in their pigeon holes in this sequence, and missing those for which there was nothing, would always produce a tour close to the shortest possible if not the shortest. As each van made its calls it would collect other books from libraries along the route. Those that were for libraries served by the van would be put in the respective pigeon holes. By continuing to work along the pigeon holes in the prearranged order the driver would deliver some books the same day that they were collected, while others would return to the node and go out again on the van the next day.

Each driver would also collect books that were not for final delivery by him. These would be sorted into two boxes: one for the other vans operating from his node and one for items to be sent to or through BLLD. At the end of each day, after the delivery vans had returned, the boxes would be unloaded. Those containing books for other vans at the node would be distributed into the appropriate van. If the node was linked directly to the BLLD, the BLLD boxes would be sent to Boston Spa on the overnight rail link.

Sorting at Boston Spa would consist of placing an item into a box that was labelled for one of the distribution vans in some part of the country. The item would either come from the BLLD stock or have been received in transit from one region to another. Groups of these boxes would then be loaded and transported by British Rail to the appropriate regional railhead.

(5) *Local government transportation*. Some local governments have a very great number of branch libraries. To allow all of them to be included in the scheme as service points would add to both the cost and complexity of the operation. Most local governments currently run their own transportation system. Clearly it would be a great saving if

they could continue to deliver to and collect from some of their libraries using their own vans.

3 ALTERNATIVE TRANSPORTATION SCHEMES

In the previous sections of this report we have set out the kinds of demands that will be placed upon a transportation system and the sort of system that will be set up to serve these demands. To summarize, a transportation system will have to provide a fast and efficient link between the BLLD at Boston Spa and some or all of the BLLD users throughout Great Britain. In addition the service should provide a link between members of the regional library systems. These requirements suggest a two-stage transportation system, with regional distribution road services linking one or more regional depots to the libraries within a region and a direct overnight rail link between Boston Spa and the regional depots. These features are common to all the options that we put forward and evaluate.

We have used as the basis of our evaluation the concept of net savings. If an item is sent by a transportation system instead of by mail then a saving is made in the cost of postage. However, against this must be set the cost of providing the transportation system. The net savings of any service are then defined as the total postal savings less the costs of providing the transportation service. We have assumed that the optimum service maximizes the net savings. We found that substantial savings could be made with all the options we evaluated. One purpose of formulating a number of options is to show the various ways of distributing these savings.

At an early stage in our evaluations we found that it is economic to serve all BLLD users in England and the majority of users in Scotland and Wales. Clearly it is more expensive to serve the more remote and sparsely populated areas (we use the word 'populated' to refer to the density of users). It will be necessary either to introduce a differential charging mechanism by which users in one area pay more or less than users in another area, or to fix a uniform charge with an element of cross subsidization implied. We have looked at both alternatives.

We then have to consider which libraries to include in the system. It makes sense to include the large users because the savings will be greatest for them. However, the marginal costs of introducing other users will be small once a system is set up and it may be economic to introduce some or all of them into the system. But which depth of service gives the greatest total savings? Is it a service serving the largest 5 percent, 10 percent or all 100 percent of libraries? The options we have evaluated cover the full range of depth of service. These options are summarized in Table 5.2 and described briefly below.

The first option is a scheme in which a number of the larger libraries are invited to participate. They will in effect join a club on payment of an annual subscription for which they will be able to return and send out items entirely free of additional charge. They can also expect to

Table 5.2   *The options summarized*

Option	% BLLD users served	Principle of participation	Finance method
1	3%	by invitation	annual price per member
2	2.7%	market forces	fixed annual price per member
3	100%	by decision of transportation organizer	prepaid charge per item
4	5–99%	market forces	fixed annual price and prepaid charge per item

receive some reduction in the price of borrowing from BLLD, in exchange for saving BLLD's postage costs.

For the purposes of evaluating this option we assumed that those invited to participate are the largest 120 or so BLLD users, together with the largest forty or so local governments. These amounted to 3 percent of all BLLD users. The annual cost of providing such a system would be of the order of $2,400 per user. In theory the potential savings to the larger borrowers will exceed this amount, especially if BLLD passes on all its savings as a reduction in the price of a request form. In practice, however, BLLD may not decide to make such a reduction. Also the potential postal savings of some users will be below the average cost of running the scheme. Thus it is likely that a differential membership fee would be charged, should this option be introduced nationally. This is similar to the arrangement in Yorkshire, where a transportation system has been in operation since 1974.

A drawback with the first option is that there may be some difficulty in selecting the users to include in the scheme. In addition a differential pricing system is likely to be contentious. Our second option avoids both differential pricing and the need for selection. In this option, membership of the club would be offered to all BLLD users for a fixed annual price. The price would be determined by finding how many users would be included when the average cost of running the system is equal to the saving to the marginal user. This point occurs when 2.7 percent of users are included. The marginal saving and average cost at this point are both approximately $2,600 per year. Thus if the scheme were offered at this price the marginal user would be indifferent as to whether or not he comes into the scheme and all users larger than the marginal user would make a saving. This concept is illustrated in Figure 5.2. This depth of service and price depends on BLLD passing on all their postal savings in the form of a reduced price for request forms. However in this case BLLD will enjoy none of the savings obtainable from the introduction of a transportation system. If

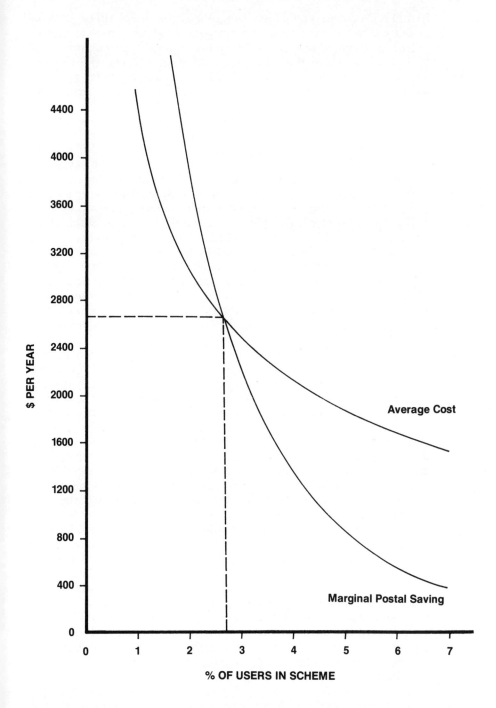

Figure 5.2   *Option 2*

BLLD does not pass on all its savings then fewer users will be attracted to the scheme and the price of participation will have to be increased.

Our third option consists of a centrally organized scheme to serve all BLLD users except those in remote locations. Unlike the first two options, option 3 would not be offered to users for them to decide whether or not to participate: the decision as to whom to serve would be taken centrally. The scheme would be financed by a fixed charge per item. There are three basic alternatives for charging for option 3.

- The first would be to sell prepaid forms at a price such that the transportation scheme would break even. This would necessitate raising the present request form price. The increased price would, however, cover the cost of return as well as delivery and would therefore constitute a significant saving for most users.
- The second possibility would be to continue selling the forms at the present price. In this case the BLLD would have to subsidize the transportation scheme by about $290,000 per year.
- The third alternative would be to sell vouchers to be used on the transportation scheme. Unlike the prepaid forms these would only pay for one journey. While the voucher system would ensure that no users pay more under the transportation scheme than under the present arrangement, it would be fairly complex to administer.

At the beginning of this section we defined the optimum level of service as that which maximizes net savings. None of our first three options achieve this optimum level. The exact point at which the optimum occurs depends on the relative levels of postal and transportation costs. The relative costs are currently such that the optimum appears to be around the 5 percent level of service, between options 2 and 3. However, as Figure 5.3 shows, the net savings curve is fairly flat for most of its length and the figures with which we have been working are not sufficiently accurate for us to say exactly where on this flat section the optimum occurs. In any case, a small change in the ratio of postal costs to transportation costs would considerably alter the optimum depth of service.

Thus we can only say that the optimum occurs somewhere between the 5 percent and the 100 percent depths of service. However, net savings at all points over this range vary only slightly, so that any scheme in this range would produce savings near to the optimum level. Because of this uncertainty we believed it would be worthwhile to illustrate the implications of setting up a scheme that served a percentage somewhere within this range. Partly as a contrast to the 100 percent level of service of option 3, and partly because we consider that there may be some merit in a more modest level of service, we selected the 5 percent level for the purposes of illustrating our fourth option.

It is not possible to finance a 5 percent level of service by charging all participants the same fixed price. This is because at this level, if all

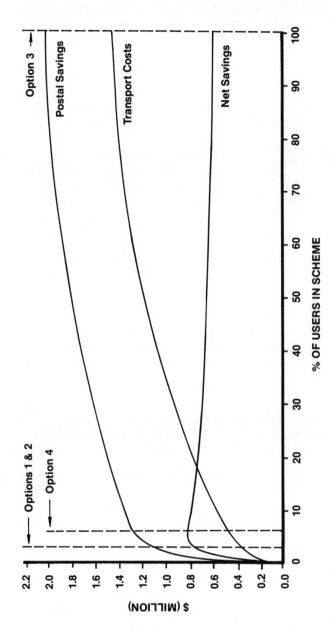

Figure 5.3   *The options*

users pay the average cost of the scheme so that it just breaks even, some of them will be paying more than they save in postage. Thus the scheme can only be financed by some kind of variable pricing system. This is the principle underlying option 4. One way in which this could be done would be to make a fixed annual charge with an additional prepaid charge per item. By setting these charges at the correct levels, and offering the scheme to all users, the option 4 target would be reached automatically with the largest 5 percent of users deciding to participate. This would overcome the problem of having to select the largest 5 percent. Table 5.3 shows various pricing policies, all of which result in a 5 percent level of use and all of which have different implications for the savings made by users of different sizes and by BLLD.

Table 5.3 *Alternative charge rate for option 4*

Price per transaction $	Fixed annual charge $	BLLD saving ($ per year)	Total user saving ($ per year)
0.29	378	7,000	797,000
0.33	353	55,000	749,000
0.40	318	131,000	673,000
0.49	271	231,000	573,000

The first row of Table 5.3 shows that the largest 5 percent of users would choose to participate if the scheme were offered at an annual charge of $378, with an additional charge of $0.29 per transaction. This charge per transaction is only a payment towards the cost of delivering and, if necessary, returning an item; it does not include an element for BLLD handling charges. These handling charges, which currently stand at $0.49 per item, are at present included in the $1.00 price per BLLD form. Under option 4, BLLD users would pay the $0.49 handling charge in addition to the transaction charge. Arrangements in the regions might vary, but provided a payment at least equal to the transaction charge was made on each regional item, several possibilities would be open. We consider some of these in the next section.

These four options are presented as illustration of the range of possibilities that is available. It should be stressed that apart from differences in the size of operation involved the only variations between the options are in methods of charging for the transportation scheme: the operational details described in Section 2 are common to all four schemes. The costs and savings of each are illustrated in Figure 5.3, which shows for the whole range of depths of service the costs of running the scheme, the postal savings to be made and the net savings (the second item minus the first item). In the next section we assess the four options in more detail.

4 EVALUATION OF THE ALTERNATIVES

Before we were able to evaluate the various basic options described in the previous section we had to work out the details of schemes providing a whole range of levels of service for many different parts of the country. We did this using the analytical techniques outlined in previous sections. Our calculations were performed separately for each English county. Insufficient information prevented us from dividing Scotland and Wales in the same way, but we were able to make some estimate of the effect of the clustering of users in these areas.

We examined each area for depths of service ranging from just 1 percent to the full 100 percent of users. This exercise demonstrated that a positive return could be obtained at any level in all but the most sparsely populated areas. By aggregating the results for the English counties, Scotland and Wales we formed Table 5.4, showing the details of schemes serving the whole country at various depths of service.

Some explanations of the column headings in this table is appropriate:

- *Percentage of users.* This shows the level of service, that is, the proportion of libraries included in the scheme, starting with the very largest and introducing successively smaller users. Because such a high proportion of inter-lending is carried out by a few very large libraries the levels of service that we evaluated do not increase by equal increments. Instead we have made a more finely graded study of the largest 10 percent of users. The unevenness of the steps should be borne in mind when reading the table, so as not to gain a false impression of the proportional increases in the various figures.
- *Number of users.* This is the actual number of BLLD users served. It should be noted that at the 100 percent level of service 4,749 libraries participate, accounting for 97 percent of BLLD membership. This is the total number of users that it is economic to serve. The remaining one hundred or so are either overseas or in remote areas of the country.
- *Percentage of users visited daily.* Visits will only be made to users when necessary. Since small libraries require visits less frequently than larger ones, bringing in small users to the scheme means that the actual number of daily visits increases but the proportion of libraries visited is reduced.
- *Percentage of BLLD items carried.* The amount of BLLD material traveling on the transportation scheme depends on the number of libraries that use it. The figure increases as more users are brought in but, since these are the smaller libraries, at a decreasing rate. The 100 percent level is never reached since even at the maximum depth of service items would continue to be mailed to users in outlying areas.
- *Number of distribution vans.* Distribution vans are those that are used solely for visiting users as opposed to linking vans, whose primary function is to connect nodes, although they may also be used for collection and delivery.

Table 5.4 *The options in context – costs and savings at various levels of service*

Percentage of users	No. of users	Percentage of users visited daily	Percentage of BLLD items carried	No. of distribution vans	No. of linking vans	No. of nodes	Total costs ($ per year)	Average cost per user ($ per year)	Average cost per transaction ($)	Postal savings ($ per year)	Marginal savings ($ per year)	Net savings ($ per year)
1	47	100	34	9	0	8	215,211	4,532	0.31	701,590	6,927	486,379
2	95	100	46	13	0	8	290,979	3,064	0.30	960,080	3,959	669,101
3	142	100	55	18	0	8	346,345	2,430	0.31	1,104,408	2,119	758,061
4	190	100	57	22	0	8	398,022	2,095	0.33	1,188,283	1,413	790,259
5	237	100	60	25	0	8	435,587	1,835	0.35	1,241,928	846	806,341
6	285	99	61	28	0	8	470,670	1,653	0.37	1,274,654	531	803,981
7	332	96	62	31	0	8	498,038	1,497	0.38	1,295,637	353	797,597
8	380	93	63	33	0	8	521,512	1,373	0.40	1,311,750	327	790,239
10	475	89	64	38	0	8	568,956	1,197	0.42	1,342,226	315	773,270
20	950	79	71	54	1	11	764,504	804	0.51	1,483,993	282	719,490
40	1,900	70	83	77	4	18	1,058,741	558	0.61	1,718,814	213	660,073
60	2,849	63	91	95	5	23	1,264,459	444	0.67	1,887,436	142	622,977
80	3,799	56	95	108	5	25	1,395,747	367	0.70	1,988,610	71	592,863
100	4,749	48	97	113	6	26	1,442,658	304	0.71	2,022,334	0	579,673

Note: On this and certain subsequent tables cost and benefit figures have been expressed to the nearest dollar or cent. The assumptions used and their derivation do not justify this degree of accuracy. The figures have been quoted in this manner to enable comparisons to be made.

- *Number of linking vans.* Linking vans are only required when the distribution vans serving a particular area operate from more than one node, making a connecting service necessary. No more than one node is needed in each region when only a small proportion of libraries are included and, as the table shows, linking vans are not required until the 20 percent level of service is reached.
- *Number of nodes.* As the depth of service increases a point is reached where it becomes worthwhile to introduce extra nodes to save mileage by the distribution vans, even though a linking van becomes necessary. This process can be seen to start around the 20 percent level of service.
- *Total costs.* Total costs are the sum of standing and running costs for all the vans and the charge made by British Rail for trunking.
- *Average cost per user.* This is found by dividing total costs by the number of libraries served. It falls continuously, demonstrating that bringing in even the smallest users could enable the price to be reduced for everyone.
- *Average cost per transaction.* This is the average cost of handling each item inclusive of the cost of returning it. This figure is found by dividing the total cost by the number of items carried.
- *Postal savings.* Postal savings represent the total savings in postage by all parties on items that would previously have traveled by mail but can now be transported by the van scheme.
- *Marginal savings.* We define marginal saving as the postal savings realized by the smallest user at any particular level of service.
- *Net savings.* Net savings are found by subtracting total costs of running the transport scheme from the postal savings which would be made.

Costs and savings at the national level
We first evaluated each of the options for the country as a whole.

Options 1 and 2. Details of each of the basic options put forward in Section 3 can be read from Table 5.4. Option 1, which we suggest could be operated at the 3 percent level of participation, results in a national average operating cost per user of $2,430 per year. Eighteen vans would be required with one node in each region except for Wales, which would be served from neighboring regions. For a map of this network see Figure 5.4. We have on this map, and all other maps, deliberately avoided naming the nodes as we wish to emphasize that there is some flexibility in their location.

Table 5.4 shows that marginal savings and average costs become equal somewhere between the 2 percent and 3 percent levels of service. By calculation they can be found to be equal at approximately $2,600 per year, when the level of service stands at 2.7 percent. Option 2 would be to offer the transportation scheme to all users at this price so as to bring in this percentage of users. This option is also illustrated in Figure 5.4.

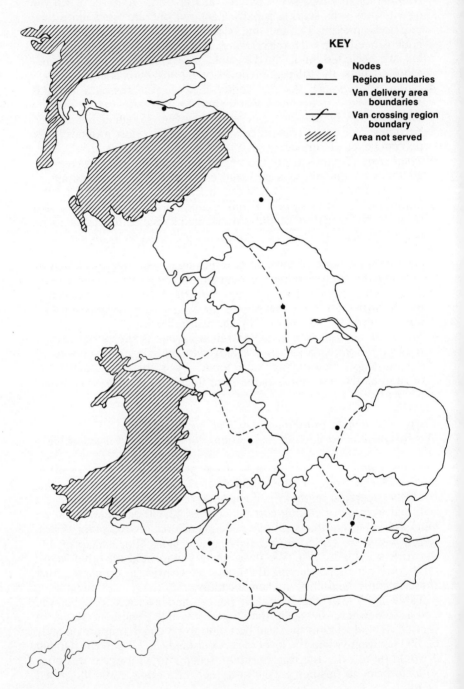

Figure 5.4   *Options 1 and 2 in practice*

Option 3. Option 3 brings in all BLLD users except those in remote locations. This option is presented in Figure 5.5, which also shows the areas that would continue to be served by mail. One hundred and thirteen distribution vans would be needed, operating from twenty-six nodes. Since some regions would have more than one node, six linking vans would also be required. In Section 3 we gave three possible ways of financing option 3: selling prepaid forms at a price such that the transportation scheme would break even; selling prepaid forms at the present price; and selling vouchers for carrying an item in one direction only. The three different methods of financing option 3 result in different distributions of net savings between participants. Table 5.5 shows the savings which would be made by various users of the transportation scheme under each pricing method.

Table 5.5   *User savings from option 3*

User	*Present cost per item ($)*	*Pricing method*					
		1		*2*		*3*	
		Cost ($)	*Saving ($)*	*Cost ($)*	*Saving ($)*	*Cost ($)*	*Saving ($)*
Requester of photo-copies from BLLD	1.00	1.20	−0.20	1.00	0.00	0.95	0.05
Borrower from BLLD	1.64	1.20	0.44	1.00	0.64	1.42	0.22
Borrower from region	0.91	0.71	0.20	0.71	0.20	0.47	0.44
Lender to region	0.91	0.00	0.91	0.00	0.91	0.47	0.44

Variant of option 3. If the transportation scheme were run by a central agency other than BLLD, and if BLLD paid a fixed charge to the agency for each item delivered on its behalf, it would find that for items below a certain weight the payment necessary to send the items on the scheme would be greater than the cost of mailing them. This is likely to be true for nearly all BLLD photocopies since their lightness makes them relatively cheap to mail. Thus although the schemes that we have put forward are designed to carry both loans and photocopies it might well turn out in practice that the greater part of the items carried would be loans.

In recognition of this we have evaluated a variant of option 3 where only loans would be permitted to travel on the transportation scheme. All photocopies would continue to be sent by mail. In all other respects the scheme would be identical to option 3 as stated above. Although total postal savings would be reduced since fewer items would be carried, there would also be a fall in transportation costs with fewer delivery stops being made.

From BLLD figures we estimated $1.67 as the current postal cost of a loan transaction. Our calculations showed that a scheme carrying loans only would produce higher net savings than any other scheme that we evaluated except for those of option 4 for loans and photo-copies (see below). The optimum level at which to run a scheme

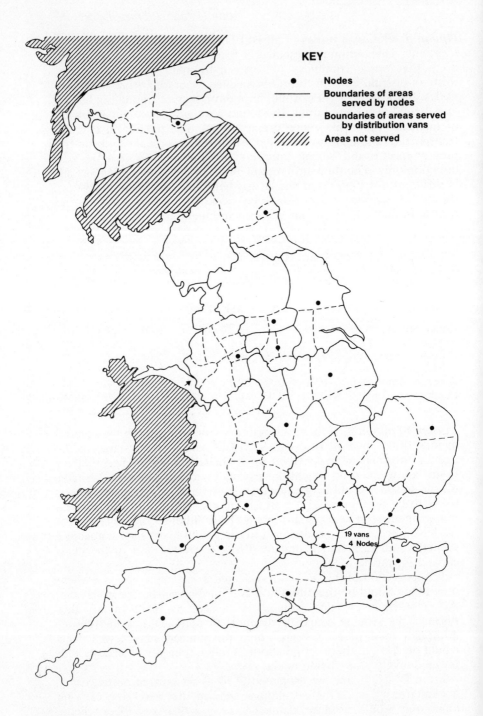

KEY

- •   Nodes
- ——   Boundaries of areas served by nodes
- - - -   Boundaries of areas served by distribution vans
- ▨   Areas not served

19 vans
4 Nodes

Figure 5.5   *Option 3 in practice*

carrying loans only so as to maximize net savings would be at the 100 percent depth of service with all users participating. Net savings to all parties would amount to $764,000 per year, while the cost of transporting a loan one way, and hence the smallest economical charge for the scheme, would be $0.51.

We have suggested previously that the largest one hundred or so users in the transportation scheme should automatically receive daily visits. With visits being made to these users in any case it would seem worthwhile to deliver photocopies to them. Thus the scheme could be organized to deliver loans and photocopies to these large users but only loans to other users. This would increase net savings above the level of the $764,000 previously quoted.

Option 4. The criterion that we have used to define the optimum scheme is that net savings should be maximized. In Section 3 we stated that because of insufficiently accurate data and the extreme sensitivity of the net savings curve to small changes in costs, we did not feel that the exact point of optimization could be calculated. Instead, our fourth option is designed to achieve any of the near optimum points between the 5 percent and the 100 percent levels of service. For the purposes of illustration we have chosen the 5 percent level. We have illustrated option 4 in Figure 5.6.

Various pricing methods would be possible. The best method would seem to be a combination of a fixed charge paid at regular intervals and a further payment per item carried, possibly charged by the sale of vouchers. Under this system it would be possible to offer the scheme to users, and correctly setting the fixed charge and the charge per item would ensure that the desired number of users would choose to come into the scheme.

A whole range of combinations of charges could be used to achieve the required level. Some of them were listed in Table 5.3. The important difference between them is that those with high charges per item carried result in smaller net savings for the biggest users than those with high annual charges.

Costs and savings at the regional level
The cost of serving a particular area of the country by the transportation scheme depends on the distribution of borrowing between users in the area, the density with which users are clustered together and the speed at which a delivery van can travel within the area. Since there is some variation in these factors in different parts of the country the costs of providing the four options would not be the same in each region. Table 5.6 illustrates these differences by listing the cost to the transportation system of one transaction in each region at various depths of service. These figures should be compared with the present postal cost per transaction of $1.00, which is of course the same in all regions. Figures for the Welsh Region are not shown in Table 5.6 as we have combined users in North Wales with those in the North West Region and those in South Wales with users in the South West.

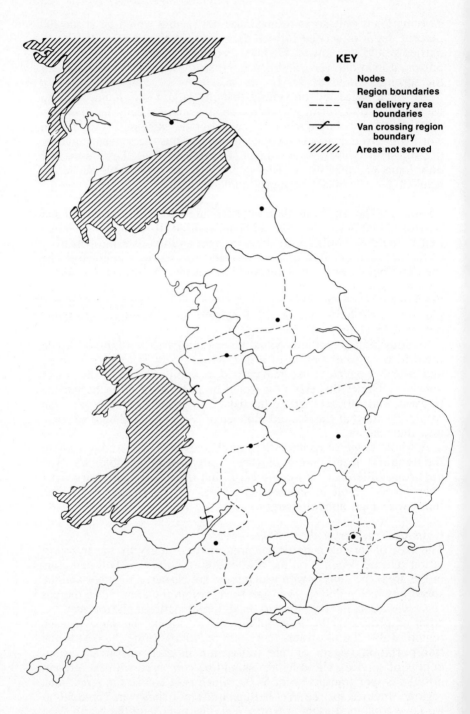

KEY

●	Nodes
——	Region boundaries
– – –	Van delivery area boundaries
∿	Van crossing region boundary
⧄	Areas not served

Figure 5.6 *Option 4 in practice*

Table 5.6 *Costs of a transaction on the transportation scheme by region (cents)*

Depth of service %	LASER * (excluding London)	London	South West	East Midlands	West Midlands	Yorkshire and Humberside	North West	North	Scotland (part)
1	26.9	13.8	43.8	51.8	33.3	34.9	28.7	58.7	35.1
2	28.0	14.2	43.5	46.2	34.4	31.3	29.8	52.9	36.0
3	30.2	15.1	43.8	46.0	34.6	35.3	30.2	52.2	36.2
4	31.8	16.2	46.7	52.2	36.0	36.4	31.6	59.8	37.6
5	33.6	17.3	48.9	53.8	37.6	38.0	33.3	61.1	39.3
6	35.3	18.2	51.1	58.2	39.3	40.0	34.9	63.1	41.1
7	36.9	19.1	53.3	60.4	40.9	41.5	36.2	64.9	42.7
8	38.2	20.0	55.1	62.4	42.2	43.1	37.6	66.7	44.0
10	40.4	21.6	58.2	65.8	44.7	48.2	39.8	69.5	46.4
20	48.9	27.6	69.1	77.5	54.9	59.5	49.1	80.4	57.3
40	58.2	34.2	80.4	89.8	67.5	70.4	60.9	91.8	70.0
60	63.3	38.4	86.6	96.2	73.1	76.4	66.2	101.1	75.8
80	66.4	40.9	90.0	100.0	76.2	79.8	69.3	107.8	78.9
100	67.5	41.8	91.3	101.3	77.5	80.9	70.4	109.1	80.2

* London and South East Region.

The three maps used to illustrate the options nationally (Figures 5.4, 5.5, and 5.6) indicate the way in which under each option the country can be divided into separate areas, with a distribution van allocated to each. It will be seen that, under some options, some of these van areas cross existing regional boundaries. When we evaluated options 1, 2 and 4 we found that the operating requirements for each region would be small. No more than one node would be needed in each and only relatively few distribution vans. Because of the small number of vans involved, and to make best use of them, we suggest that in options 1, 2 and 4 it would be best to serve the peripheries of some of the existing library regions with vans based in neighboring regions. As an example of this, in options 1 and 2 users in South Wales would be served from the South Western Region. To run option 3 would require several more nodes than the other options. This would inevitably introduce an extra delay into the system with items traveling between nodes within a region. This extra delay could be minimized by connecting some of these new nodes to Boston Spa either directly by rail, or with a direct van connection to the railhead. This would, however, add to the overall cost of running the system and impede movement of items within the region.

5   CONCLUSIONS

In the preceding sections of this report we have examined a wide variety of options for introducing a transportation scheme for handling items on inter-library loan. It appears that savings of the order of $\$^2/_3$ million could be made by the library sector if a transportation system is introduced. Such a system would take the form of a van distribution system linked to the BLLD at Boston Spa by rail. However, it is not sufficient to design a transportation system simply to maximize the savings to the library sector. Two other considerations are important. First, it is desirable that the scheme can be offered to users at a price such that no user has to pay more than at present; and secondly, this price must be such that the organizers of the transportation system do not operate at a loss. A further consideration relevant to the design of the transportation system is who should run it.

Let us first assume that the transportation schemes are organized by the regional library bureaus as an additional service to their members. We have illustrated, in option 1, how a scheme can be offered to a certain number of users and financed by subscription from them. There are difficulties in introducing this sort of scheme, especially for the small user for whom the average cost of the scheme may be greater than his current expenditure. However, by careful research, and setting of appropriate differential prices, these difficulties can be overcome.

Alternatively the transportation system could be organized by a central agency. Certainly the most attractive way of running such a scheme is to serve all users nationally except those in remote locations. Such a scheme is best financed by the sale of prepaid request forms in the same way that BLLD uses at present. However, we have shown that to avoid running the transportation system at a loss the form price would have to be increased from its present level of $1.00 to $1.20. This will not represent a true price increase for most users as the new price covers the cost of return. However, those users that receive a large proportion of photocopies might find their costs increased. Users within the regional systems could also participate in this sort of scheme by using the BLLD form for their transactions.

There are two ways in which a national scheme could be improved further. First, it is really not economic to serve the small user who never borrows more than one item at a time. If these users are eliminated the scheme would be easier to operate and would yield higher savings. The second way in which a national system may be improved is to restrict it to the transportation of loans only. Photocopies, being generally lighter than loans, can be carried more economically by mail. However, our calculation of these extra savings are dependent on a number of assumptions that may not be justified.

We have been impressed throughout our study with the lack of information on which we could build a firm set of conclusions. We are sure of our basic conclusion that a transportation system is cheaper than the present postal arrangements. However, more information is needed on which to base a fully operational national system. We see this information being obtained primarily by introducing and monitoring a pilot transportation system in one area of the country, and we suggest that this should be the next undertaking.

6

Discussion

SUMMARY OF RESULTS

The study presented in Chapter 2 gives the results of an evaluation to find the number and locations of standby ambulances that would be needed to meet nationally recommended response-time standards for emergency ambulance services in a new health authority. The study found that a minimum of six ambulances were needed during daytime and five during nights and on weekends and holidays. However, for various reasons, it was recommended that the new health authority initially deploy eight ambulances at seven locations and possibly reduce the number of ambulances as experience was gained with a new dispatch and control system then being implemented. By the time we visited the authority in 1978 there were 40 percent fewer ambulances operating on the day shift and 20 percent fewer on evenings and at nights than there were prior to the study. This is a study in which the testing and subsequent modification of the original solution appears to have played a major role in achieving a successful implementation. In addition to reducing the number of ambulances required to serve the area, the study also resulted in a number of other benefits, such as standardizing the documentation and collection of data and providing managers with ideas for large cost savings in other areas of ambulance administration.

Chapter 3 presented a study which examined how a county social services department could increase the number of hot meals delivered to the elderly or handicapped in their homes to five per week at minimum cost. This involved determining the number of kitchens needed to prepare the meals and how large they should be, where they should be sited and which area they should serve. The study recommended a phased expansion of the meals-on-wheels service, which included opening ten new kitchens within an eight-year planning period and closing seven of the nineteen existing kitchens. The recommendations were well received but were only partly implemented because of the difficulty in finding enough volunteers to carry out an expanded service. This study illustrates well the importance of developing an accurate and complete problem definition. The recommendations of the study could not be fully implemented because an important constraint, a limitation on the availability of volunteers, was left out of the problem definition.

Chapter 4 presented the results of a study to develop a new points scheme for ranking applicants for government-owned housing. The primary objective of this study was to develop a set of needs factors and points for each factor that would give highest priority to those applicants who were considered to be in greatest need. Devising the new points scheme was an integral part of a large, two-year research and development program which also included the development of a computer information system. The new points scheme and computer information system have been successfully implemented and have resulted in a number of benefits. In addition to providing a fairer system of assessing applicants and allocating housing, the new points scheme and computer information system together provide the housing department and the city council with current data for making decisions concerning a large system which includes over 100,000 housing units. This study illustrates a practical and successful way to formalize and make more objective some very difficult decisions.

To determine whether the transportation costs of inter-library loans could be reduced, and to encourage the development of a coordinated national system of regional transportation networks, the British Library commissioned the feasibility study described in Chapter 5. The study concluded that a transportation system would be cheaper than the current method of mailing items between libraries and had the potential for saving up to $\$^{2}/_{3}$ million per year in transportation costs. Two pilot transportation systems were subsequently established and both adequately demonstrated the savings to be achieved by operating a van transportation system. The two trial schemes are now operating on a permanent basis, and other library regions have established or have plans to establish systems for delivering inter-library loans by van. The development of such a large system presented a number of unusual problems, some of which were not recognized until alternative solutions were tested through the implementation of the two pilot transportation systems.

DESCRIPTION OF METHODS

All the studies in Part One involve the allocation of scarce resources: resources for dealing with medical emergencies (Chapter 2); food, kitchens, delivery vans and volunteers to prepare and deliver meals (Chapter 3); city-owned housing of various sizes and locations (Chapter 4); and, finally, library books and the vans to deliver them (Chapter 5).

Consequently there are similarities in the types of models constructed and the methods used to derive solutions in these studies. One of the major subdivisions of operations research models and methods is sometimes called mathematical programming, and many of the methods that fall into this category are associated with resource allocation problems. For example, mathematical programming includes shortest path analysis, nonlinear programming, linear programming and the traveling salesman problem, each of which is used in one of the studies in this part.

The interested reader will find descriptions of the general types of models that were used and how solutions are derived from them in most operations research textbooks, a selection of which are listed in the general references at the end of this book. In this section we briefly describe the models in nonmathematical terms. Where possible we provide specific references for the models used in these studies.

Shortest path and queueing models
Planning Emergency Ambulance Cover in West Glamorgan (Chapter 2) employs two well-known operations research models – the shortest path model and a multiserver queueing model. The shortest path model was used to develop a table of travel times between different locations in the service area. To do this, a set of nodes (locations on a map) were identified which represented population centers, major road junctions, existing and potential locations for ambulance stations, and hospitals. A small group of the ninety-four nodes identified in the West Glamorgan service area is shown on Figure 2.1. These nodes are interconnected by a road network and the next step was to estimate the time it would take an ambulance to travel between adjacent nodes. Finally, using a method for solving the shortest path problem, a table of shortest travel times could be developed between all pairs of nodes. Part of this table is reproduced as Table 2.1.

Next, a computer model was developed which measured the percentage of calls for service that would be satisfied within various times, given the number and locations of ambulances, the distribution of calls, time of day, estimated activation time, method of operating the service (that is, single- or multi-tier) and average service time. The main component of this model was a multiserver queueing model which assumed that calls had an exponential probability distribution. Having obtained data on the distribution of calls for service and their frequency (see Figure 2.2), the model was used to evaluate many different plans for providing emergency services by changing the number of ambulances used and their standby locations. Groom (1977) gives the mathematical formulation of this model.

Nonlinear programming
A nonlinear programming model was used to obtain the results presented in *Meals on Wheels in Worcestershire* (Chapter 3). The county was divided into areas (parishes) and the inputs to this model were: the number of recipients in each area; the average number of meals each recipient was to receive each week; the locations and capacities of existing kitchens and possible sites and capacities of new kitchens; the costs to build, equip and run these kitchens; and the shortest distances between the kitchens and the areas to be served.

Given these inputs, the model found the kitchens that should be used to serve each area which would minimize the total time needed to deliver the meals. By using the model, which was computerized, to evaluate a number of different arrangements (groupings) of kitchens, it was possible to find the number of locations of kitchens and the recipients to be served from each which minimized the cost of preparing and serving the meals. The model was able to take into account geographical barriers, varying travel times on different types of roads and the effects of traffic density on travel times.

Linear programming

A linear programming model was used to obtain the distribution of points described in *Developing a Housing Points Scheme* (Chapter 4). In order to construct this model it was first necessary to develop an agreed list of needs factors – the factors to which points would be assigned – and a means of measuring how an applicant scored on these factors. For example, one of the needs factors was 'overcrowding' and one of the ways used to measure an applicant's score on overcrowding was the number of bedrooms the applicant was currently lacking. Next, a sample of 152 applicants who were representative of the wide variety of people on the current waiting list was selected. A panel of judges then subjectively ranked this sample of applicants in terms of overall need for housing. The method of paired comparisons was used to obtain this ranking.

The ranking of applicants and the scores that each achieved on each needs factor were the inputs to the linear programming model. The model then derived the points (weights) that should be applied to each of the needs factors. It did so by minimizing the difference between the ranking that would result from the points derived from the model and the ranking based upon the subjective judgments of the panel. Wilson (1976) gives the mathematical formulation of the model used in this study.

Traveling salesman problem

The delivery system described in *A National Transport System for Inter-Library Loans* (Chapter 5) uses vans to transport books between libraries and distribution points in each region, which are connected by rail to the British Library Lending Division in Yorkshire. A single van provides regular service to a group of libraries, calling on each in turn and returning to the distribution point from which it started. There are many routes for linking the group of libraries served by a single van. As implementing a transportation scheme was dependent on whether the new system was cheaper than mailing inter-library loans, it was important to find the route that minimized the distance traveled by each van and hence minimized the transportation cost of the system.

This problem is known as the 'traveling salesman' problem in operations research. Although methods exist for finding the optimal tour (see Little *et al.*, 1963), in this study what was needed was the length of the routes in order to determine the costs of the various alternative distribution systems being considered. To obtain these lengths, a method for approximating the length of the optimal route was used (see Beardwood *et al.*, 1959). First the total number of libraries in a region that would participate in a given distribution system was determined. This number was adjusted by using the Poisson distribution to obtain the average number of libraries visited each day. Then it was assumed that one van would visit all these libraries and the minimum distance for a single tour was found. This provided the information for calculating the minimum number of vans that would be needed to serve all the libraries in the region. The libraries were then grouped and the average minimum distance traveled each day by each van was found, using once again the method for approximating the length of the optimal route. This information – the number of vans and the average distance traveled each day – was used in a model to determine the total cost per user of the transportation system. Details of these methods are given by Houghton and Nixon (1976, appendix 2).

ANALYSIS OF PROBLEMS

Applying operations research to health and social services presents difficulties that are not found in other areas of government. We believe one reason for this lies with the fact that solutions to problems in these areas have a more immediate bearing on the public than solutions to problems in many other areas of government. This is not to say that other studies in this book do not deal with problems which greatly affect the public. However, in many cases the effect is not immediately apparent, or as important as it seems with applications in health and social services, whereas several of the problems dealt with in Part One can literally be of life or death importance. Because these problems so clearly affect the public, and because the approach taken is necessarily quantitative and objective, the operations research analyst can easily appear to be unsympathetic to human problems and unknowing about social services or medical practice. Furthermore, although skilled analysts are aware of the human factors which exist in a social welfare problem as well as in other areas, they sometimes cannot find a way to incorporate these factors into the mathematical model. They should, however, make it clear that they recognize that these factors exist and that they will have a bearing on the solution to a problem.

It is thus extremely important for an analyst to develop a close working relationship with professionals in the health and social service area being studied and to have access to their knowledge about the problem. These professionals need to be consulted throughout a study, but it is especially important for them to be involved during the problem identification and problem definition phases. This close cooperation existed in each of the studies in Part One. In addition, staff in each of the organizations for which these studies were conducted provided data or made it possible for the analysts to collect the data needed to complete the study. These efforts not only helped to bring the studies to a successful conclusion but also enabled the staff of the health and social agencies involved to understand the quantitative methods used, how the results should be interpreted and the part that assumptions played in the solution process.

A related difficulty in working on health and social service problems concerns how the analyst incorporates a measure of the quality of service provided by a social welfare program. Practitioners in these areas naturally tend to be very concerned about service quality and they may be anxious that an operations research study which appears to be chiefly concerned about the *cost* of providing a service will ignore the *quality* of that service. Occasionally these fears are warranted, but usually they are not. An understanding of how the analyst has defined the problem, and especially the relationship between the criteria on which a solution will be based and the constraints placed on obtaining feasible solutions, can help overcome such fears. For example, the criterion used to select the best number and locations of ambulances in Chapter 2 was to minimize the cost of the system, but quality of service, measured by response time, was certainly not ignored. Those alternatives which did not meet the response-time standard were eliminated. Only then did the cost criteria (in terms of numbers of personnel and ambulances) enter into the selection process.

Health and social services include a large number of functions at all levels of government and there is a wide range of other possible operations research applications to problems in these areas. We conclude this chapter with a listing of some other models that have been applied or could be applied to health and social services. No attempt has been made to provide an exhaustive collection of references. The ones that follow are intended to suggest possible areas of application and the interested reader might find these useful as a starting point for understanding additional applications.

In the area of health Grundy and Reinke (1973) suggest applications to problems in recruitment and training, manpower scheduling and disease control. A number of possible applications of operations research to problems in the mental health field, such as satellite facility location, nurse staffing, appointment scheduling, warehouse operations and data processing, are discussed in a handbook for administrators who manage mental health systems (Halpert *et al.*, 1970). The proceedings of a conference on systems aspects of health planning (Bailey and Thompson, 1975) contains many examples of systems analysis. Some of the topics covered are determination of acute care bed requirements, medical information systems and computer simulation studies of alternative population screening policies. Horvath (1967) gives examples of two interesting operations research applications in the medical field. One involves developing staffing policies to overcome variable demands for hospital facilities and the other concerns medical diagnosis. Jennings (1972) applies inventory control methods to a blood bank to overcome stockouts, high operating costs and losses from outdated supplies. Palmer (1975) reviews and assesses a number of models for planning and operating health services.

There have also been a number of applications in the field of education. For example, operations research has been used to develop course schedules, decide on the types of transportation that should be offered, determine inventory policies for school supplies and forecast enrollments. In addition, models have been developed for assigning students to schools to achieve a specified level of racial balance (see, for example, Belford and Ratliff, 1972). Weiss (1975) discusses a wide range of decision problems in education and reviews models that have been developed to solve some of these problems.

The resource allocation problem described in Chapter 2 is similar to the types of allocation problems faced by police and fire protection agencies. A book on deployment problems associated with fire protection (Walker *et al.*, 1979) includes applications to allocating fire companies, locating fire houses and evaluating dispatch policies. In *Urban Police Patrol Analysis*, Larson (1972) describes a number of operations research applications and models including a police patrol allocation algorithm, a simulation model of the dispatch patrol system and travel time models. Additional operations research applications to drug law enforcement, prosecution management, court scheduling, information systems and other topics are contained in a book on law enforcement, justice and societal security (Brounstein and Kamrass, 1976) and Gass (1975) discusses a number of models that have been used in law enforcement and criminal justice.

In the area of social services Brotherton *et al.* (1972) use operations research to determine the resources needed to provide social services for the elderly. And in the field of library management *Operations Research: Implications for Libraries* (Swanson and Bookstein, 1972) suggests a number of possible applications.

In addition to these references, the methods used and the problems tackled by other studies in this book could generate ideas for applications to problems in health and social services. Cost-benefit analysis (Chapter 9) can be a useful method of evaluating social welfare programs. The study presented in Chapter 13 describes the problem of determining the most cost-effective level of checking invoices before they are paid; but the same concept could easily apply to the checking of applicants for health and social services. Chapter 14 is an example of the types of results obtained by simulating a service facility and Chapter 15 concerns the relocation of staff after a reorganization, with special emphasis on communications problems.

Part Two

Transportation and Environmental Problems

Part Two includes four studies involving transportation and environmental problems. Each chapter begins with a discussion of how the results of the study were used.

Transportation and environmental issues are often related. Although not every environmental problem also concerns transportation it is generally true that every transportation problem has an environmental impact. For this reason environmental impact studies are now routinely performed on new transportation projects, as well as on most public works projects. In fact, since the passage of the National Environmental Policy Act of 1969 such studies have been required in the United States during the planning of projects, in order to receive federal funding.

There have been many beneficial effects of the coming of the automobile, such as enabling vital services to reach more people more quickly, but there have also been many harmful results, such as noise, congestion and pollution. Overcoming these harmful results without creating new environmental problems is the subject of Chapter 7, 'Economic and Environmental Evaluation – Highway Planning'. This chapter includes a study which evaluates a set of alternative bypass routes for a small town on a major road, taking into account factors such as impact on land use and on noise and safety as well as the cost of the project.

Building new roads, however, does not solve most environmental problems. Some people now believe that putting the roads we already have to more effective use is a better solution, especially if we are also to cope with shortages in fuel. One approach, and a major concern of most urban areas today, is to develop and maintain a viable public transportation system. Chapter 8, 'Public Transportation – Bus Operations', includes the report of a study which addresses a problem common to many governments: how to maintain or improve local bus services during a period of rising costs and decreasing patronage.

Environmental problems often deal with uncertainty, especially in regard to their long-term impacts on society. Flooding is an environmental problem about which there is an unusual amount of uncertainty. Chapter 9, 'Capital Investment Decision – Flood Relief', includes a study which examines the case for building a flood relief scheme on the basis of the probability of flooding, the estimated losses in property and the cost of the scheme.

Finally, the refuse disposal problem addressed in Chapter

10, 'Regional Cooperation – Locating Refuse Treatment Plants', also had its uncertainties. These were associated with the changing nature of refuse, increases and shifts in population and the amount of refuse disposal capacity that would be needed in the future. The study found the best number and location of refuse treatment plants for a group of local governments facing a severe shortage of sites for disposal of untreated refuse. Minimizing the transportation costs of refuse collection and disposal, as well as the environmental concerns for land reclamation, disposal area hygiene and public amenity, were all at the heart of this problem.

The studies included in Part Two are a small sample of the types of transportation and environmental problems to which operations research has been applied and in Chapter 11 we reference other applications for further reading. Chapter 11 also discusses some common features of the problems solved by the studies presented in Part Two and presents a brief description of the mathematical models and methods used to obtain their results.

7
Economic and Environmental Evaluation – Highway Planning

Faringdon is a small stone-built seventeenth-century market town, situated at the edge of the Cotswold Hills in the south-west of England. The town is surrounded by attractive countryside and the area is popular with tourists and hikers. The center of the town is a conservation area with several of the buildings listed for historical preservation.

This pleasant country town with its attractive rural environs is the focus of several major roads. The main road (route number A420) from Swindon to Oxford passes through the center of Faringdon and roads number A417 and A4095 also run through the town. The roads in the center of Faringdon along which traffic on these routes must pass are narrow and twisty; at places so narrow that traffic can pass in only one direction, while vehicles going in the opposite direction must wait. In recent years there has been a marked increase in private and commercial traffic in the town, which has given rise not only to considerable congestion but also to a noticeable deterioration in the town's environment. As a result the local community considered that a bypass was urgently needed and in 1973 the Berkshire County Council, which was then responsible for Faringdon, commissioned an economic and environmental evaluation of a set of possible bypass routes.

The study was conducted by Graham Faulkner and Gerald Miller who examined five alternative bypass routes, one to the north of Faringdon and four to the south. These routes were evaluated in terms of construction costs, road-user benefits and their quantitative and qualitative impacts on the environment. Each of the five alternative bypasses enabled traffic along the heavily traveled A420 route to avoid Faringdon, while two of the alternatives (routes 2 and 4) could incorporate extensions that would also permit traffic on the A417 to bypass the center of town. The study found that only two of the alternatives, route 2 *without* the extension for the A417 traffic and route 3, were justified economically; that is, had positive road-user benefit to construction cost ratios. Although both these alternatives enabled traffic along the A420 to bypass Faringdon, traffic along the A417 would still need to pass through the town center.

The benefit to cost ratio of alternative bypass 2 (*without* the extension) was found to be slightly higher than the benefit to cost ratio of alternative 3. However, alternative 3 was considered to be more acceptable on environmental grounds. Consequently, Faulkner and

Miller concluded that a bypass following alternative 3 should be constructed. After the bypass was completed and in use, they suggested that the volume of traffic and environmental conditions in and around Faringdon should be reassessed and, if conditions warranted, it would then be possible to build an extension to enable traffic on the A417 also to bypass Faringdon. The results of the study were submitted in 1974 to Oxfordshire County Council, which had by then become responsible for Faringdon following a local government reorganization.

On July 12, 1979 the Faringdon bypass was opened. The route finally selected by Oxfordshire County Council was a combination of two of the routes analyzed by the study: route 2 *with* the extension, and route 3. Coming into Faringdon from the south-west, the new bypass leaves the A420 slightly to the north of the proposed alternative route 3, then follows route 3 to where it would join the extension for the A417 traffic. From this point it follows the proposed route 2, rejoining the A420 to the east of Faringdon.

The study team had concluded that route 3 was the most acceptable alternative, with particular reference to environmental considerations. However, after reexamining the traffic survey data and conducting further studies, the Oxfordshire Highways Department justified the extension for the A417 traffic. The decision on the final alignment of the new road was based on traffic, economic and environmental factors and also on public opinion. Several public meetings were held to discuss the proposed bypass and information from the study report was widely circulated to people living in the areas that would be affected. By including the extension, which runs in part along a disused railway line, the new bypass incorporates the major advantages of route 2 – enabling traffic on the A417 as well as the A420 to bypass the center of Faringdon – while also retaining many of the environmental advantages of route 3.

We visited Faringdon prior to the completion of the bypass and there could be no doubt one was needed. Oxfordshire County Council is conducting its own before-and-after study to assess the impact of the new scheme. The results of the study will not be clear until the scheme has been in operation for at least two years but members of the highways department have no doubt that it has been a success. Moreover, much of this success is attributable to environmental improvements. Much of the work of the follow-up study is directed towards measuring factors such as reduction in the noise, disturbance and fumes associated with heavy traffic in narrow and congested streets.

This study is a good example of cost-benefit analysis. It illustrates two types of cost-benefit criteria: first-year economic rate of return (the ratio of road-user benefits for the first year and the capital cost of the project); and the ratio of net discounted benefits over thirty years to discounted construction cost. However, the study is particularly interesting for its handling of the qualitative environmental impacts of the alternative schemes.

Too often the qualitative aspects of a decision are ignored because any evaluation of them must be subjective. In their report Faulkner and Miller carefully identified the qualitative environmental impacts. In this way the county council and the public were made aware of a number of important aspects of the proposed bypass routes and could make their own subjective comparison, even if the alternatives could not be objectively ranked in terms of these impacts. We believe this approach helped to broaden discussion of the proposals beyond the immediate quantifiable considerations and that it consequently improved the final outcome.

A condensed version of *Which By Pass for Faringdon?*, the report prepared by Faulkner and Miller, follows. It begins with a brief background to the study. Section 1 examines the impact of traffic on Faringdon in terms of congestion, public safety and noise pollution and Section 2 describes the proposed alternative bypass routes. An economic evaluation of the alternative routes is presented in Section 3. This analysis considers road-user benefits and construction costs. Section 4 of the report contains the environmental evaluation and Section 5 presents conclusions and recommendations. All costs and user benefits have been expressed in dollars at 1970 prices. The average exchange rate in 1970 was 0.4174 pounds sterling per dollar.

Which By Pass for Faringdon?

GRAHAM FAULKNER and GERALD MILLER

INTRODUCTION

There has been considerable public feeling that the narrow roads in Faringdon are unsuitable for heavy traffic and, in fact, the first road scheme for diverting traffic from the town center of Faringdon was proposed in 1947. The recent increases in traffic volume have only reinforced the feeling of the local community that a bypass is urgently needed. In 1970 the Ministry of Transport decided that an inner relief road would not solve the town's traffic problem and concluded that 'the provision of a bypass clear of the town was undoubtedly the primary need'. Subsequently the Department of Environment placed a Faringdon bypass on the list of principal roads to be planned.

In July 1973 the Faringdon Rural District Council produced a report entitled *A Facelift for Faringdon* which concludes that any improvements made to property would soon be lost if traffic continued to use the town center as a major thoroughfare. These comments echo the feeling that emerged from a public meeting held in Faringdon in June 1973 to discuss the proposed bypass scheme. The main conclusion drawn from members of the public was that a bypass was needed, and it was needed soon. The exact alignment of such a road was seen as being of secondary importance.

In this report we look at the present situation in Faringdon, consider why a bypass is necessary and evaluate, both quantitatively and qualitatively, the alternative routes that have been proposed. In all, six possible bypass routes have been suggested. Routes number 1 and 2 were proposed by the county council and presented to the general public along with a scheme (route 3) suggested by Faringdon Rural District Council at the public meeting in June 1973. Following the meeting routes 4, 5 and 6 were suggested by various units of local government and members of the public. Details of the routes are given in Section 2.

For the purposes of this study we have assumed that the road network in and around Faringdon will remain unchanged and that the only modifications would be those proposed in the bypass schemes. Finally, we consider the alternative routes only as general 'corridors' although we examine the important distinctions between routes in some detail. Only when a general route has been chosen is it realistic to consider details of alignment and design.

1   IMPACT OF TRAFFIC

In this section we consider the impact that traffic has had on the town of Faringdon and the main factors that combine to make a bypass an urgent priority. We outline the problems of traffic congestion, public safety and noise nuisance that are a function of the development of Faringdon as a main thoroughfare.

Traffic volume

In order to describe the trips of travelers on the existing roads in and around Faringdon, a roadside interview of a sample of travelers was undertaken in September 1973. The major information obtained was the trip origin and destination, the purpose of travel, the type of vehicle and the number of occupants. With this data it was possible to estimate the expected traffic on each of the proposed bypasses. The survey also enabled data to be gathered about the present conditions of traffic flow in the area. This survey provided information needed for the analysis of the economic viability of each of the alternative bypass routes. Data were collected at eight sites (see Figure 7.1). Counts were made on all major roads – A420, A417 and A4095 – to assess the volume and composition of traffic entering Faringdon. Similar counts were also taken on the roads around Faringdon, on the A420 into Shrivenham and on route B4508, which bypasses Faringdon to the south.

In summary, these data indicate that a large volume of traffic uses the main A420 route between Swindon and Oxford which passes through the center of Faringdon. Furthermore, contained within this overall large volume of traffic is a high proportion of trucks and other commercial vehicles. It is these vehicles that create the noise and dirt within the center of the town, especially as they climb the hills in low gear on leaving Faringdon. The narrow streets with steep gradients

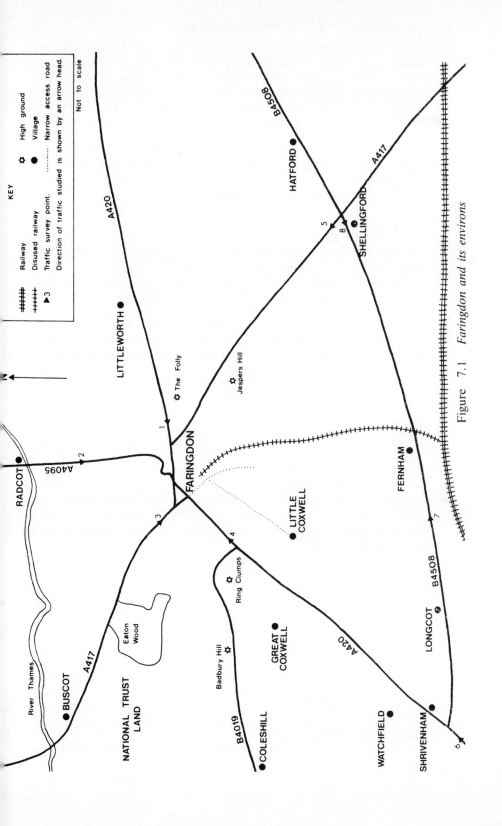

Figure 7.1 *Faringdon and its environs*

(1:20) in the center of the town are unsuitable for carrying large volumes of traffic, especially heavy and medium goods vehicles. Traffic flow through the center is controlled by traffic signals, as the roads are only wide enough to allow one vehicle at a time to pass. Any impedance to the traffic flow, such as trucks stopping to unload, parked cars or pedestrians, soon creates extensive congestion. As more and more traffic uses the A420 conditions can only deteriorate unless heavy goods vehicles are diverted away from the center of the town. These traffic characteristics also create two major problems for the residents of Faringdon: risks to the safety of people and property and a noisy and generally unpleasant environment.

Pedestrian safety
We gathered data on pedestrian flows and noise in the center of Faringdon in September and October 1973. The sites at which these measures were taken are shown in Figure 7.2.

The traffic counts around Faringdon and the pedestrian counts in the center of the town indicate that a potential danger exists of serious injury to person and property. The traffic flows through the town are large and the narrow streets are busy with pedestrians, a significant proportion of whom are vulnerable when crossing the street (including the elderly, children, mothers with babies, and so on). In the opinion of the Berkshire County road safety officer there exists a threat to public safety which can be eliminated only by the removal of through traffic from the center of Faringdon.

Noise nuisance
The terms 'noise' and 'sound' are often considered interchangeable, but this is misleading. Sound is a form of energy that can be specified explicitly in terms of its main parameters, that is, intensity, frequency and duration. Noise implies a human reaction – the sound is unpleasant, annoying or unwanted. Therefore when talking about traffic noise we are faced with the dilemma of relating the precise sound measurements that can be made to the more subjective human reaction to the sound.

The Department of Environment has laid down a standard for noise levels based on the intensity of sound (measured in decibels), its distance and its duration over an eighteen-hour period from 6.00 a.m. to midnight. The standard is 68 decibels measured at a distance of 1 meter (3.3 feet) from the facade of a building. If this standard is exceeded for 10 percent of the time over the eighteen-hour period, a resident becomes eligible for a government grant for insulation. Moreover, research shows that low ambient noise levels with irregular traffic flows can be more annoying than a consistently noisier environment, where the sound level remains relatively constant. For example, a highway, although producing consistently higher sound intensities than a traditional urban street, may be regarded as more tolerable because the sound is steady.

Sound levels in and around Faringdon were recorded at the sites

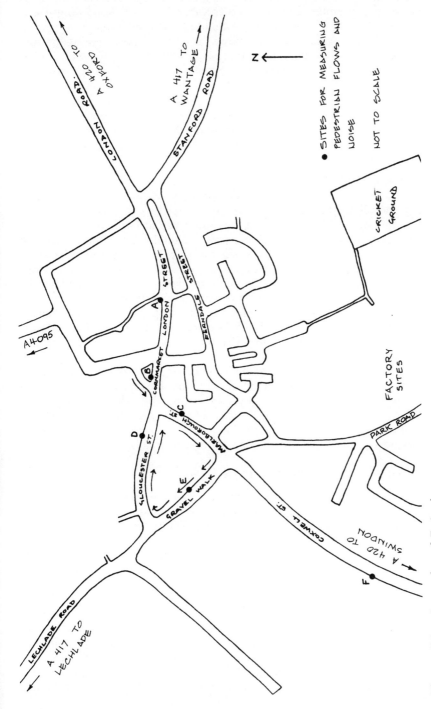

Figure 7.2 *Street plan of Faringdon*

used for pedestrian counts (see Figure 7.2) on five separate days between September 27, 1973 and October 12, 1973. Recordings were made one meter in front of the buildings at each site.

The results of these surveys show that those parts of Faringdon that are adjacent to major roads (that is, London Street, Coxwell Street, Marlborough Street, Gloucester Street and Gravel Walk) are subjected to extremely unfavorable conditions with respect to traffic noise. The sound levels are high (on average in excess of 85 decibels over the eighteen-hour period) and the flows are interrupted by narrow streets and gradients, thus producing peaked sound curves. The data confirm local feeling that traffic is a major source of disruption to life in Faringdon.

Other impacts
Apart from the problems outlined above, which we were able to quantify and measure, there are several other deleterious effects of traffic in Faringdon. Traffic flows of the type observed in Faringdon cause considerable nuisance; heavy trucks produce unpleasant fumes which can be damaging to health and which can discolor stone and brickwork. Equally, vibrations from heavy traffic can damage buildings and disturb local residents. It is impossible to assess how much damage the dirt and vibrations have had on the health and happiness of local residents, nor is it possible, in a study of this scope, to assess the damage to property caused by traffic. It is, however, clear that Faringdon is ill-equipped for and ill-at-ease with the type of traffic presently passing through the town.

Our studies of the existing environment in Faringdon thus lead us to conclude that the opinions stated by the Faringdon Rural District Council in 1973 are essentially correct and that 'the solution to the town's traffic problems largely rests in the bypass and until this is in being it seems as though Faringdon will have to suffer the ever increasing flow of through traffic, with all that it entails'.

2 PROPOSED ALTERNATIVE BYPASS

In this section we describe the proposed bypass routes and outline the main characteristics of each route as they would be apparent in traveling along them from west to east. The future bypass would be a two-lane road of total width 7.3 meters (23 to 24 feet) and the design and standard of the road would be independent of the actual route chosen. Landscaping and other detailed design features which are a function of the actual alignment chosen are not included at this stage of the evaluation.

A total of six bypass routes have been proposed for Faringdon but one of the schemes, which entailed the upgrading of route B4508, has already been rejected following preliminary engineering investigations. Of the five remaining routes, one is to the north of Faringdon and the other four to the south. The routes are shown in Figure 7.3. A brief description of the main features of each of the alternative bypasses follows.

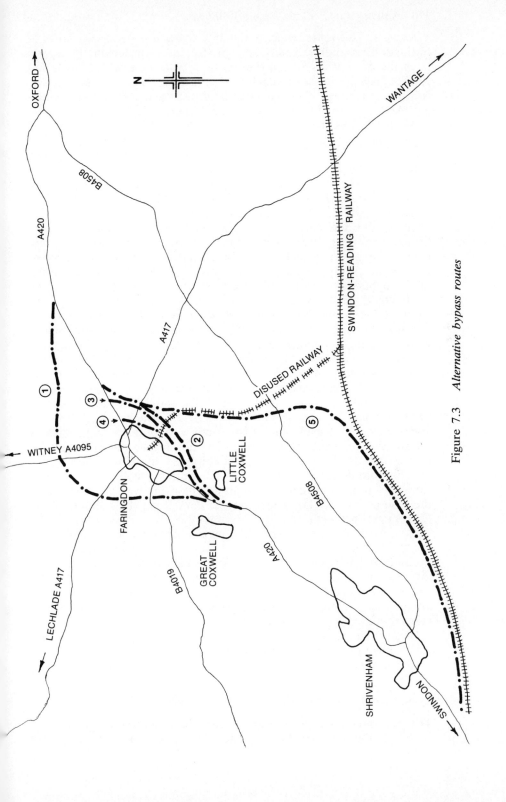

Figure 7.3   Alternative bypass routes

Route 1. This route, which is the only one that passes to the north of Faringdon, is approximately 8.9 km (5.5 miles) in length. It departs from the present A420 near the junctions with the roads to Great and Little Coxwell, crosses route B4019 on a bridge near Highden Farm, continuing through National Trust land, with junctions at routes A417 and A4095, to rejoin the A420 some 3.3 km (2 miles) to the east of the town near Barcote Manor. Because of the hills to the north of Faringdon this route would involve a fairly sharp curve near the intersection with the A4095 and a cutting at the point where it passes beneath the existing B4019.

Route 2. The second alternative route leaves the A420 at the same point as route 1 and runs south of the town, passing north of Wicklesham Lodge Farm and swinging north-east to cross route A417 near the Old Berkshire Kennels. The route rejoins the A420 at Wadley Lodge, one mile east of Faringdon. This scheme incorporates a link from the bypass adjacent to the disused railway line and connecting to Park Road. With this link the A417 would be closed on the town side of the bypass and traffic traveling from the Wantage direction to the town would use the bypass and Park Road link. The total length of this route including the link along Park Road is 7.7 km (4.8 miles).

Route 3. This route incorporates a realignment of the A420 south-west of Faringdon and, running south of the town, passes through the gravel pits and across Sands Road to climb Jespers Hill. The route then crosses the A417 and, unlike route 2, would allow access to the A417 in both directions, that is, to Wantage and Faringdon. It rejoins the A420 0.8 km (half a mile) east of the town. The total length of route 3 would be approximately 4.4 km (2.7 miles).

Route 4. On leaving the A420 south-west of Faringdon, route 4 follows the same alignment as route 3 until it reaches the gravel pits. It then swings north-east, crosses Sand Hill Lane, the disused railway line and Sanford Road to rejoin the A420 near the Folly. This route is similar to route 2 in that it provides a bypass link with the A417 along the disused railway line connecting to Park Road. It is about 4.0 km (2.5 miles) in length.

Route 5. This route also acts as a bypass for Shrivenham, leaving the A420 11.3 km (7 miles) to the south-west of Faringdon and following the railway line from Bourton to Alfred's Hill. It takes the route of the disused railway line north-east of Farnham, passing through Cole's Pits to follow the line of route 2 and rejoins the A420 at Wadley Lodge, 1.6 km (1 mile) to the east of Faringdon. Route 5 is about 14.5 km (9 miles) long.

These then are the overall alignments and main features of the routes which have been proposed. In the next two sections we evaluate each of the schemes on economic and environmental grounds.

3 ECONOMIC EVALUATION

The economic concept used to evaluate the proposed bypass schemes is called the cost-benefit principle. This principle as employed in highway project evaluation is broadly similar to that of the private businessman choosing to invest in those opportunities that bring him the highest return on his capital. Unlike commercial investment, however, the return on road investment is in the form of benefits to road users, not profits. In this analysis we calculate the changes in road-user costs following a proposed improvement and weigh the benefits against the construction cost of the scheme.

Two methods are employed. One involves finding the first-year economic rate of return (ERR) by dividing the road-user benefits for the first year of the improvement by its capital cost and expressing this as a percentage. The other calculates the costs and traffic benefits of a road scheme over an assumed thirty-year life and discounts them to the present. The effect of discounting is to remove the time dimension from the economic analysis. Discounting weights the costs and road-user benefits (in different time periods) according to the discount rate laid down by the Treasury for use throughout the public sector (currently 10 percent). The economic worth of a scheme is then expressed by the ratio of the net discounted (or present value of) benefits to discounted construction costs (NPV/C), which operates as a ranking device similar to the ERR.

Schemes can be ranked by their NPV/C ratios. A ratio of zero represents a scheme in which the user benefits exactly equal the construction and maintenance costs, and a scheme with a ratio of 1 has benefits that are twice the cost of the project. An NPV/C ratio greater than zero can therefore be regarded as economically justified, whereas a negative NPV/C ratio indicates that it is not economically justifiable to implement the scheme now. The public's money can be better spent in other ways.

Benefits of road schemes
The user benefits of a road improvement scheme consist of cost savings to road users, comprising the vehicle occupant's travel time savings, savings in vehicle operating costs and savings in accident costs. The savings in time and vehicle operating costs derive directly from the changes in speed and distance traveled. The accident savings result from lower accident rates on the improved roads.

The time savings are generally the most significant. Time is categorized as either working or non-working and given an average value. In the case of working time, empirical studies have indicated that a rate of approximately 25 per cent of the wage rate is applicable. Savings in vehicle operating costs consist of the costs of fuel, oil, tires and general vehicle wear and tear. Savings in accident costs as a result of safer roads can be obtained from road accident statistics.

The benefits of a scheme are found by calculating the difference in user costs between the existing network and the proposed improved network over the assumed life of the project. We used a computer program which simulates the movement of a complete year's traffic on each network, allowing for congestion encountered on each link and the delays at all major junctions. The vehicle operating costs, travel time cost for the occupants and the costs of accidents are determined for the existing network and the new network each year over a thirty-year period. Network and traffic volume information is required only for the first or base year of the evaluation. For future years, traffic growth based on national trends and subsequent changes in the network speeds are computed automatically by the program. The annual user benefits are obtained by subtracting the user costs on the improved network from the user costs on the unimproved network. These annual benefits throughout the thirty-year period are discounted to the present, that is, expressed as an economic benefit at present monetary value.

Costs of road schemes

The costs of a road improvement scheme that we need to consider are the estimated costs of construction, including the purchase of the land. These estimates are based upon engineering studies of the types and quantities of materials and labor required to build the road, bridges, drainage facilities, and so on. For this study the cost estimates were made by the Oxfordshire County Council Department of Planning and Highways. Table 7.1 presents the estimated costs for each route in 1974 prices.

Table 7.1   *Construction cost estimates*

Route	Cost (1974 $)
1	2,668,000
2 with extension	1,535,000
2 without extension	1,326,000
3	1,152,000
4	1,300,000
5	3,466,000
Shrivenham bypass	1,129,000

Cost-benefit analysis

The five alternative bypass routes are combined into two groups for the assessment. The first grouping consists of the routes that bypass Faringdon (routes 1, 2, 3, 4) and the second includes route 5 and route 3 from the Faringdon group plus an assumed local bypass for Shrivenham. By comparing route 5, which in fact bypasses Faringdon and Shrivenham, with route 3 and a Shrivenham bypass, the costs and benefits will be comparable.

The results of the analysis for the Faringdon schemes are presented in Table 7.2. Two versions of route 2 are investigated: one *with* the Park Road extension and the existing A417 closed to Faringdon traffic; and the other *without* the Park Road extension and with the A417 open. Hereafter when route 2 is referred to without qualification it is route 2 *with* the Park Road extension that is being discussed. For this

Table 7.2 *Summary of cost-benefit results for routes 1 to 4 (bypass open in 1978)*

	Route 1	Route 2 with extension	Route 2 without extension	Route 3	Route 4
Benefits:					
transit	598.460	-110.823	1,023.035	707.943	-455.295
junction	762.895	710.162	640.347	638.062	710.142
accident	-67.953	-96.600	82.984	-30.114	-229.209
total user benefits	1,293.402	502.739	1,746.366	1,315.891	25.638
Costs:					
maintenance	65.839	35.838	34.613	29.522	28.808
construction (C)	1,621.066	932.899	805.952	700.214	790.072
total costs	1,686.905	968.737	840.565	729.736	818.880
Net present value (NPV)	-393.503	-465.998	905.801	586.155	-793.242
NPV/C ratio	negative	negative	+1.124	+0.837	negative
1st-year benefit as % construction cost	1.6%	-1.5%	8.5%	6.5%	-6.3%

Notes:
(a) The figures are in $ (except ratios).
(b) Construction costs occur in 1977.
(c) Benefits and costs are discounted.
(d) All costs and benefits are in 1970 prices.

assessment the construction costs occur in 1977 and traffic flows over the new route in 1978.

A second analysis in Table 7.3 presents the assessment of route 3 together with a Shrivenham bypass, compared with route 5. In this assessment construction costs occur two years later, in 1979, and traffic flows on the new roads in 1980. This delay is a realistic estimate of the additional time that will be required to build route 3 and a Shrivenham bypass or route 5, the longest alternative scheme.

Discussion of results

Table 7.2 shows that only two schemes, route 2 *without* the Park Road extension and route 3, have positive NPV/C ratios and are economically justified as alternative Faringdon bypasses. The other alternatives have negative net present values and are not economically justifiable.

It is instructive to compare route 2 *with* the Park Road extension and the existing A417 closed to Faringdon traffic and route 2 *without* the extension and with the A417 open. The junction benefits are lower *without* the extension as there are fewer junctions. The travel benefits as well as the accident savings are negative on route 2 *with* the extension and positive *without* it. This is because with the A417 closed to Faringdon traffic all the movement to and from the Wantage area would be along the bypass and into Faringdon on the Park Road extension. This traffic would travel farther than it does on the existing network and thus the user travel and accident costs would be greater than with the A417 remaining open.

Table 7.3 shows that route 5 has a negative net present value, indicating that the benefits of one long bypass for the two towns do not justify the costs. However, route 3 together with a local Shrivenham bypass produces a positive net present value and a positive NPV/C ratio.

By comparing route 3 in the two analyses it can be seen that including a Shrivenham bypass produces greater user benefits. There are two reasons for this. First, the two-year delay in opening the bypass increases the benefits since traffic grows each year. Secondly, there are the additional user benefits associated with the local Shrivenham bypass. However, we must emphasize that the assumptions made concerning the Shrivenham bypass are based upon less than complete data. A detailed consideration of Shrivenham was outside the scope of this study, although the results suggest there is a case for a comprehensive analysis of the area with a view to the building of a local bypass at a later date.

So far we have made an assessment only of three quantifiable user benefits of a new road scheme: time savings, vehicle costs and accident costs. In the next section we perform an environmental evaluation on the alternative schemes and attempt to assess them on both quantitative and qualitative environmental considerations.

Table 7.3 *Summary of cost-benefit results for route 3 and a Shrivenham bypass and for route 5 (bypass open in 1980)*

	Route 3 with Shrivenham bypass	Route 5
Benefits:		
transit	3,382,074	1,232,293
junction	750,899	828,287
accident	−161,479	−291,117
total user benefits	3,971,494	1,769,463
Costs:		
maintenance	50,757	84,882
construction (C)	1,145,657	1,740,389
total costs	1,196,414	1,825,271
Net present value (NPV)	2,775,080	−55,808
NPV/C ratio	+2.422	negative
1st-year benefit as % construction cost	+19.4%	+3.0%

Notes:
(a) The figures are in $ (except ratios).
(b) Construction costs occur in 1979.
(c) Benefits and costs are discounted.
(d) All cost and benefits are in 1970 prices.

4 ENVIRONMENTAL EVALUATION

Evaluating road schemes in terms of their impact on the environment is difficult. The essence of environmental considerations is that they are subjective: different people have different conceptions of what is attractive and what should be conserved. Added to this there is natural self-interest associated with the planning of new roads. People will agree that a bypass is needed but do not want it near where they live or work. For these reasons, simple quantitative comparisons of alternative schemes, based on an enumeration of the number of acres lost, the number of trees to be felled or the number of planning applications affected, are inappropriate. They do not answer questions about which land is more environmentally valuable, which trees are the most attractive, or whether development is desirable.

In this section of the report we quantify those aspects of the environmental impacts of the alternative routes that can be meaningfully measured. Where such measurements proved impossible a systematic description of each alternative, listing the environmental benefits and disadvantages, is presented.

It should be remembered that only on very rare occasions can roads be built to the satisfaction of all those who live in the area. However, the answer is not 'to stop community developments that make life more comfortable, convenient and pleasant. To do that would simply deprive many people of the opportunities of a better environment. The answer must be to plan new developments so as to minimize the disturbance and disruption they can cause' (HMSO, 1972, pp. 1–2). In considering the bypass schemes proposed for Faringdon we have tried to assess not only the adverse environmental effect that each would inevitably have on the area, but also the improvement to living and working conditions in Faringdon itself.

Quantifiable impacts

Four categories of environmental impacts have been quantified; land take; traffic reduction in Faringdon; noise levels on the bypass; and severance of links such as footpaths and tracks.

Land take. One of the most important environmental impacts of any new rural road is the amount of land that it requires. Although the actual area of land required for each route would depend in part on the earthworks involved (that is, cuttings and embankments) and on the amount of widening and upgrading of existing roads, in general it can be assumed that land take is proportional to the length of the route requiring new land. The results for each route are presented in Table 7.4. Route 4 has the least environmental impact with respect to the actual amount of land taken and route 5 has the most adverse affect.

Two aspects of land take that are important in the Faringdon area are the possible loss of National Trust land and of farming land. Route 1 would require 2.80 hectares (692 acres) of land owned by or covenanted to the National Trust which is a body that aims to conserve areas

Table 7.4   *Land take*

Route	Length requiring new land	Ranking
1	8.9 km	4th
2	5.6 km	3rd
3	4.4 km	2nd
4	4.0 km	1st
5	14.5 km	5th

of outstanding natural beauty. Route 1 would also have a particularly adverse effect on farming, and consequently causes concern to the Ministry of Agriculture. Of all the routes, the Ministry would prefer route 3, which tends to follow the line of existing farm boundaries and requires a relatively small amount of top-quality farm land.

Reduction of traffic in Faringdon. Whereas land take can only be seen as detrimental to the environment, the reduction in traffic flows within Faringdon is an environmental benefit. Estimates of daily flows associated with each bypass route can be related to base flows at various sites within the town and a percentage reduction in traffic flows calculated.

In our surveys, we estimated traffic flows in Faringdon for August 1973. We found that flows in London Street are substantially larger than those in any other street in Faringdon. These figures show that the majority of traffic in the town is using the A420 Swindon to Oxford Road (that is, London Street and Coxwell Street) and that it is these high volumes that a bypass should be primarily designed to reduce. Moreover, very little traffic on the A420 would end its journey in Faringdon. The majority had destinations further afield.

In Table 7.5 the percentage reduction in traffic using the A420 is compared for each alternative route. Routes 2 and 4 are clearly the most efficient schemes in this respect: both remove 75 percent of the traffic from London Street and Coxwell Street compared with a 60 percent reduction with the next best route, route 1. Considering the overall situation in Faringdon based on the flows predicted at each of the five main sites, the differences in effectiveness between routes 1 and 2 and 4 are very small.

Table 7.5 *Predicted traffic reduction*

Route	Reduction on London Street and Coxwell Street	Ranking of bypasses	Reduction throughout Faringdon	Ranking of bypasses
1	60	3rd	58	1st
2	75	1st	54	2nd
3	49	4th	43	4th
4	75	1st	54	2nd
5	49	4th	43	4th

Predicted noise levels. Using data from our 1973 surveys it is possible to predict traffic volumes on each of the bypass routes in 1993, based on national trends. Using these predictions we were able to estimate eighteen-hour average sound intensities as recommended by the Department of the Environment. For the purposes of the comparisons presented here we have assumed an average speed of 75 km/hour (approximately 50 m.p.h.) on the bypass and have assumed that the number of heavy vehicles will remain a constant 20 percent of total traffic.

The figures presented in Table 7.6 are the maximum noise levels at 30 meters (about 100 feet) from the edge of the roadway. Routes 2 and 4 will have maximum eighteen-hour average sound intensities of 71 decibels at this distance at the point near the Park Road extension, but where there are no buildings within 100 meters (330 feet). Thus we can safely conclude that none of the routes would cause significant noise nuisance. Noise levels along the Park Road extension would also be in the region of 71 decibels, which could affect the forty or so houses along the road. However, it is difficult to make precise predictions in this case, as much would depend on detailed engineering and design work.

Table 7.6 *Predicted noise levels at 30 meters from the bypass in 1993*

Route	Maximum predicted volumes (vehicles per day)	Estimated 18-hour average sound intensity (decibels)
1	8,020	68
2	14,320	71
3	6,820	68
4	14,320	71
5	10,760	69
Park Road extension	7,500	71

The provision of a bypass would reduce the amount of traffic using the center of Faringdon. However, it is difficult to estimate what the reduction in noise level would be, or even if there would be one. The data gathered in Faringdon suggest that even with relatively small traffic flows and relatively small numbers of heavy goods vehicles high noise levels can be expected. The only conclusion that can be drawn is that future noise levels in the center of Faringdon should not be any greater with the advent of a bypass, although they may not be sufficiently reduced to be perceived by local residents.

Severance. As well as problems of severance within farms associated with land take, severance of footpaths and roads can be a serious environmental disadvantage. To assess the extent of the impact we counted the number of paths and roads each alternative route would cut. We present the results in Table 7.7.

Table 7.7 *Severance of footpaths and roads*

Route	Number of footpaths cut	Ranking of bypasses	Number of roads cut	Ranking of bypasses
1	11	4	7	4
2	6	2	4	1
3	4	1	4	1
4	6	2	4	1
5	11	4	10	5

Summary. Table 7.8 summarizes the quantifiable environmental impacts. In each case the rankings are in order of least environmental damage.

Table 7.8 *Ranking of quantifiable environment impacts*

Route	Land take	Effect on farms	Traffic reduction	Noise on bypass	Severance of footpaths	Severance of roads
1	4th	5th	1st	1st	4th	4th
2	3rd	2nd	2nd	4th	2nd	1st
3	2nd	1st	4th	1st	1st	1st
4	1st	3rd	2nd	4th	2nd	1st
5	5th	4th	4th	3rd	4th	5th

Qualitative impacts

In the last section we were able to rank the alternative routes in terms of their impact on certain aspects of the environment. However, there are environmental impacts that cannot be quantified, but are no less important. In this section we describe the major environmental benefits and disadvantages in a qualitative way. The classification of impacts as benefits and disadvantages is based in part on the consensus of opinion expressed in letters received following a public meeting in June 1973. We consider each route in turn.

Route 1. Environmentally, the main problem with any northern route is the impact that it would have on the countryside. What is now an attractive view would be drastically changed by a bypass. Much of the land is owned by or covenanted to the National Trust, who regard it as belonging to the public. In terms of disruption and accessibility route 1 would isolate a number of farms from Faringdon; and because of engineering difficulties created by the hills to the north of the town there would have to be a large amount of earth-moving during construction. In addition, it would be necessary to build a bridge where the bypass would pass under route B4019.

Route 1 does have one substantial environmental advantage. Since the vast majority of residential and industrial development is to the south of the town, a northern route would cause less of a change in the town's character than would a southern route. Schools and recreational facilities lie to the south, as do the majority of the outstanding plans for new construction. A northern route would not interfere with any future development of Faringdon, but equally it would not help to contain it. A southern route on the other hand could form a natural boundary to further developments.

Route 2. We shall consider route 2 in two parts: the southern section (that is, the A420 bypass); and the upgrading and widening of Park Road to carry the A417 traffic. Route 2 (*without* the extension) covers only the first part whereas route 2 *with* the extension covers both.

The southern A420 section would involve disturbance to farm life and disturbance to road users during its construction. Apart from the problems of land take discussed earlier, route 2 would pass quite close to a number of farms. Some disturbance to road users at the eastern end of route 2 would occur where it joins the A420. The other major environmental consideration relates to future planning and development within Faringdon. Several applications for new construction are pending along this route. On the other hand, a southern route such as route 2 could form a natural boundary to the development of Faringdon.

The extension of Park Road has a completely different environmental impact from the other routes. It is the only section of any of the routes that passes through a residential area. This section would directly affect some of the people living in Faringdon. The main considerations with this section of road are the increased accessibility that would result, against the disruption to the lives of the residents.

This area of Faringdon already has some industrial development. The road itself is fairly narrow and this scheme would necessitate a wider road. This extended and widened road would improve accessibility to and from the industrial site, but would result in approximately forty houses along Park Road being very close to a busy main road. Although this section of route 2 would result in a deterioration of the environment in Park Road, it would ultimately improve conditions in the center of Faringdon. Route 2 *with* the Park Road extension has the potential to remove all traffic from the center, even heavy traffic destined for Faringdon's industrial site on Park Road.

Route 3. This route is in many respects similar to route 2. However, the slight differences between the routes lead to considerable differences in their environmental impacts. One environmental disadvantage of route 3 is that it passes through local gravel pits which contain unique fossiliferous sponge gravels. Otherwise route 3 is environmentally superior to route 2. It tends to pass along farm boundaries, with consequently less damage to farm life, and like route 2 it forms an efficient southern boundary to the town's expansion. The main environmental disadvantage relates to route 3's efficiency as a bypass. Although it can remove all through traffic using the A420 from Faringdon, it does not relieve the town of through traffic on the A417. Heavy lorries traveling to the industrial site on Park Road would still have to travel through the town center.

Being sited away from the town and entailing no upgrading or improving of existing roads, route 3 would cause little disturbance to road users or local residents during or after construction.

Route 4. This route can also be considered in two sections: the road to the south of the town, which is designed to relieve the A420; and the upgrading of Park Road to provide a more suitable road for the traffic using the A417. The southern section is very similar to routes 2 and 3 but passes closer to the town. Several residential areas would be affected by it. In addition, the southern section passes through the local gravel pits containing valuable geological deposits.

In summary, it would seem that on environmental grounds the southern section of route 4 passes too close to the town and leaves little scope for future expansion. On the positive side, it is relatively short and would require little farm land. The other section of route 4, along Park Road, follows exactly the same route as the extension discussed for route 2 and therefore has the same environmental impact.

Route 5. This route is by far the longest. Despite this, its land take is not a major problem as approximately half the route lies either along disused railway lines or adjacent to the line. Using an existing alignment also minimizes the likely severance to farms. In a sense the old railway already forms a natural boundary to farm land. Nevertheless, along the sections of the route that diverge from the railway line the environmental impact is considerable. The route passes through several coppices of trees and cuts a number of footpaths and tracks. Although well away from Faringdon itself, this route passes very close to several farms and cottages.

Even though route 5 would not require much farming land, its visual impact and disruption to the rural environment would be severe because of its length. Moreover, being so far from Faringdon it has little utility as a boundary to future development and may be inefficient as a local bypass. People starting or ending their journeys near to the center of Faringdon would surely take the much shorter route through the center of the town.

Summary. Integrating the qualitative and quantitative elements of an environmental evaluation of alternative road schemes into an overall index is difficult. It requires some form of subjective interpretation of the relative importance of the qualitative aspects. It requires, for example, a decision as to whether the loss of farm land is more or less damaging than the loss of National Trust land. Such subjectivity means that there can be no unique solution. There is no one route that will be environmentally 'better' than all others.

Based on the quantitative evaluation, route 3 has the least damaging effect on the environment. However, it does have environmental disadvantages, especially with respect to the amount of traffic that would remain in Faringdon and its encroachment on the gravel pits and surrounding countryside. The extensions along Park Road, although damaging in terms of the disruption they would cause to residents, do remove far more traffic from the center of the town, and ultimately provide the potential for restricting the flow of traffic in the town center, for example, by pedestrianization.

We conclude, therefore, that route 3 does the least damage to the environment but that routes 2 and 4 with the planned improvements to Park Road have the greatest potential for significantly improving the environment in Faringdon itself. The overall conclusions of the combined economic and environmental evaluations are presented in the next section.

5   CONCLUSIONS AND RECOMMENDATIONS

In this study we have investigated the economic and environmental implications of five alternative bypass schemes for Faringdon: a northern route (route 1); three short southern routes (routes 2, 3 and 4), two of which (routes 2 and 4) also provide an alternative route for traffic using the A417 by improving the existing Park Road; and a much longer southern route (route 5) which bypasses both Faringdon and Shrivenham.

Route 1 was shown to be economically and environmentally impractical as a Faringdon bypass. A short southern route without extensions to Park Road was shown to have benefits to road users that justified the cost of construction. Of the three southern alignments considered, route 3 was shown to be preferable on a number of environmental grounds. The schemes incorporating improvements to Park Road to divert A417 traffic from the center of Faringdon were shown to entail capital costs that could not be justified in terms of user benefits. Since route 5 bypasses both Faringdon and Shrivenham, it was compared in a second analysis with a scheme for a local bypass around each of the towns. In this second analysis route 5 was shown to be impractical on both economic and environmental grounds.

The cost-benefit analyses of each of the five schemes proposed indicate that route 2 *without* the extension or route 3 would be the best economic proposition. There are however several factors in addition to user benefits that are not considered in the cost-benefit evaluation but are vitally important in the planning of rural roads. These are the factors that have been considered in this report under the general heading of environmental impacts.

New roads have benefits (and disadvantages) for people other than those who will eventually drive along them. In Faringdon a bypass will reduce delays to through traffic; and it will reduce the adverse effect (for example, noise and dirt) of heavy traffic on the town and its inhabitants. To concentrate on one objective in isolation from the other, however, could result in a planning decision that solves only part of the problem and may in fact make the problem worse. In Faringdon, for example, it might be possible to produce considerable benefits to road users by simply widening the A420, thus allowing traffic to pass more quickly through the town. However, the resulting net effect on the town could only be seen as a deterioration. A bypass should improve the situation both for road users and for local residents.

Unfortunately the cost-benefit analysis could not consider both criteria simultaneously. It could not trade-off capital costs against both environmental and user benefits. However, it is possible to supplement the economic evaluation with an assessment of non-users' benefits and environmental impacts.

In section 3 we showed that only two routes (routes 3 and 2 *without* the extension) produced positive net benefit-to-cost ratios and were therefore the only justifiable schemes in terms of user benefits. We also argued that routes 2 and 4, *with* extensions to Park Road, were the most effective in removing traffic from Faringdon, although they show low economic rates of return. These results suggest a paradox. Those routes that have substantial benefits to road users do little to improve the situation for local residents; and those routes that improve conditions in Faringdon are not warranted in terms of user benefits. In fact none of the routes proposed have positive benefits for both road users and local residents.

Our cost-benefit analysis based travel benefits and accident benefits in part on the change in the journey time and distance traveled. Table 7.2 shows that all the routes, except routes 2 and 4, have positive transit benefits, that is, for the volumes of traffic predicted on the bypasses over thirty years there would be overall savings in travel time and costs to road users. However, routes 2 and 4 have negative transit benefits because traffic using the A417 would in fact have a longer journey if it used the Park Road extension than if it traveled through Faringdon.

The magnitude of the increased cost to road users of the Park Road extension can be seen by comparing the total user benefits of route 2 *with* and *without* the extension. *Without* the Park Road extension, traffic on the A417 would still pass through the center of Faringdon, whereas with routes 2 and 4 access into Faringdon along the A417 from Wantage would be blocked. The overall difference in cost of a southern route *with* and *without* the Park Road extension, including both reduction in user benefits and increased construction costs, would be $1,371,799 over thirty years (the difference in net present value between route 2 *with* and *without* the extension). This figure represents the additional cost of removing traffic from the A417 as well as from the A420.

We therefore conclude that, initially, a short southern bypass should be built, the exact alignment of such a route being carefully chosen so as to minimize the impact that it would have on the environment. Of the three southern alignments considered here, route 3 is the most acceptable on environmental grounds. At the time of writing we conclude that the traffic using the A417 Lechlade – Wantage road should continue to travel through Faringdon; the question of traffic flows within the town can be reconsidered when the bypass is operational. Should the traffic volumes still be sufficiently high to cause adverse noise conditions it would then be possible to build an extension to route 3 along Park Road, thus removing additional traffic from the town center of Faringdon. Eventually, consideration should be given to introducing pedestrianization or restricted vehicle access to the town center.

8

Public Transportation – Bus Operations

Huddersfield, a city of approximately 144,000 people is in the county of West Yorkshire about twenty-five miles north-east of Manchester. In 1976 a major two-year study of bus operations in Huddersfield was completed for the West Yorkshire Passenger Transport Executive. The study involved three main phases. In the first, a series of surveys was carried out, giving a comprehensive review of travel needs in the area and the role of the bus system in meeting those needs. Next, investigations led to recommendations for immediate improvements in the bus network. Finally, studies were made of the likely effects of secular trends and national and local policies over a longer time period. The study team, headed by Andrew J. Daley and Andrew Last, produced a three-volume report, *Huddersfield Bus Study*, each volume covering one of the main phases of the study. In addition, a short report summarizing the entire study was prepared.

Information obtained during the first phase of the study was used to construct a set of computerized models for predicting travelers' behavior. Once calibrated and verified, these models were used to evaluate a number of alternative bus networks in terms of their effectiveness in satisfying travel demands. The results of these evaluations enabled the study team to make recommendations for short-term improvements in the bus network and in operating frequencies. Two sets of recommendations were produced, one to satisfy each of the two distinct objectives of the study of short-term improvements. These objectives were to provide: (1) the best available level of service for no additional subsidy; and (2) the current level of service for minimum subsidy. One of the findings of this phase of the study was that the current level of service could be maintained at a saving of over 6 percent in the annual cost of operating the system.

In reviewing the impact of the various recommendations of the *Huddersfield Bus Study* it was important to bear in mind that this extensive study of bus operations was begun in 1974. There had been hope at the time the study was initiated that improvements in the bus system could be implemented by providing the best available service for no additional subsidy (short-term objective 1). However, poor economic conditions, including double-digit inflation, plagued the United Kingdom between 1974 and 1976. By the time the results of this study were submitted to the West Yorkshire Passenger Transport Executive in 1976 it had become essential that West Yorkshire, like most local governments in the UK, find ways to reduce the rate at which their expenditure was increasing. Therefore it is no surprise that the Passenger Transport Executive, in 1976, approved changes in the bus network and operating frequencies that would reduce the subsidy, while still providing the current level of service (objective 2).

We spoke to Mr Brian Eastwood, district manager for the Kirklees area of the West Yorkshire Passenger Transport Executive, in October 1979 and learned that implementation of a major route network reorganization scheme was proceeding towards a target date in 1980. Because of the length of time that has elapsed between the original study and the implementation date of major service changes in Huddersfield, more recent surveys on passenger loadings and travel patterns updated from 1974 will be taken into account. The revised pattern of services will correspond closely to those recommended in the short-term study, taking the opportunity for improving operational efficiency by the amalgamation of services and the removal of duplication. New links are to be provided to meet increased demand in some areas, and routes deleted where demand has declined. The net effect of the proposed changes will be a slight decrease in overall mileage to achieve savings in operating costs, while as far as possible maintaining a level of service matched to the changing patterns of demand in the 1980s.

Looking back on it now, we can see clearly that the main value of the original study was in the provision of such a comprehensive and detailed data base. As Mr Eastwood said, 'The study got us started'. Without the evidence of the study it is doubtful whether the case for significant changes in the bus network could have been justified, even though in the event the short-term recommendations were modified to take account of more up-to-date information.

The medium-term recommendations, although less specific, have also had a fair measure of success. Nevertheless the changed economic climate brought about cuts in local government services from which the planning section of the transportation function suffered particularly badly. The study recommended greater consultation and liaison between land use planners and transport planners in the Huddersfield area and this has recently been achieved. In particular, options have been exploited in accordance with the study's recommendations for an improvement in the penetration of bus services in Huddersfield center by coordination of bus routing and traffic management, including a number of bus priority measures.

Finally, in the context of forced economies, it is interesting to note a slightly unusual aspect of this study: the setting of two objectives to be met by the recommendations for short-term improvements. The first objective, which we could call 'idealistic', called for the best available service for the current level of expenditure. The second objective, which we would call 'realistic', was to provide the current level of service at reduced cost. The decision to set dual objectives, we believe, reflects the dilemma faced even in 1974 by public transportation authorities. Patronage depends on a variety of factors, each of which interacts with the others. As patronage has declined, bus operators have had to increase fares, reduce services or obtain larger public subsidies. Although the situation in practice is more complex than this, the dilemma is clear: each of the possible alternatives is intrinsically unattractive. In this study it was decided to explore all the possibilities fully before reaching a conclusion on the most practicable, if not necessarily the most desirable, course of action. Time proved this decision right. At the start of the study it was confidently hoped the idealistic solution would be selected. By the end of the project it had become clear that the prevailing economic climate demanded a more realistic approach.

The report that follows is based on the summary report of the *Huddersfield Bus Study* and is, we believe, of particular interest because of the way it describes in general terms the development and use of the models for investigating alternative bus networks. The report is divided into four sections. The first section presents the context in which the study was carried out and summarizes the results of extensive surveys on transportation needs in the area. Section 2 gives the findings of the study of short-term improvements. In this section we have incorporated parts of Volume 2 of the main study and also parts of a subsequent report, *Bus Operating Costs in Huddersfield* (Daly *et al.*, 1977). Section 3 summarizes the study of potential medium-term developments in the bus system. It focuses on economic trends, local developments and policy options available to local planners. The final section of the report is a summary of conclusions and recommendations. All costs and user benefits have been expressed in dollars at 1976 prices. The average exchange rate in 1976 was 0.5541 pounds sterling per dollar.

Huddersfield Bus Study

ANDREW J. DALY and ANDREW LAST *et al.*

1 THE CONTEXT

A comprehensive review of the Huddersfield bus network was particularly appropriate in 1974. This was the year that the bus operation and its planning passed from local control to the West Yorkshire Passenger Transport Executive, a county-wide organization. Practical considerations in the local transportation system also made a comprehensive review essential at that time. Road improvements and pedestrianization in and around the town center and the construction of the M62 highway had greatly altered traffic conditions in the town, and the opening of the new bus station had brought a change of operating patterns in the town center. Finally, the need for a comprehensive review was indicated because the bus system in Huddersfield had developed by a series of amalgamations and routes that had previously operated in competition with each other were now the responsibility of one operator.

A comprehensive review of a system as complicated as a bus network requires reference to a large amount of essentially local information. Accordingly the first part of the study was devoted to the collection, assimilation and analysis of the local data that would give the study team the necessary understanding of local conditions and problems. Wide ranging surveys, based on extensive home interviews but also including roadside interviews, postcard rail and bus surveys and more detailed surveys of the bus system, were therefore carried out to assess the current situation. The findings of these surveys are summarized in the remainder of this section.

Population and transportation

Transportation systems and land use patterns in Huddersfield are strongly influenced by the unusual local topography and industrial development. The town's regional setting between the main conurbations of Lancashire and Yorkshire has brought about the predominantly east–west orientation of the inter-urban transport systems seen in the canals, railways and highway networks. The industrial development is concentrated in the river valleys, whereas residential development has spread up the valley sides and, more recently, to the flatter areas to the north and east of the town center.

The population living in the study area was estimated from the home interview survey as 143,600. Employment at the time of the survey in 1974 was close to the national average, but a higher than average proportion of women were working part-time, largely in textiles.

An analysis of the journeys made by those living in the study area shows a predominance of trips to be between the traveler's home and place of work or education. Just over half of all the trips made (taking more than five minutes) fall into those categories. This predominance means that the pattern of trips over the day is highly peaked, with 46 percent of the trips being made during the morning and evening peak periods (6:30 to 9:00 a.m. and 3:30 to 5:30 p.m.). Another important time for trip making is around midday.

The overall use of different transport modes is shown in Table 8.1. Most notable is the very low use of 'other' modes, particularly trains and bicycles. The use of different modes is associated with trip pur-

Table 8.1　*Percentage of all trips made by study area residents by each mode*

Mode	Car (driver)	Car (passenger)	Regular bus service	Special bus	Walk	Other modes
% trips in 24-hour period	31.5	12.7	33.0	1.3	19.6	1.9

poses, as nearly half the education trips are made on foot and most others are by bus; and more than half the shopping trips are by bus. For other purposes the car predominates, although many people go to work by bus.

The role of the bus system
The movements described in the previous section take place on a transport system that has many different components. The bus system, which was the main concern of the study, must realistically be examined in the context of these other opportunities available to the traveler.

The road system in Huddersfield is fairly extensive and free from congestion. The main radial roads and the inner ring road are broad and well aligned, offering good communication within the study area and connections with regional highways. Minor roads, however, are often narrow, steep and twisting. The bus network is necessarily complicated because of the steep hills and the scattered land use patterns. Most of this network is covered by buses of the Kirklees District of the Passenger Transport Executive, but an important contribution is made by the local subsidiaries of the National Bus Company. A total of about 180 buses are in service in the evening peak.

Nearly all of the routes serve the town center, either passing through it to link two suburban parts of the town, or terminating there, usually in the bus station. The dominance of this small area as an attractor of trips, the preference of these trips for the bus and the role of the center as an interchange for through trips mean that this central orientation must be retained as a major feature of any bus system. Nevertheless there are many important requirements for bus travel outside the town center which, for example, attracts very few education trips.

To the east of the center there are large residential areas served by bus routes using Wakefield Road. These routes usually either terminate in the town center or run through it to the New Hey Road. Analysis of the survey showed that although this cross-town movement was extremely important, linking in particular some of these residential areas with a large school complex, other movements to and from these areas were also important and were not met by the existing routes. Two such requirements were for access to the industrial areas on Manchester Road and Leeds Road. Another requirement was for a cross-town service from Almondbury to the west of the study area. A more detailed analysis of the existing routes showed an exceptionally high frequency on Wakefield Road – nearly one bus a minute at peak, including National Bus Company routes – that was not matched in every case by the demand. Particular attention was drawn to routes 17, 30 and 88/89, some of which have been adjusted since the survey.

The northern part of the study area is served largely by buses running along Leeds Road and Bradford Road. Most routes are cross-town, providing links to Meltham, to Honley and the Holme Valley, to

Newsome, to Crosland Moor and to Longwood. We identified no significant demands not currently met, but detailed analysis led us to question the cross-town value of the 66/67 indirect route to Meltham and the 20/21 link to Newsome. The north-western part of the area is served via New Hey Road and Halifax Road. In general these services cover the requirements for travel revealed by the survey and show a close match between demand and capacity. Thus few substantial changes in this area are indicated.

The routes serving the Colne Valley in the west of the study area are inextricably intertwined, leaving the town center by Manchester Road or through Paddock and criss-crossing up the valley to their terminuses. The cross-town routes are the well-used 40/41 and 60/61 services and the less used 66/67. This part of the study area is farthest from Huddersfield town center, and the centers at Golcar and particularly Slaithwaite are to some extent independent. The complex pattern of routes is difficult to analyze clearly but it seems that most of these routes have a limited amount of spare capacity.

The southern part of the study area, in the Holme Valley, is served by a wide range of parallel roads. These are good cross-town links to the northern part of the area and this provision generally matches the travel requirements. Detailed analysis of the routes seems to indicate a lower demand than is provided for, but the steep hills in this area require a wide spread of routes to reduce difficulties of pedestrian access.

Conclusions from a survey of this type are essentially detailed, so that we can draw out few general points. One such point, however, is that nearly all the significant requirements for travel are met by existing routes, but one or two possibilities for extended service were revealed. Some spare capacity in existing frequencies was indicated although often local circumstances would make its redeployment difficult. A fundamental problem for bus operation is the extremely peaked pattern of demand, caused by working and school hours, which requires very careful matching of peak capacity to demand to avoid excessive costs.

2 SHORT TERM IMPROVEMENTS

In commissioning a study of improvements in the Huddersfield bus system which could be implemented immediately, the West Yorkshire authorities set the study team the specific objectives to recommend a network and operating frequencies that would give:

(1) the best available service for no additional subsidy
(2) the current level of service for minimum subsidy.

A third objective, seeking a very much improved service with additional costs, was abandoned because restrictions on public expenditure imposed in 1975 made its implementation in the short term unrealistic. It was anticipated that the commissioning authorities would select the most appropriate service level for implementation in the light of the financial circumstances prevailing at the end of the study.

The method adopted to meet these objectives was based on the use of computer programs (code-named TRANSEPT) that had been developed by the Local Government Operational Research Unit in previous studies and were further enhanced for this work. These programs permit the rapid and detailed assessment of proposals for new bus networks, which can thus be evaluated without the need for practical trials.

The TRANSEPT programs were used to assess successively the currently operated network, then a series of networks designed by the study team. Three of these networks were based on radically different concepts of network design: one aimed to give maximum frequencies by concentrating on major routes; one gave maximum penetration to ultimate origins and destinations by utilizing as many roads as possible; and the third tried out a large number of new cross-town linkages. The fourth new network tested was a synthesis of these three, incorporating also many of the best points of the existing network. The final network, which forms the basis of the recommendations, was a further development of the synthesis network, adapted to facilitate the direct implementation of as many as possible of the recommendations.

Considerable attention was devoted to the assessment of the existing network, which achieved four important steps. First, it enabled the calibration of some of the behavioral models used to predict travel demand. Secondly, the assessment revealed a number of errors in the representation of the network and the demand for travel in the town which could be corrected. Thirdly, the accuracy with which the computer model replicated the observed patterns of bus use indicated the accuracy likely to be obtained in the assessment of other networks and hence the level of confidence with which the recommendations could be accepted. Finally, the assessment of the existing network gave a basis for the comparative assessment of alternative networks.

The assessments of the six networks considered a number of different aspects of their performance. First, estimates were derived of the contribution of the network to the overall transportation system of the town, the number of travelers who would use it and the extent to which car use would be affected. Next, the impact on the operator was estimated, comparing likely revenue with the costs incurred. Finally, the benefits to the users of the network were calculated as a measure of the service given.

These assessments were used in the process of network development, to ensure that the later networks tested gave improvements over the earlier ones and over the existing network. This process of improvement led us finally to the network (network 6) that forms the basis of our short-term recommendations. The final stage leading to the formulation of the recommendations was an investigation of the appropriate levels of service on this network at different times of the day.

The TRANSEPT model gives a very detailed representation of

the bus system and careful work is necessary to set up the computer model. This work is described very briefly in the next section. We then go on to describe the procedure used to develop the recommended network, and finally summarize the short-term recommendations.

Setting up TRANSEPT

Setting up the computer models for this study was a fairly lengthy process involving two major stages: calibration and verification. For calibration it was first necessary to estimate the parameters of the submodels that forecast the times that bus passengers will spend in the various phases of their journeys: walking, waiting and traveling in the bus. These times can then be used to calibrate the models that predict which routes bus travelers will choose and how many travelers will actually go by bus, rather than by car or walking.

The prediction of travelers' behavior in TRANSEPT is based on generalized costs. The generalized cost of a journey is a measure of the dislike of travelers for that journey. It includes not only the actual money cost of the journey, but also takes account of the times taken in the various phases of the journey – walking, waiting and traveling time – weighted by the dislike of travelers for each phase. The first step in setting up the model is to obtain accurate estimates of these costs and times. The analysis of survey data showed that the important modes of travel in Huddersfield are car, bus and walking, together accounting for over 96 percent of all trips made. Thus these are the alternatives we represented in the behavioral model.

The generalized cost function used for the bus mode in this study was more complicated than that used for the car and walk modes. This complexity arises partly because in a bus study we wish to model most accurately the behavior of bus users, but also partly because complexity is intrinsic to bus travel. A bus journey has components of time spent walking, waiting and traveling in the bus, as well as the fare, and each of these must be modeled accurately. To ensure accurate modeling of bus generalized costs, it was necessary to undertake two local surveys. The first covered bus running times, permitting the prediction of the times buses would take for any journey in the network. The second was a survey of bus passengers waiting times. The availability of these estimates of costs and times enabled us to calibrate the models predicting travelers' behavior and then to apply those models to give estimates of the numbers using each bus route at present, or with alternative operations. It was also necessary to develop a model for predicting choices in this study, estimating the numbers of travelers making a given journey who will go by car, walk, or use each of a number of bus routes.

When the various behavioral models had been calibrated we were able to verify the accuracy of the representation of travelers' behavior. The verification process requires first that we check that the qualitative representation of travelers' behavior is reasonable. This somewhat subjective check can then be supported more objectively by a quantitative verification, in which we compare the predictions made by the model with observations made on the streets of the town. The most stringent such test is to compare the number of passengers using a route as predicted by the model with the observed number, and this was the test we generally used.

Overall the agreement between modeled and surveyed passenger movements was excellent. Moreover, the model's representation of the levels of patronage on routes tallied well with the opinions of the operators' staff. With the representation of behavior also appearing satisfactory, we were confident in proceeding to use the model for the assessment of alternative bus networks.

Developing alternative networks

Information gathered from our surveys indicated that certain important movements in the town were not directly catered for by the existing network and one of the considerations in designing alternative networks was naturally to attempt to serve these movements. This information was reinforced by many helpful suggestions and much useful advice from the local operating staff, who also passed on to us proposals they had received from the public. At each stage in the design process, reference had to be made to the local topography, which determines the roads that are usable by buses and the difficulty of pedestrian access from residential or industrial areas to proposed routes.

The most valuable input to the design process at each stage, however, was the TRANSEPT analysis of previous networks in the process. The TRANSEPT output gives a wealth of detailed information on the effectiveness of routes in satisfying demands for travel, and this is invaluable in designing different patterns of routes for the same area of the town. The nature of this information makes it possible to design greatly improved networks after testing some initial ideas. In designing alternative networks, we worked in a three-stage process. First, we assessed a wide range of initial ideas. Then we selected from these assessments those ideas that had proved most successful. Finally, we refined the network developed to achieve maximum practicability.

The initial ideas tested were based on three radically different – and somewhat abstract – concepts of network structure. These three concepts were embodied in networks 2, 3 and 4, the existing network being analyzed as network 1.

- Network 2 aimed to give maximum frequencies on the main radial roads. To this end a number of existing services were simplified and the most direct path chosen for every route.
- Network 3 was designed to penetrate to the greatest extent possible the residential, industrial and shopping areas of the town. This network is thus in a sense the antithesis of network 2 and would generally offer lower frequencies.

• Network 4 was intended to investigate fully the possible benefits of cross-town linkages. This network minimized the use of the bus station, since in general only center-terminating routes use it.

With these overall approaches to network design, it was possible to design a wide range of alternative routes for suburban and town center operation and, after analysis by TRANSEPT, to select the best features of these networks for refining into the recommended network.

When these three networks and the existing one had been tested we were able to select their best points and put them together as network 5. In designing network 6, we took account of a wide range of operational considerations to facilitate the direct implementation of our recommendations. This network includes a number of marginal services, excluded from network 5, but providing a service to otherwise isolated areas. It thus gives a much more practical basis for recommendations that are to be implemented.

The following section describes the process of assessment and gives the results that led us to recommend network 6.

Assessing the networks
Assessing the merits of one bus network against another is complicated by the number of factors that must be taken into account. A network that performs well, say, financially may give a poor performance in serving its users or in attracting car-owners.

In addition to the operational assessments that form the main input to the design of new networks, TRANSEPT can give an evaluation of the performance of each network on several other criteria. For example, estimates are made of the likely diversions of travelers to and from car use or walking and the overall benefits given to bus users by the network. Of particular interest is the financial performance of the network, and facilities are available in TRANSEPT for estimating both revenue and cost for a network. In this study we found little variation in the proportion of travelers using buses or in the revenue, so that the main financial changes are in the cost of operating the network, which is largely determined by the number of buses needed in the peak.

The performance of the six networks tested is shown in Table 8.2, which shows the minimum requirements of buses for evening peak operation (3:30 to 5:30 p.m.) and the user benefits measured in dollars per hour. The minimum level used, which ensures that the frequency on each route is *just* sufficient *on average* to carry passengers wanting to travel, is to some extent an artificial measure, as on a number of routes fluctuations in demand would lead to too many passengers being left behind to be acceptable. Thus this minimum level is simply a useful concept for preliminary analysis, indicating which networks are likely to have most scope for saving, rather than the size of the savings that can be made.

Table 8.2 *Comparison of minimum number of buses required and benefits in the evening peak*

Network	Minimum number of buses required	Total modeled benefits to bus users ($/hour)
1 (existing)	123	61,625
2 (high-frequency)	99	62,744
3 (high-spread)	104	62,903
4 (cross-town)	96	63,971
5 (synthesis)	87	63,724
6 (recommended)	88	63,473

The figures in Table 8.2 show that substantial reductions can be made in the number of buses operated in the evening peak without consequent reductions in the modeled user benefits. The benefit figures, which are based on savings in time and cost, should be treated with caution for two main reasons. First, the generalized cost coefficients used in estimating these benefits are not fully consistent with those used for predicting traveler behavior. Most important is the absence from these figures of distributional effects. For example, comparing network 6 with network 1, we find an overall improvement in service; but a small number of travelers will find a much reduced service. It is difficult to argue that small gains for a large number of people can be added together and offset one for one with large losses for a small number. Secondly, some of the more detailed service changes recommended are not reflected fully in the model. This applies particularly to the assessment of network 5, which has less route mileage than some other networks, but which appears to offer quite good service.

The table shows that there is most potential for saving buses with network 5 and 6. We went on to investigate the possibilities for using network 6, which is preferable to network 5 as explained above, to meet the specific project objectives.

Defining service levels for implementation
The minimum service level used in the previous section gives the frequency on each route that will just carry the average number of passengers wanting to travel. Clearly fluctuations of demand throughout the peak period will cause this minimum level to be inadequate from time to time. For implementation we require higher and more realistic service levels. The objectives of this study required us to make recommendations for two specific service levels:

(1) the best possible service for the present subsidy
(2) the current service for minimum subsidy.

These two service levels are called level 1 and level 2 respectively.

To meet the objectives of the study it was necessary to extend the investigation in two ways. First, we considered improving the service on network 6 above the minimum. By increasing the peak output from 88 to 110 buses we estimated that the present service level (level 2) would be matched (to meet objective 2); and by increasing output further to 134 buses we could give an optimum service (level 1) at the present subsidy level (meeting objective 1). Secondly, we compared the operation of network 6 with that of the existing network in the morning peak (6:30 to 9:00 a.m.) and offpeak (11:00 to 2:00 p.m.) hours. The results of these investigations are shown in Table 8.3.

Table 8.3 *Comparison of numbers of buses and service levels on networks 1 and 6*

	Number of buses on service routes	Total modeled benefit to bus users ($/hour)
Morning peak (6:30 – 9:00 a.m.)		
network 1		
level 1	127	52,309
network 6		
level 1	127	53,343
level 2	110	53,240
Offpeak (11:00 – 2:00 p.m.)		
network 1		
level 1	96	24,910
network 6		
level 1	96	25,533
Evening peak (3:00 – 5:00 p.m.)		
network 1		
level 1	134	62,587
network 6		
level 1	134	65,841
level 2	110	65,005

It can be seen from Table 8.3 that the modeled benefits of network 6 show substantial improvements over network 1. These benefit figures should be treated with caution, however, since apart from the technical difficulties of reducing the various measures of service given by a bus network to a common basis, they cannot reflect the effects of an unequal distribution of the benefits. Nevertheless we can conclude that the substantial savings offered by level 2 operation can be achieved without a reduction in the overall level of service. Alternatively, an implementation can be made at level 1 that will substantially improve the service without additional cost.

The number of buses used for level 2 is 110 in both morning and evening peaks. This level is chosen to achieve a slight improvement in overall measured service and because it is probably near the minimum operable level. In effect it is an example of what can be achieved if financial savings are required. We have not made level 2 recommendations offpeak, since the cost and service balance offpeak is totally different from that in the peak and large-scale cost savings cannot be made.

The recommended network
In the previous sections we described the derivation and assessment of network 6, our recommendation for short-term implementation. In this section we outline the main changes that this network would bring.

The proposed changes, although affecting much of the network, are not radical. The route mileage of network 1 and network 6 are almost identical. Such changes as have been recommended are in the way the bus routes use the road network, particularly the cross-town linkages offered to passengers. Two main groups of changes are proposed to cross-town routes.

First, three new routes are included in the network that serve the demand, identified in the survey, between the residential areas in the east of the town and the industrial areas and schools in the west. These routes would link Almondbury and Lindley, Kirkheaton and Marsden, and Grosvenor Road and Slaithwaite, all via the town center. The TRANSEPT analysis confirms that these routes would be well patronized and could be run economically.

Secondly, a number of long low-frequency routes have been eliminated and replaced by services terminating in the town center. In this category are the 66/67, 20/21 and 92/93 routes. These routes carry no significant cross-town traffic and the demands can be more effectively and flexibly met by the recommended center-termination service.

In several areas we have recommended simplification of the network to allow the concentration of resources on principal routes. Of particular importance in this category are the 1–5 Golcar services, but we have also recommended simplifying the 6–9 Slaithwaite routes and the 10-14 Brackenhall–Holme Valley links. Simplification will also result from the omission of a number of routes that closely parallel other services. Such routes are the 60, the 76 to South Crosland (the Netherton service would remain), the 79 and 95. The 88/89 would also be omitted and the Fernside area served via Almondbury. Care has been taken to preserve accessibility and in some important areas, particularly Brackenhall, Honley and the town center, accessibility to the network would be improved.

In the town center we have made few recommendations for changes, since in many cases existing arrangements are the only possibility. One change we do recommend, however, is that the inbound buses that currently pass behind the bus station should instead use Market Street, stopping there to set passengers down if required. This would improve access to the town center and eliminate an awkward and potentially dangerous right turn.

No recommendations are made for changes in the operation of National Bus Company subsidiaries, whose route patterns and frequencies are usually determined outside the Huddersfield study area. These routes do, however, provide additional facilities within the study area, and care has been taken to avoid inefficient competition.

Cost analysis

In this section we summarize the results of an analysis of the costs of operating buses in Huddersfield under the present network and under the recommended network.

Recall that the objectives of the short-term study were to recommend a network and operating frequencies that would give:

(1) the best available service for no additional subsidy (level 1)
(2) the current level of service for minimum subsidy (level 2).

These objectives necessitated financial assessments of a network in order to determine the subsidy required for these different service levels. The subsidy is defined as the difference between the cost of operation of the network and the revenue received from it.

For level 1 we found that holding the number of buses constant also held constant the cost of operation. In fact none of the cost headings showed a change of more than a half of 1 percent. Revenue, on the other hand, was predicted to rise by 4 percent as a result of increased patronage on the recommended network, mainly from those who presently make their journeys on foot. Partly because there is so slight a change in the cost and partly because, as a result of public expenditure cuts, interest shifted more to level 2, we do not give further figures for level 1.

For level 2, however, the cost reductions are substantial following the reductions in vehicle requirements. These reductions were concentrated in the morning and afternoon weekday peak periods, no recommendations being made for reductions at other times. The estimated costs are summarized in Table 8.4. This shows that the bulk of the saving would be in crew costs, but much of this saving would be in reductions in premium rates for split shifts, rather than in cutting the number of staff employed. Other substantial savings come from time-dependent variable costs (vehicle servicing, and so on) and vehicle replacement costs. Altogether the total cost saving is just over half the present subsidy.

Table 8.4 *Operating costs of present and recommended network (level 2)*

Cost heading	Operating costs of present network ($ per year)	Estimated operating costs of recommended network (level 2) ($ per year)	Estimated net cost saving ($ per year)
Crew costs	3,421,200	3,129,000	292,200
Other time-dependent costs	1,886,200	1,810,600	75,600
Mileage-dependent costs	382,100	366,700	15,400
Vehicle replacement costs	719,800	614,500	105,300
Other variable costs	20,600	17,500	3,100
Fixed costs	1,404,000	1,404,000	0
Total costs	7,833,900	7,342,300	491,600

Thus the recommended network offers the operator very substantial savings in cost, without damage either to the service offered or to the revenue collected. This change will not solve many of the longer-term problems of the bus system (discussed in the next section), nor will it eliminate the current subsidy requirement. It does, however, give an opportunity to maintain an acceptable standard of service to the traveling public while achieving the cost savings necessary in the present economic circumstances.

3 MEDIUM-TERM DEVELOPMENTS

In contrast to the short-term investigations reported in the previous section, the goal of the medium-term study was not to make specific recommendations. Rather we aimed to indicate likely trends that would continue to influence bus operations and to outline various policy options available to planners seeking to make full use of buses in the overall transportation system.

Three specific areas are described in this section. First, we discuss the national economic trends in income, car-ownership and restraint on public expenditure, all of which will inevitably affect bus operation in Huddersfield but over which local planners can exert no control. We go on to consider the likely impact of the specific local developments that can be projected for the near future. Finally, we sketch out some of the policy options that are available to local planners and that seem to us to offer realistic prospects of improving the bus system. Throughout this study we have used 1986 as a planning year, but this should be taken as a general indication of the time scale of the problems under discussion rather than as a specific year when specific events will come about.

Economic trends

The most noticeable national trend affecting the bus industry in recent years has been the policy of severe restraint on public expenditure adopted by the government since the oil crisis in 1974. This policy has come at a time when bus companies were increasingly in need of subsidy after a long period of declining demand, fundamentally the result of rising car-ownership. The conjunction of these two pressures, which it seems reasonable to project as continuing for some years, require severe economies to be made by the bus industry. In West Yorkshire the 1975/6 budgeted general fares support was $6.4 million and although the council argued in their 1975/6 submission for continuation of support at that level (in real terms), it seems realistic to consider the options should the government not sanction this level of support.

Fare increases are the most obvious means of reducing a subsidy requirement; and indeed fares have been raised in Huddersfield as throughout the area. There is a limit, however, to which fares can be raised, where the loss of patronage and hardship caused by a further increase will outweigh the increase in revenue. Near this limit more attention should be paid to more sophisticated fare structures. Discriminatory fares, for example, would have two objectives. First, they would attempt to raise the fares for those who are willing to pay (for example, commuters) and retain low fares for passengers who could not afford increases (for example, offpeak travelers and senior citizens). Thus the maximization of revenue would be combined with minimization of hardship. Secondly, discriminatory fares would aim to encourage traveling habits in the population that are convenient for the bus company. Two examples of this approach are offpeak fares and prepaid passes, which can speed the boarding of passengers. Service cuts are another obvious means of reducing expenditure, but clearly they also reduce the service offered and also the passenger revenue.

In the short-term study we described another means of cutting the subsidy requirement without reducing the service or revenue, by a comprehensive review of routes and frequencies. Since economy measures are required, and since a full investigation of fare increases was beyond the scope of our study, we assumed as the basis for the remainder of the medium-term study that this option would be selected, that is, that the recommended network 6 would be implemented at the much cheaper level 2. We also considered the probable effect of the long-term trend of increasing family income. The main impact of increased income on the bus system is through increased car-ownership. Although some members of car-owning households do make trips by bus, they obviously do so to a much lesser extent than members of households without cars. Projections were therefore made of changes in car-ownership to 1986 and their likely impact on bus patronage.

Techniques for forecasting car-ownership are still the subject of much technical debate. For example, different projection methods can show a rise in the number of cars per head in Huddersfield from the 1974 figure of 0.20 to anything between 0.28 and 0.32 in 1986. Rather than entering the technical debate, we chose to investigate the likely effect of the extreme figure of 0.32 as showing the most drastic impact on the bus system. Somewhat surprisingly, the 60 percent increase in the number of cars owned in Huddersfield has a rather small effect on the level of bus patronage. Our best estimate of the loss of revenue was 9.3 percent in the evening peak, with a somewhat higher proportion being lost during offpeak hours. Thus perhaps the worse effect of increased car-ownership would be further to increase the difference between peak and offpeak service levels. This would clearly pose great problems for the bus system, unless measures can be adopted to spread peak loads over a longer period.

Local developments
The preceding section was concerned with the impact of national trends on the bus system in Huddersfield. Here we look at the effect of purely local developments. In this case we shall be looking for more detailed conclusions than were possible in the previous section, since developments scheduled before 1986 are usually intended for sites already specified.

In planning terms Huddersfield, however, is likely to prove an unusually static town over the next decade. Little expansion is likely – indeed a slight decline in population is projected – and major developments in transport systems are unlikely to be added to those completed in the previous decade. Nevertheless some commitment to development on a local scale exists and in this section we consider its likely impact on the bus system.

The most apparent such development is the building of new housing and the demolition of old. Information on demolition is difficult to obtain but a certain amount of data is available on the location of building developments, although the timing of completion is uncertain. Four sites are projected each to contain more than 200 new houses by 1986, and are likely to require adjustment to the bus services to meet their needs. Simple amendments to network 6 are likely to prove adequate to serve two of the largest developments. The existing network would be more difficult to adjust. Most difficulty, however, will be given by two other large schemes, for which access roads present problems. In general the smaller schemes will be moderately well served by existing or slightly extended routes.

Changes in school catchment areas, particularly for secondary schools, have very important effects on peak-hour bus services. Two main changes are proposed: to expand Newsome Secondary School and to convert King James Grammar School to a second high school for children from areas to the east of the study area. The former, associated with a nearby housing development, is likely to present few transport problems, but the latter development could cause considerable difficulty.

Industry is the most difficult type of development to predict, both in location and timing. It seems likely that most such development will be adjacent to existing premises and service by bus will continue as at present. Shopping development is likely to continue to be concentrated on the town center, although a center at Birkby is also projected. Some office development is also expected in the town center.

Policies and options

Having considered in the two preceding sections the trends and developments not under the control of the local bus planners, we now look at the options that they can control to improve bus services. These policy options obviously have to be linked with the policies of other planners, particularly those concerned with roads and land use. These three policy areas come together most strongly in the town center.

In planning for the town center a number of objectives and constraints are in conflict. Pedestrianization of a number of the main shopping streets has already greatly improved the pedestrian environment and for this reason there is advantage in closing more streets to traffic. This objective conflicts with the need for traders to get deliveries to their shops, although it would not cause problems for through traffic. For the bus system there are three main considerations. First, to provide an attractive service it is necessary to gain bus access very near the main shopping and office areas. Secondly, bus routes through the town center must be reasonably direct to keep down running times. Finally, enough space must be provided to allow buses to set down and pick up passengers at appropriate points.

While it was beyond the scope of this study to make detailed recommendations for radical changes to traffic patterns in the town center, we were able to formulate some proposals that are worth further investigation. These proposals aim at improving accessibility and reducing running time, principally for the routes using Wakefield Road. Tests using TRANSEPT indicated that the practical advantages and difficulties of the proposals to the operator would prove more important than any benefits or disbenefits to travelers.

A further policy variable relevant to town center planning is the price charged at car parks, and tests were carried out using TRANSEPT with much higher prices than are current. These tests showed that very high prices, of the order of $2 per day, were necessary to achieve appreciable transfers of peak-hour car users to buses. The impact of such charges, however, would be more widespread, affecting Huddersfield's status as a shopping center. It is therefore at the county-wide level that such proposals should be evaluated.

A problem that has been mentioned both in the short-term study and in the medium-term is the difficulty of coping with the peak. All possible measures should clearly be taken to reduce the magnitude of this problem, which is likely to increase. Flexible working hours are gradually becoming more widespread, but support from the local governments should be used to accelerate this trend. Attention should also be given to the possibilities for staggering school hours and the cooperation of education departments should be sought to this end.

SUMMARY OF CONCLUSIONS AND RECOMMENDATIONS

An extensive series of surveys was carried out as the first stage of this study, giving a comprehensive analysis of travel requirements in Huddersfield on which this and other studies could be based. These surveys revealed that 143,600 people lived in the study area and that they made 290,000 trips on a typical day, mostly between their homes and places of work or schooling. Nearly half these trips were made during the morning and evening peak periods. Most trips were made by car but a third were by bus and a fifth by foot. Very few trips were made by other travel modes. The bus network as operated in 1975 offered a wide variety of routes to the traveler, most converging on the town center, but covering most of the suitable roads in the study area. A number of the routes were run at low frequencies and several of these carried very few passengers. High-frequency routes were better patronized, but some of the peak-hour frequencies were not matched by demand.

To investigate the potential for short-term improvements, a computer model was set up using the TRANSEPT computer programs. This model gave an accurate assessment of passengers' reactions to proposed bus services and was used to evaluate a series of possible alternative networks. The final network, which we recommend for implementation, should allow cost savings to be made without cuts in the overall level of service. Alternatively, an improved service could be run without increasing the subsidy requirement.

The main changes recommended to achieve these improvements are:

(1) reorganization of the Wakefield Road routes, introducing three new cross-town services;
(2) replacement of several long, low-frequency routes by center-terminating services;
(3) simplification of operations in a number of areas.

Care has been taken to preserve ease of access to the bus network and in Brackenhall, Honley and the town center, improvements in this respect are recommended.

Looking into the future, we considered the effect of national economic trends on bus operations in Huddersfield. Restraints on public expenditure for the next few years will require significant savings in bus subsidy and the best way of achieving these savings will be the implementation of our short-term recommendations. If national income and car-ownership continue to rise bus patronage will clearly be reduced, but unfortunately the reduction will be more than proportionate outside the peak hours. Measures should be considered that try to persuade passengers to travel offpeak.

Local developments in Huddersfield will also require changes in the bus network. Housing developments projected for the next ten years can in general be served by simple amendments to the network recommended for the short term; there would be greater problems in changing the current network. Industrial and other developments are more difficult to predict, but it seems likely that existing or recommended routes can serve the new developments without amendment. We recommend consultation between land use planners, transport planners and the bus operators, to minimize future difficulties.

Finally, we considered options that might be exploited to improve bus services by coordination of bus routing and traffic management. The potential for such improvements was found to be largely in the town center, where issues were raised beyond the scope of this study. A package of proposals is recommended for further investigation.

9

Capital Investment Decision – Flood Relief

Towcester, a small town with a population of almost 3,000 located about sixty miles north-west of London, has long been susceptible to flooding. In August 1969 after several hours of very heavy rain, the town suffered a severe flood covering about a square mile and affecting 170 properties. Flooding occurred again in 1970. Although drainage improvements had been made in preceding years, local opinion began to favor further improvements. Therefore in 1970 Towcester Rural District Council contracted with a firm of consulting engineers to design a flood relief scheme. In order to obtain a grant from central government to pay for part of the construction cost, it was necessary to show that the scheme was economically justified. Thus the council commissioned a cost-benefit study of the proposed scheme.

The study was conducted by Richard F. Carter and Robert E. Wraith and two reports were produced: a summary report, *Evaluating Flood Relief in Towcester* and a technical report, *Cost-Benefit Analysis of Towcester Flood Relief Scheme*. Carter and Wraith found that the benefits of the scheme to the community, in terms of reduction in the costs of flooding both to property-owners and to community services, were very small in relation to the cost of constructing the scheme, which was estimated at around $660,000. As a result the ratio of benefits to costs proved to be 1:18. In spite of the fact that the proposed flood relief project was not justified in terms of its quantifiable benefits, Towcester nevertheless went ahead with a modified scheme in 1978.

The job of widening and straightening Silverstone Brook and lining it with concrete where it flows through Towcester began during the first week of August 1978. Reconstruction of several bridges over the brook had begun earlier and was nearing completion as work on the brook began. Thus seven years after the cost-benefit study was completed Towcester was getting its flood relief scheme. The scheme is more modest than the one originally planned. However, inflation has had an impact on its cost, which came to approximately $1,440,000 in 1978, compared to the 1970 estimate of nearly $660,000 for a larger project. The Northamptonshire County Council has shared the cost of the scheme with the district council. The county council has paid for the raising and widening of the bridges over Silverstone Brook.

The study concluded that the scheme was not justified on the basis of the quantifiable benefits to property-owners and community services, but that it could be justified on the basis of the need to locate a new housing development in Towcester. In fact it was determined after the cost-benefit study was completed that the 134 acres set aside for new houses were not on the flood plain and hence would not be affected by flooding as originally thought. Thus the developers of this land were granted planning permission by the county planning department and went ahead with the development. A number of houses were built before work on the flood relief scheme even began and by 1983 the development is expected to include over a thousand homes. Why then, with a benefit to cost ratio of only 1:18, was the Towcester flood relief scheme built?

The main reasons were the benefits that were not quantified – the relief for residents from the fears associated with flooding and the general environmental improvements that would result from reducing the likelihood of flooding in the town. In the conclusion to their report Carter and Wraith note that some residents of Towcester had expressed fears that they might drown in a flood. This is a very real and powerful concern and it had a strong influence on the Towcester Rural District Council. Therefore when it came to making a decision the Council was swayed more by these immeasurable benefits to the community than by the low benefit-cost ratio.

The Towcester Rural District Council and the Northamptonshire County Council were largely committed to providing flood relief for Towcester even before the cost-benefit study was commissioned and did not change their minds as a result of the study's analysis. The rural district council commissioned the study in order to provide an economic justification for the scheme they had proposed. If the scheme had been justified purely on economic grounds, the council had hoped to receive a grant from the Ministry of Agriculture to pay for part of the cost. But the scheme could not be justified on economic grounds and in fact, since little agricultural land was affected by flooding in the area, it was unlikely that the ministry would have covered much of the cost of the project if the results had been different.

Since Towcester went ahead with a project that could not be justified in terms of its benefits and costs, it seems reasonable to conclude that the study was pointless. We believe, however, that the study was needed and that it did serve a useful purpose. Most important, it helped to clarify the issues surrounding the project and to identify the benefits, both quantifiable and nonquantifiable, for flood relief. When it came time for the Towcester Rural District Council and the Northamptonshire County Council to make a final decision, it should have been clear to all concerned that the flood relief scheme was being built largely to overcome community fears, rather than as a means of preventing property loss.

Evaluating Flood Relief in Towcester is a good example of traditional cost-benefit analysis. It estimates the benefits and costs of a project over a number of years – the lifetime of the project – and through the device of discounting represents those benefits and costs in present monetary values. This having been done, the results can be presented in a way that is easy for the decision-maker to understand – a ratio of total benefits to total costs. Furthermore in this study researchers Carter and Wraith recognized the existence of a number of economically immeasurable benefits, and it was these benefits that proved to be the most important factors in deciding to go ahead with the scheme. We believe this study points up the need to identify such intangible factors and to bring them to the attention of decision-makers, even if they cannot be included directly in the method of analysis.

There follows a combined and condensed version of the summary and technical reports submitted to the Towcester Rural District Council in 1971. The first section presents the background to the study and describes the approach taken. The benefits of the proposed scheme are analyzed in Section 2 and the costs of the scheme are summarized in Section 3. Section 4 gives the conclusions. All costs have been expressed in dollars at 1970 prices. The average exchange rate in 1970 was 0.4174 pounds sterling per dollar.

Evaluating Flood Relief in Towcester

RICHARD F. CARTER and ROBERT E. WRAITH

1 INTRODUCTION

In August 1969 a combination of several weeks of fine weather followed by some hours of very heavy rain caused a severe flood in Towcester. The next year flooding again occurred, probably because of blockages in sewage pipes. As a result of these floods the Towcester Rural District Council commissioned a study of the town's drainage works by a firm of consulting engineers. In their reports (Howard Humphreys & Sons, March and July 1970) the consulting engineers proposed a flood relief scheme which would completely eliminate flooding from a five-year storm, that is, a storm of an intensity that would normally be expected once in every five years. The scheme would also alleviate flooding from storms of greater intensity and it was estimated to cost $660,000. An alternative scheme which would completely eliminate flooding from storms of greater intensity (those likely to occur once every twenty years) was considered, but finally rejected as being too expensive.

But even the more modest scheme represented a very substantial item of expenditure for a local government with Towcester's resources. However, in certain circumstances the Ministry of Agriculture is prepared to give a grant of up to 50 percent of the total cost of a flood relief scheme. The ministry specify that in order to be considered for a grant the scheme must be economically justified. In other words, the cost of alleviating flooding in Towcester must be justified by the economic benefits achieved. Thus the rural district council commissioned the cost-benefit analysis presented in this report. The objective of the study was to examine the costs of and benefits expected from a scheme to prevent the flooding of the low-lying areas of Towcester occasioned by a storm of an intensity to be expected once in every five years. In fact, as will be seen, it was necessary to modify slightly the scope of the study so as to include all of the likely costs and benefits, by considering storms of all intensities to be expected in Towcester.

At present there are some 94 properties including industrial and commercial premises and approximately 120 mobile homes on two sites which are affected to a greater or lesser degree by flooding. In addition to the existing properties there is a further area of land estimated at 134 acres which is included in the town development plan for residential development. The eventual development of this land may exacerbate the present situation by the creation of large impervious areas.

Method of approach

For most of the categories of benefit considered, the method of approach adopted was based on determination of the costs to the community of the August 1969 flood. Then, using the calculations produced by the consulting engineers of the likelihood of floods of different intensities, we predicted the costs which would be likely to occur as a result of flooding, (1) if the scheme was built and (2) if it was not. Subtracting the former costs from the latter thus gave the costs averted by the scheme, that is, its benefit to the community.

The one category in which this method was not employed was the effect on plans to develop for housing an area of land on either side of Silverstone Brook. Since this development cannot take place if the flood relief scheme is not built, the comparison here is between the cost to the community of development in Towcester with that of development in the next best alternative site(s).

It is important to make clear that the costs and benefits to be considered are the costs *to the community as a whole*. This does not mean that we discount personal costs, but we count them only when there is a net loss to the community. Thus, for example, if a shopkeeper in the flooded area loses trade to a neighboring shopkeeper who is not affected by flooding, the net cost to the community is nil, although it certainly is not nil to the individual shopkeeper. Also we count costs only when they are genuine resource costs. For example, we do not count the time of ambulance personnel, since flooding is only one of the emergencies which they are in any case employed to deal with.

The provisional analysis of the *benefits* which would have to be quantified was as follows.

(1) *Benefits to owners of public and private property* – the effect of prevention of flooding on:

(a) property values;
(b) direct or indirect loss and/or damage to private individuals,

industrial and commercial concerns, agriculture, schools, libraries and other public property;

(c) relief for residents from the fear of flooding;

(d) environmental improvements.

(2) *Benefits to community services* – the benefits to the community of the avoidance of costs resulting from the immediate effects of flooding and the disruption and/or damage to public utilities, including costs incurred by:

(a) police and welfare emergency services;

(b) fire department and air force mobile equipment and labor for pumping, drying out and so on;

(c) temporary rehousing, social security payments and welfare (food, bedding, clothing and so on);

(d) emergency communications and rescue operations;

(e) local community organizations and other voluntary help;

(f) sewage disposal, water supply, main drainage and refuse collection;

(g) telephone, mail, electricity supply and roads.

(3) *Effects on planned new development* – the increased availability of land for new homes within the town. The county comprehensive plan for the area provides for the development of approximately 134 acres (1,664 dwellings). Of this, approximately 95 acres (1,268 dwellings) would not be possible because of refusal of planning permission if the scheme were not undertaken. If this land is not capable of development because of the flood problem then other land would have to be found, since Towcester has been earmarked as a center of development.

Costs presented no problems since the proposed scheme was a straightforward engineering job of laying a second drainage pipe and straightening out and lining with concrete the bed of an offending stream. There were no hidden or consequential costs of the kind which scientific analysis might be expected to disclose. Accordingly the study was primarily an exercise in quantifying benefits, though as both costs and benefits arose at different times it was necessary to reduce them to a common time basis and this was done by the device of discounting.

2 BENEFITS OF THE SCHEME

In this section we describe how we estimated the cost to the community of the 1969 flood. We then describe how these costs are used to estimate the benefits likely to accrue in the future from the proposed flood relief scheme. The benefits are discussed under the three headings outlined in Section 1: benefits to property-owners, benefits to community services and benefits to new development.

Benefits to property-owners

In the event, the benefits of the proposed flood relief scheme to owners of property in the flood-affected area proved to be very small compared with the effects on the planned new development in the town. This fact was of interest in itself, since at the outset of the study it was generally thought that benefits to property-owners would be the most important and that the justification of the scheme might prove to rest on them.

In estimating the benefit to the owner of a particular property, whether public or private, it is important to avoid falling into the trap of double-counting. If the property is liable to frequent flooding its value on the market will be lower than an otherwise identical property that is not so liable to flooding. If the property is actually flooded the owner suffers costs of various natures. But in calculating the total cost to the owner of having a property that is subject to flooding, rather than one that is not, we should not add the two effects, because one reflects the other. This means that there are two alternative methods of estimating the benefit of removing the danger of flooding: either to calculate the total reduction in value of properties that are liable to flooding; or to estimate the effects of flooding if it occurs.

To identify the loss in value of a property that is subject to flooding, it is necessary to compare the property with one that is identical in all other respects, for example, its condition, position, accessibility for transport, shopping, recreation and so on. This matching of properties is extremely difficult and although some studies have attempted it the results are rarely satisfactory.

The alternative method, which is the one we adopted in this study, is to identify for the property first, the frequency and intensity of flooding, and secondly, the amount of the cost incurred directly or indirectly as a result of the flooding. If this is done (1) assuming that the scheme is not constructed and (2) assuming that it is constructed, subtraction of the latter from the former will give the cost which will be averted by the scheme. In other words, this is the benefit to that property of introducing the scheme. Summing these figures over all properties gives the total benefit of the scheme to property-owners.

The analysis fell into two stages. It was first necessary to calculate the actual cost of flooding and then to estimate the benefit (that is, the prevention of comparable losses) over the lifetime of the flood prevention scheme.

Losses in the 1969 flood. The first problem was to find out how much damage was caused by flooding in Towcester. We decided that as the consulting engineers had based their calculations on the August 1969 flood it was best to base our calculations on the same flood. Thus we decided to find out the costs incurred by interviewing (in a house-to-house survey) the people affected. Since the number of properties actually flooded was not large (about ninety houses, fifty mobile homes and a small number of shops and business premises) and because we thought that the damage incurred was likely to differ widely from one property to another we decided to attempt as full a coverage as possible, rather than carry out a sample survey. Accordingly, during February 1971 we questioned those owning or occupying property in the area flooded in August 1969. A number of follow-up interviews took place later to cover some of the properties missed during the main part of the survey. We asked householders to tell us what the flood cost them in terms of property and possessions damaged or lost, of repairs or maintenance rendered necessary and of any other costs which they incurred.

In evaluating the answers to these questions care was needed. Clearly, in estimating values of private possessions some people over-estimated the value of things lost and others underestimated it. There was little we could do about this except to hope that the two effects canceled each other out. Another problem is caused by the need to replace some things, carpets, for example, when the old ones would have been good enough for some time to come. Where insurance was paid the amount was taken as an estimate of the value of the replaced object. Where insurance was not paid we somewhat arbitrarily took half the replacement cost for the new object. Next, people were asked, if householders, whether they suffered any loss of earnings and, if traders, whether they suffered any loss in stock or trade. Because the flood took place on a Sunday and was mostly cleared up before the next day few people suffered any loss in earnings. From the evidence collected, however, it seemed unlikely that losses in earnings would in any case represent a substantial figure, because flooding is most unlikely to last longer than about twelve hours. (The August 1969 flood went down within ten hours.) Losses in stock to traders were counted but losses in business were not. Finally, people were asked how long they took to clear up afterwards. This question was very difficult to answer. However, enough firm answers were received to provide the figures we needed.

Table 9.1 summarizes the main findings of the survey. The percentage of households and businesses interviewed was high but that for mobile homes very low, mainly because many of the original occupants in 1969 had moved.

The household survey told us the amount of damage that had been incurred in about half the affected properties. We needed to extend the findings to cover all properties in the affected area. To do this we examined the results of the survey to see if we could obtain a relationship between the severity of the flooding and the amount of damage suffered. As a measure of the severity of flooding we used the depth to which it occurred and examined the correlation between this and the total cost of damage suffered and the time taken to clear up afterwards. We did this separately for shops, private houses and mobile homes.

With private houses no simple relation was shown. Instead a more reasonable hypothesis was found to be that up to a certain depth the cost would be constant (corresponding to carpets being cleaned, for example); and that over this depth, damage would be at a higher level

Table 9.1   *Findings of survey on August 1969 flood*

Type of property	Number in flooded area	Number interviewed	Coverage (%)	Total losses recorded ($)	Average loss per property ($)	Average time taken to clear up afterwards (hours)
Private houses[1]	89[2]	55	65	9,876	180	28
Shops[3]	18[4]	12	67	14,776	1,231	58
Mobile homes	53[5]	7	13	1,291	184	33
Other businesses	10	10	100	23,600	2,360	—
All properties	170	84	49	49,543	590	33

Notes:
[1]   Includes a church hall, the Catholic church, the band rehearsal room and the football supporters' club, as well as houses.
[2]   Includes seven now unoccupied.
[3]   Includes shops, showrooms, bed and breakfast establishments, cafes and the cinema.
[4]   Includes two now unoccupied.
[5]   Estimated.

(corresponding to more structural damage). For shops and mobile homes we had less data and the assumptions were simpler. For the former we took the average cost per foot of flood water; and for mobile homes the average cost per home flooded. These results are summarized in Table 9.2.

Table 9.2   *Estimated costs of flooding*

Type of property	Estimated cost of flooding ($)	Estimated man-hours to clear
Private houses		
(a) flood depth less than 6 ins	89	25
(b) flood depth above 6 ins	295	30
Shops	659 (per foot of flooding)	60 (per foot of flooding)
Mobile homes	189	33

The figures thus produced were then used to estimate the total damage that would have been caused had all properties been occupied in August 1969. This entailed estimating the damage in properties for which costs were not known and adding this to the costs already ascertained. The total estimated losses of the August 1969 flood are shown in Table 9.3.

Table 9.3 *Total estimated losses to all properties from flood*

Type of property	Total estimated losses ($)	Total man-hours lost[1]	Total economic loss[2] ($)
Private houses	19,795	2,939	23,322
Shops	23,209	2,198	25,847
Mobile homes	8,517	1,798	10,674
Other businesses	23,600	—	23,600
All types	75,121	6,935	83,443

Notes:
[1] Includes allowance for time lost during flood as well as cleaning up afterwards.
[2] Total losses plus valuation for time lost at $1.20 per hour.

Table 9.3 also shows the effect of putting a monetary value on the time of those affected by the flood. There is much conflicting evidence on the value people place on their leisure (that is, 'non-working') time. We used a value of $1.20 per hour, a figure based on evidence produced by the Department of the Environment.

Losses in future floods. So far we have shown the costs accruing to property-owners as a result of the 1969 flood. We now convert these into the costs that are likely to accrue as a result of future flooding. Then, as explained earlier, the benefit of the scheme is given by the difference in costs with and without the scheme.

As part of their study of the town's drainage works the consulting engineers carried out calculations, based on past data, of likely levels of flooding for different intensities of rainstorms, expressing the latter in terms of the return period for the different storms. The August 1969 storm was calculated as having a return period of seventy-five years. Using these calculations and the results of our survey, we estimated the likely costs at each level of flooding. The results are given in Table 9.4.

Finally, from the probability of occurrence of each intensity of flood, these figures were converted into a single measure: the annual expected value of losses through flooding of all kinds. This is the amount of damage which, *on average*, will be caused in any given year. This does not mean that it will be caused *every* year, but that if we take a sufficiently long period, losses will average out to this value. Without the flood relief scheme, expected annual losses are $2,717. With the scheme they are $2. Thus we see that the annual value of costs *averted* by the flood relief scheme, that is, its benefit to property-owners, is $2,717 – $2 = $2,715. Capitalizing these figures over sixty years at a discount rate of 10 percent this amounts to a total benefit of $27,100.

Benefits to community services
When flooding occurs the community organizes rescue and other assis-

Table 9.4 *Estimated losses to property in Towcester for different intensities of storms*

	Return period of storm (years)	Estimated losses to all properties ($)	Annual expected value of losses for all levels of flooding ($)
	1	0	
	2	218	
Without	3	922	
the	5	2,130	
flood	10	7,135	
relief	30	27,919	2,717
scheme	50	48,196	
	60	64,354	
	70	79,299	
	75	83,443	
With the	below 60	0	
flood	60	268	
relief	70	393	2
scheme	75	982	

tance for those affected. The prevention or alleviation of flooding removes the need for this assistance and to the extent that this frees real resources, the community benefits from the flood relief scheme. This section describes how we valued the resources employed by the various community services during the 1969 flood.

Costs in the 1969 flood. The costs in the 1969 flood were very small although the net was cast wide in the search for any potential benefit of flood prevention. The costs to the emergency services included: the costs, additional to routine costs, of ambulance and police; the cost of a temporary emergency control office; and the costs of pumping and drying, undertaken by the fire department, the Royal Air Force and a local hospital. The total for these emergency services came to $1,682. The costs to welfare organizations included: social security payments (used as a proxy for distress caused by the flooding); temporary rehousing (in hotels and boarding houses); the costs to the county welfare department; and the cost of bedding distributed to flood victims and not recovered. This came to a total of $635. The costs of voluntary assistance included out-of-pocket expenses and time of Women's Royal Voluntary Service members and many local people, both in organized groups and individually and came to $1,620. For public utilities, calculations were made for repairs, making good, or additional burdens on drains and sewers, refuse collection and an electricity substation. The total cost was $264. Finally, for roads and road users, the time and extra running costs incurred by travelers in making detours, based on traffic flows obtained from the county

Table 9.5 *Resource costs to community services in August 1969 flood*

Service	Cost ($)
Emergency services	1,682
Welfare organizations	635
Voluntary assistance	1,620
Public utilities	264
Roads and road users	2,413
All services	6,614

highway department, and the costs to the department of repairing roads came to $2,413. These figures are summarized in Table 9.5.

Costs in future floods. As with losses to property-owners, the consulting engineers' calculations were used to estimate the likely costs to the community services of floods of different intensities. We made the reasonable assumption that the resources employed were proportional to the number of houses flooded. By calculating the number of houses affected at each intensity of flood, we arrived at an estimate of the cost to community services at each intensity (see Table 9.6). Then, again from the probability of occurrence of each of these floods, we estimated the annual expected value of costs both with and without the flood relief scheme. With the scheme, annual costs were $0.22; without it, $304.76. Therefore the annual benefit of the scheme to community services is $304.54, which capitalizes to a net benefit of about $3,100.

Table 9.6 *Estimated costs to community services for different intensities of storms*

	Return period of storm (years)	Estimated cost to community services ($)	Annual expected value for costs for all flooding ($)
	1	0	
	2	48	
Without	3	141	
the	5	261	
flood	10	736	
relief	30	2,995	304.76
scheme	50	4,504	
	60	5,295	
	70	6,301	
	75	6,614	
With	under 50	0	
the	50	0	
flood	60	20	0.22
relief	70	20	
scheme	75	59	

Benefits to new development

Effects on the county plan. Under the comprehensive plan for Northamptonshire County the population of Towcester is expected to increase during the next fifteen years by about 3,000 over its estimated 1976 population of 2,900. It is intended that most of this population increase should be housed in a series of new developments on land near Silverstone Brook, much of which is subject to flooding. This land comprises some 134 acres (planned for 1,664 dwellings), for 95 acres (1,268 dwellings) of which planning permission would not be granted if the flood relief scheme were not built. Hence one benefit of the scheme would be to enable this development to take place, and to measure accurately the benefit of the scheme it was essential to evaluate the costs of the alternative locations of this development. To do this it was first necessary to find an alternative to Towcester for the development. To the planners, however, there was no acceptable alternative, measured in planning terms, because for most reasons Towcester was ideal. This may have been a good argument in planning terms, but in economic terms it was less satisfactory. It was therefore agreed with the county planning department to adopt a hypothetical alternative. This alternative would be to assume that the development planned for Towcester would be split up into small parcels and situated in the villages in the rural area around Towcester itself.

A number of consequences followed from this decision. These consequences; and their effects on costs, are as follows.

(1) *Value of land used.* For design reasons, houses can be built at higher population densities when built in larger parcels than when built in small ones. The county planning department suggested that whereas they were able to build at over thirteen dwellings per acre in Towcester, if the development was built in smaller lots, they could only achieve seven or eight dwellings per acre. This would mean that instead of using 95 acres, a total of about 181 acres would be needed. The value of the additional 86 acres absorbed would then be counted against an alternative outside Towcester. But what is the value of agricultural land? The market price cannot be taken, as this does not reflect the true value, mainly because agricultural subsidies inflate the cost of land. What we want is the total social benefit of using land for agricultural purposes. This has already been the subject of considerable research and we based our calculations on the results of this work. We estimated the social benefit of land in the Towcester area at about $2.88 per acre per year, or $31.63/acre capitalized over sixty years. This figure was the same for both alternatives.

(2) *Sewage disposal.* Because in almost all the possible sites for expansion in the villages the sewage network is at or near capacity, new pipes and sewage treatment facilities will have to be provided. It is much less economic to do this in a number of packets than all in one. Provision of off-site sewerage for the 1,268 dwellings in Towcester was calculated by the consulting engineers at $337,822. Detailed figures for the on-site sewerage have not yet been produced, but the proposed

developers for the site estimated from current figures in comparable sites that the cost would be about $239,590 for the whole site. Thus the total cost of sewerage provision in Towcester is $577,412, or $455 per dwelling. By contrast, the provision of sewerage for two small schemes in neighboring villages will cost an average of $1,582 per dwelling, and this figure was used in the calculation.

(3) *Refuse collection.* The rural district council estimate that their present refuse collection equipment will be sufficient if the houses are built in Towcester but that if the alternative is adopted an extra collection vehicle will be needed. We estimate that the additional cost will be about $12,000 per year.

(4) *Other factors.* The Towcester alternative is favored for a number of other reasons. Shopping facilities, schools and recreational facilities already exist in Towcester whereas extra facilities will need to be provided elsewhere. None of these effects has been quantified because it is not possible to do so without more definite alternatives. However, they all work in favor of development in Towcester and because of this the cost we calculate for the alternative to Towcester is bound to represent a lower limit to the real cost. The resulting figure should be considered as indicative only.

Assuming the houses will be built in phases between 1973 and 1986, using the costs we have just discussed and discounting the future costs at a rate of 10 percent, we calculated the total cost for each alternative. In Towcester the total cost came to $436,000; for the alternative site it was $1,054,000. On this basis there was a net benefit to the community of building the new development in Towcester of $618,000. This figure was nearly enough to justify the flood relief scheme on its own.

Benefits to other projected property. Several properties were either being built or were planned and it was necessary to make some allowance for these. It was not possible to carry out a calculation like the one made for property already in existence, as damage to the properties in question could not be estimated with any accuracy. The projected community center, for example, is not comparable with any of the properties affected in the 1969 flood.

One measure was the cost of raising the buildings above flood level by means of a concrete pier. For the properties in question this came to a total cost of $18,000. If the owners were prepared to pay this it would be a measure of the worth to them of avoiding floods. But they had not paid it, so the worth of avoiding floods must be less than $18,000. On the other hand, the worth must be greater than zero, or the owners would be indifferent to flooding, which they obviously are not, so it must lie between zero and $18,000. There was some evidence that the true figure lay nearer the former than the latter, so rather arbitrarily a figure of $6,000 was taken.

The total benefit of the flood relief scheme to new development was thus about $624,000.

3 COSTS OF THE SCHEME

The costs of the scheme were calculated by the consulting engineers, and are set out in Table 9.7. The total capital cost was calculated at $659,000 at 1970 prices.

The $659,000 is taken as a straight cost to the community. In considering projects where the amount of money to be raised is very large the method of raising it, whether by loan or grant, must be considered, because the possible methods affect income redistribution in different ways. But the cost of this scheme, although large for a relatively small local government like Towcester, is very small compared with many central government schemes and its income redistribution effects are negligible.

Table 9.7 *Capital cost of Towcester flood relief scheme*

	Capital cost ($)
Silverstone Brook	
1 Widen, straighten and regrade the stretch of the brook between route A43 and the edge of the present town development	105,500
2 Concrete line the brook between this point and through the town as far as the Mill Stream.	203,700
3 Reconstruct and/or modify existing bridges upstream of the Town Bridge	74,300
	383,500
Wood Burcote Brook	
1 Construct duplicate culvert from the Plessey Factory to the Mill Stream	263,500
2 Widen, straighten and regrade the stretch of the brook between the Plessey Factory and the first culvert	12,000
	275,500
Total	659,000

4 CONCLUSIONS

Is the scheme justified?

Table 9.8 summarizes the findings of the study. The total measured benefit of the flood relief scheme to the community is estimated at $654,200 and the total cost of the scheme is $659,000. Thus on these figures the scheme shows a small net loss. But we have already stated that the effects on the county plan for new housing development in Towcester have been underestimated, so that the first conclusion we reach is that if the alternative that we have used for development in Towcester is a realistic one the scheme is justified.

But our alternative is a hypothetical one. It may be that it could never be realized. A better alternative may be to situate the development in Northampton, the largest city in the county, or outside the

Table 9.8   *Total benefits of flood relief scheme*

Source of benefit	Total benefit ($)
Benefits of reduced flooding to property-owners	27,100
Benefits of reduced flooding to community services	3,100
Benefits to projected property:	
(1) under county plan	618,000
(2) other projected property	6,000
Total	654,200

county altogether. In this case the benefit of the Towcester alternative, which here makes up almost 95 percent of the total benefit of the scheme will disappear. So justification of the scheme depends entirely on whether the alternative to development in Towcester is valid or not.

The second conclusion we draw is that the total benefit to the community of the almost complete removal of the possibility of flooding in Towcester, estimated at $36,200 (excluding the benefits to projected property under the county plan), is very small in comparison with the total cost of $659,000. The ratio of benefits to costs is only 1:18. It is likely that a more modest scheme would have a better benefit-cost ratio, but this would involve a higher risk of flooding and it may be unacceptable. If such a scheme were adopted the council would be taking the decision to allow a few people to suffer more frequent flooding so that the rest of the inhabitants of the area could pay less in taxes. This would not be an easy decision for the council to take.

Sensitivity analysis
An exercise of the kind we have attempted here is full of assumptions. It is important to know which of these many assumptions will have a significant effect on the conclusions if they turn out to be wrong. Normally an analysis of how sensitive the conclusions are to changes (an increase or decrease) in the values of the various benefits and costs is carried out in such a study, but in this case it is less relevant as the conclusions depend more upon whether we should include the benefit of new development in Towcester than upon the actual value of these benefits.

Consequently we have only performed one sensitivity analysis for this study. We determined how large the losses would have to have been in the 1969 flood to ensure that the scheme was justified, even ignoring the effects of the county plan. Assuming that losses in floods of lower intensity are correspondingly greater, we estimate that losses to property-owners and community services combined in the 1969 flood would have had to have been about $1,900,000, or over twenty times as high as they actually were, and the costs of floods of lower intensity proportionately higher, to justify the scheme without including the benefits of the county plan. This is a measure of the discrepancy between the costs of the scheme and the direct benefits it is likely to yield.

Unquantifiable factors

Finally, there are some factors that we have not been able to quantify. These include relief for residents from the fear of flooding and environmental improvements.

We have measured the benefit to the community of the flood relief scheme in economic terms. The economist assumes that people act as rational beings. But people do not act in this conveniently rational way. They are naturally afraid of the dangers of flooding. Their fears may worry them and intrude on their everyday lives. At meetings held in Towcester to discuss the problem of flooding many people, especially those living in the mobile homes, expressed alarm at the possibility of drowning, particularly if a flood occurred at night without warning. It is impossible to put a value on these fears. All we can do is to evaluate, as we have done here, the value in economic terms of the removal of the likelihood of loss of personal possessions. For rather different reasons the possibility of a death in future flooding cannot be allowed for. There are ways of putting a value on a human life and if the probability of a death occurring were known the *economic* loss could be estimated. But in the past no deaths, fortunately, have occurred.

The benefits of improvements in environmental conditions is also impossible to quantify in monetary terms, despite attempts by cost-benefit analysts. We can only say that, on top of the benefits we *can* calculate, extra ones, non-quantifiable, will be obtained. How great these benefits are we cannot say, although if the effects of the county plan are ignored they must be at least $618,000 for the scheme to be justified.

10

Regional Cooperation – Locating Refuse Treatment Plants

Toward the end of the 1960s the local governments in the Tyneside/ Wearside area of north-east England recognized that they were facing a severe, long-term refuse disposal problem. The problem resulted from two basic trends. First, the increased use of packaged goods was resulting in much greater amounts of paper, cardboard, plastics and tin cans per household. Because of this change in the nature of refuse it was predicted that the volume of refuse produced in the area would more than double between 1970 and the year 2000. Secondly, suitable sites for dumping refuse near to towns were being rapidly filled in, so that increasingly distant holes had to be used, with a consequent rise in refuse collection costs.

In 1966 twenty-one local governments in the Tyneside/Wearside area took steps to examine their refuse disposal problems jointly. The need was certainly most urgent. One of the larger authorities, South Shields, estimated that it had approximately two years' space remaining in its disposal site and was being forced to take drastic measures to conserve what little space remained. Other local governments in the area were experiencing similar problems.

After an initial examination of the situation the governments concluded that regional cooperation was not only necessary but also urgent. Through the cooperative spirit fostered by the recently formed North Regional Planning Committee, the short-term problems were quickly resolved – agreements were reached whereby those local governments which were running out of disposal sites were permitted to use sites of neighboring authorities. But what about a long-term solution? Were refuse disposal treatment methods such as composting, incineration, or pulverization needed? If so, what type of method was best, how many treatment plants were needed, and where should they be located?

To answer these questions, the committee commissioned a study of the area's long-term refuse disposal problems. The purposes of the study were to identify the most economic methods of organizing the disposal of refuse within the region. The study was conducted by John A. Green, Neil S. Lister and Brian Whitworth, who developed and used a computerized mathematical model of refuse generation, collection and disposal for the region. They determined that refuse disposal treatment plants were indeed needed and found the best number, location and phased installation of these plants.

In their final report, *Refuse Disposal in the Tyneside/Wearside Area,* Green, Lister and Whitworth recommended that either six incinerators or six pulverizers should be eventually built to serve the region. Six treatment plants were found to be the most economic number of facilities, based upon forecasted amounts of refuse, the best locations found from the mathematical model and the actual sites that were available on which to build plants. Using very conservative cost estimates for the present method of dumping untreated refuse, the study found that a system of refuse treatment plants would be more expensive than the present system up to 1990, *assuming* disposal sites could be found. After this date, however, a system of treatment plants was projected to be cheaper. In fact, using more realistic estimates of the cost of the present system, it was shown that treatment plants would provide a cheaper system immediately.

The study also found that six pulverizers were cheaper than six incinerators, by about $400,000 per year over the period 1971 to 2000. But it was pointed out by the research team that incineration was a better method of treating refuse than pulverization for two reasons. First, it created more hygienic disposal sites, hence greater public amenity, and secondly, it used up disposal site space at a much slower rate because it produced a more dense refuse. In their final report, however, Green, Lister and Whitworth fall short of recommending one method of treating refuse over another. They considered that the final choice involved some value judgments which should be made by the local governments in the region.

Regardless of the method of treating refuse that is adopted, *Refuse Disposal in the Tyneside/Wearside Area* makes it clear that solving the long-term refuse disposal problems in the region will depend upon the continued cooperation of the local governments which had joined together to form the North Regional Planning Committee. Each treatment plant recommended by the study would be used by more than one local government; in most cases three governments would share a plant. The study concludes that continuing to cooperate by building and sharing refuse treatment plants and reappraising this policy in light of actual experience would be the most economic arrangement for the governments in the Tyneside/Wearside area.

Green, Lister and Whitworth submitted their final report to the North Regional Planning Committee early in 1967. Eleven years later we spoke with David W. Jackson about how the report's recommendations were used. At the time the study was conducted Mr Jackson was a member of the North Regional Planning Committee in his capacity as cleansing superintendent for Sunderland. He had also served as chairman of the study's steering committee, and when we spoke to him about the implementation of the study's recommendations he was director of waste disposal for the Tyne and Wear County Council. In the intervening years the treatment and disposal of refuse had become a county function, while the collection of refuse remained with the local jurisdictions within the county.

Mr Jackson informed us that in 1967, following up the results of the study, the North Regional Planning Committee and the constituent local governments which it represented decided on a plan to build five incinerators over a period of six to eight years. Four of these were to be at locations recommended by the study. The fifth, which was planned for Newcastle, would be built instead of the two incinerators recommended for Newcastle in the final report and would have a location which differed from the study's recommendation.

The first incinerator was completed at the end of 1971 and the fourth in 1973. Construction of the fifth, the one to be located in Newcastle, was postponed in order to find a suitable site that would enable the plant to be linked to a new housing development for the purpose of providing residential heating. In 1974 refuse disposal became a county function and early in 1975 Mr Jackson found that there was no need to build the fifth incinerator. By operating the four existing ones on a twenty-four hour per day basis and using the two existing refuse transfer stations in Newcastle, it was possible to get by with the four existing incinerators.

By 1978 plans were under way to build a reclamation plant (completed in 1979) on the site in Newcastle earmarked for the fifth incinerator. This plant produces prepared refuse in the form of pellets which are used as fuel in the Newcastle district heating station, providing heat for housing and public buildings. The county council plans eventually to convert one of its four incinerator plants into a second reclamation plant and possibly phase out the remaining three incinerators, converting them to transfer stations.

The initial decision to build incinerators rather than pulverizers was made because the region lacked suitable refuse disposal sites close to the more heavily populated areas in the region. Treating refuse by incineration would help to conserve the sites that were still available and, therefore, reduce the cost of transferring the treated refuse from the plants to the disposal sites. The last three incinerators built had the same design. This resulted in considerable construction cost savings and subsequently has meant that fewer spare parts have been needed to be stocked because three of the plants can share spares. As a result the costs of construction and maintenance of the plants have been 5 percent lower than the cost estimates used in the study. Mr Jackson also noted that the quantity of refuse projected by the study was right on target.

Refuse Disposal in the Tyneside/Wearside Area helped twenty-one local governments jointly to solve an acute problem. The study showed that joint action, that is, the sharing of refuse treatment plants, would be approximately 10 percent cheaper than for each local government to continue to dispose of refuse individually. We believe one of the major benefits of the study was that it helped to clarify issues and to promote mutual cooperation and joint action. But this could not have been accomplished without the computerized mathematical model.

This study illustrates how a mathematical model of a very complex system is used to derive and analyze a large number of solutions that would have been virtually impossible to explore without such a model.

The model needed to describe the system of generation, collection, treatment and disposal of refuse for a region with a population of approximately 1,200,000 (in 1971). The system consisted of a large number of collection rounds which served a complicated distribution of population. Included in the model were all the relevant costs associated with the problem, such as the capital, maintenance and operating costs for the various types of refuse treatment plants under consideration, the refuse collection costs associated with operating various numbers of plants at various locations and the costs of disposing of treated refuse.

A number of different systems were studied through the model. First, the cost of disposing of untreated refuse, the system of disposal used in the region at the time of the study, had to be determined. Then the model was used to assess the costs of a system of one, two, three and more treatment plants properly located to minimize collection and disposal costs. Calculations could be made for various dates in the future by simply using forecasts of the amounts of refuse that would be generated then. Thus the computer model enabled a number of options to be investigated in a short time and was used to show the North Regional Planning Committee that, in fact, plants were needed. In doing so it promoted cooperation by demonstrating how a joint system of refuse disposal would benefit the communities in the region.

The final report of the study follows. All costs have been put in dollars at 1966 prices. The average exchange rate for 1966 was 0.3580 pounds sterling per dollar. The report is in four main sections. Section 1 gives the background to the problem. Section 2 describes the alternative refuse treatment and disposal methods that were considered. The third section analyzes these methods in terms of their costs and the projected amounts of refuse they will need to handle. It answers the questions: 'should plants be installed?', 'is the whole area suitable for plants?', 'how many and what type of plants are needed?' The final section describes the most economic location of refuse treatment plants for the region in terms of the proposed possible sites on which they could be constructed.

Refuse Disposal in the Tyneside/Wearside Area

JOHN A. GREEN, NEIL S. LISTER and BRIAN WHITWORTH

1 BACKGROUND TO THE PROBLEM

The long-term refuse disposal problem facing the local governments in the Tyneside/Wearside area originates from two basic trends.

First, the nature of refuse is gradually changing, so making disposal by the present method of controlled dumping without first processing or treating the refuse more and more difficult to achieve without nuisance to the public. The main features of the change in refuse are an increase in the amount of paper, cardboard, plastics and tin cans and a decrease in the amount of ashes. The predicted net growth in the volume of refuse produced in Tyneside/Wearside is from 2¾ million cubic yards of crude refuse per year in 1971 to 6¼ million cubic yards per year in 2000.

Secondly suitable sites for dumping refuse near to towns are being rapidly filled in, so that increasingly distant holes must be used, with a consequent rise in refuse collection costs.

The compounded effect of these factors has been to strain established refuse disposal methods and resources to the point where further adaptation is becoming difficult and expensive. Controlled dumping without transfer, which is the most commonly used method of disposal in Britain, has the advantages of simplicity and low costs. The collection vehicle discharges its load into a suitable disposal site where the refuse is flattened and covered with soil or some other suitable covering material by a bulldozer. It is apparent that the system will only operate economically if the disposal site is close to the collection round. For this reason, in a particular area only a certain number of sites are economically suitable for simple controlled dumping.

The growth in refuse production is causing suitable sites, reasonably near to built-up areas, to be used up at an ever-increasing rate. As nearby sites are filled activities must be transferred to sites which are progressively farther from the collection areas. Increasing urbanization and rising land values have also accelerated the rate at which disposal sites are being pushed outward into the countryside. The symptoms are seen in steadily rising costs and increasing difficulty in dealing with peak workloads. There must come a time when costs reach the point where previously uneconomic methods of refuse disposal must be seriously considered as long-term alternatives to controlled dumping without transfer. Many local governments, not only in the Tyneside/Wearside area, believe that they are dangerously close to this point.

Before considering solutions to the economic problem, it must be noted that there is also a social problem posed by the practice of controlled dumping which has nothing whatever to do with the problem of transporting refuse. The changing composition of refuse has made the control of disposal sites more difficult and this trend is likely to worsen. Public reaction to the existence of these sites will probably harden as urbanization spreads, perhaps even to the point where dumping at economically suitable sites will cause increasing public objections. This can be an absolute barrier to the continuation of controlled dumping.

In consequence, there are three major questions to be answered.

(1) How to use the collection vehicles and teams more effectively by either reducing or stabilizing their haul distances?
(2) How to use and conserve disposal sites efficiently?
(3) How to ensure that public nuisance from dumping is kept tolerably low?

2   ALTERNATIVE DISPOSAL METHODS

Of all the major alternative methods of disposal which could replace it, controlled dumping without transfer is unique. It requires only one fleet of vehicles whereas all other methods call for two fleets as well as plants.

Refuse disposal plants offer some advantages which are quite independent of the actual type chosen. The productivity of the collection vehicles can be improved by allowing them to discharge their loads at some central point where the refuse can be collected together and transported to the final disposal site by bulk-haulage vehicles. This process is described as transfer without compaction. Also, throughout this report the central point, or any fixed installation, is called a 'plant'. To prevent nuisance the plant will be some form of building with a certain amount of equipment for handling and controlling refuse. Transfer without compaction permits distant sites to be used for controlled dumping but does nothing to improve the objectionable nature of the dump or the use of disposal site capacity. Because of the voluminous nature of the refuse, the vehicles for the second stage of haulage also tend to travel with poor payloads.

One solution is to consider the installation of some form of mechanical plant which makes refuse denser: a treatment plant. If a reduction in the weight of refuse can be obtained at the same time as an increase in density, so much the better. The provision of treatment will not only provide the same advantages as transfer without compaction but, in addition, will improve vehicle payloads and the utilization of disposal site capacity. The nature of the refuse after treatment may also be such as to reduce the chance of public nuisance at the final disposal site.

Several kinds of plant for the treatment of refuse are available commercially and their operation will be considered below. But the basic questions are now reduced to the decision whether or not to install plants since plants provide facilities for better utilization of collection vehicles, make better use of disposal sites and can reduce public nuisance. If plants are to be used, the questions what type, how many and where follow. Also, since the problem may be common to neighboring local governments, to what extent does common ground exist between governments for the shared use of plants and disposal sites?

Methods of refuse treatment

It has been said that the object of treating refuse is primarily to make it denser. All the methods described here are intended to do this. Another important feature of some plants is that they convert refuse to a more hygienic material which the public may find less offensive.

An added and important bonus in any refuse plant is the ability to reduce the weight of refuse economically. This can be done by extracting from the refuse the salable material like paper, rags and tin cans. In this report no allowance is made for any income from salvage but all plants, except both types of transfer plants, are regarded as being equipped with magnetic salvaging units for tin cans.

Incineration is unique in that it achieves a considerable weight reduction over that obtained by salvaging. In this case the weight is lost as flue-gases and so can be said to be disposed of. The cost of controlling flue-gases adds significantly to the price of an incinerator. The building which houses a plant can also be made artificially expensive by emphasis on its appearance. There is no standard way to judge the cash value of appearance. Consequently it has been necessary to assume that buildings will be erected to high industrial standards and no more. Departure from this standard can easily double the cost of a plant. No cost-allowance has been made for service facilities, for example, canteens.

Finally there is the question of the capital costs of plants. The lifetime of a plant is approximately twenty years and in order to spread the expenditure evenly over this working life the actual capital cost of a plant has been regarded as a loan repayable over twenty years at 6 percent. The method of accounting used in the calculation of weekly costs treats the loan and interest as repayable in a number of equal instalments.

Because most plants represent a significant investment they should be used as intensively as possible. A working day of two eight-hour shifts is much cheaper than single-shift working and has been taken as normal. Three shifts work out only slightly cheaper so it is assumed that the third shift is held in reserve.

Main methods of refuse treatment are as follows.

Incineration. Modern refuse burns quite readily. Properly controlled, the ash and clinker obtained can be virtually sterile and unrecognizable as refuse. The conversion should reduce the weight of material by at least 50 percent and the volume by about 90 percent. Incinerator ash can be dumped with a minimum of nuisance and uses disposal site capacity very efficiently. The flue-gases from an incinerator must comply with the Clean Air Act and equipment to meet this need is taken as standard.

An incinerator burning about 200 tons of refuse in two eight-hour shifts (100 tons per shift) costs about $1,400,000 and will serve a population of about 180,000. This assumes that the plant comprises basic essential equipment and buildings only and that the site is ideal.

Pulverization. Violent mechanical agitation of refuse will break it down into denser material. The product is thoroughly mixed and of more uniform composition than crude refuse. There is no loss of weight but a volume reduction of at least 50 percent is normal. A proportion of this volume reduction is the result of the destruction of glass containers and the consequent elimination of the voids which they create in crude refuse. The breakdown of organic material in the refuse when it is finally dumped is accelerated and the initial settlement in the dump is more rapid. There is some risk that the accelerated bacterial process will cause putrefaction and smell if pulverized refuse is dumped in thick layers without covering. Shallow dumping is therefore recommended and can be especially useful in areas where the surface soil is sterile or very poor.

Of the many different machines available, the majority fall into one of two distinct classes: 'dry' pulverizers, which subject dry refuse to the action of an enclosed, rotating swing-hammer; and 'wet' pulverizers, in which water (or sewage sludge) is added to the refuse before or during a tumbling-and-slicing process in a revolving cylinder. Wet pulverizers have slight advantages over dry, but only at the expense of increasing the effective weight of refuse.

Although there are some immediate advantages in the use of disposal site capacity by pulverized refuse, after a relatively short time in the dump it is not significantly more dense than compacted crude refuse which has been given a year or two to settle. In the long run, therefore, the capacity of a disposal site is the same for both kinds of refuse except for the fact that pulverized refuse is claimed not to need covering material. As a result, approximately 20 percent of the site's volume, which would otherwise be filled with expensive (but essential) material like topsoil, could become available for refuse disposal. But compared with incinerator ash, which offers savings of up to 60 percent in the long run, pulverized refuse does not make the best use of disposal site capacity.

A major pulverizer handling 200 tons of refuse in two eight-hour shifts costs about $400,000 and serves a population of about 180,000.

Composting. The question of the use of composting as a method of refuse disposal is a vexed one. Pulverized refuse, especially when mixed with sewage sludge, forms a very useful compost provided that 'contraries' (glass, metal, plastics, and so on) are removed from the original refuse. Unsalable contraries must be dumped in the usual way and may amount to 25 percent of the original weight, or more if the market for salvage is poor.

In general terms, the capital costs of composting plants are the same as those for incinerators. Actual costs per ton are roughly the same provided that the compost can be sold. If no firm market can be found for the compost it must be disposed of wastefully and expensively by dumping.

Transfer with compaction. Simple transfer was mentioned briefly in a previous section. A refinement of this system is to install hydraulic equipment in the plant, or in the bulk-haulage vehicles, which compresses the refuse and makes it denser. No weight reduction results but volume reductions of 50 percent or more are possible. Newcastle County Borough currently operates a system of this type. The costs of major transfer/compaction plants are very similar to those of major pulverizers; the reduced running costs are more than offset by increased transportation charges.

The product of this process is of course still crude refuse and must be disposed of by controlled dumping, but this method does extend the range at which controlled dumping can be used.

Social aspects of controlled dumping
In choosing between alternative methods of disposal, the difficulties of achieving adequate control of the dumping of untreated refuse cannot be overstressed. No dump can be regarded as controlled unless it is run on the lines laid down by health authorities. Among other things this involves adequate sealing of the refuse with inert material, and material of this nature is both costly and difficult to obtain in adequate quantities.

There is undoubtedly increasing public resistance to the use of disposal sites for untreated refuse. When this is allied to the need for conservation of disposal sites within reasonably short haul range of urban areas, it is a factor which must receive serious consideration despite the present relative financial advantage of continuing to dump untreated refuse. With pulverized refuse nuisance from stray paper is definitely reduced, although not entirely eliminated. It is difficult to generalize about the possibility of smell from pulverized refuse. Some methods of pulverization when used with certain dumping procedures undoubtedly cause smell, but this is by no means true in every case. Incinerator ash is virtually sterile and odorless and, for obvious reasons, should be completely free of nuisance from blown paper.

It is difficult to put a cash value on amenity and aesthetic considerations or to make accurate long-term predictions as to the value of conservation of existing disposal sites. One simple approach is to set a price on controlled dumping which permits an acceptable standard of operation and to compare the total costs of this method of refuse disposal with the cost of methods not so likely to cause nuisance. If controlled dumping is more expensive overall than more hygienic methods, such as incineration, it can justifiably be abandoned. If not, the whole question of the value of public amenity must be considered in relation to the difference in cost between controlled dumping and its alternatives. This is the approach used in this report where for the purposes of comparison controlled dumping is assumed to cost $0.93 per ton of refuse. This sidesteps the economic questions of site conservation for the time being, but conservation must always be part of a long-term policy and must become increasingly important if present trends continue.

Land reclamation and refuse disposal
Land reclamation has many meanings. In this report it refers to the improvement of the environment by the filling in of undesirable holes and depressions caused by past industrial activity. Land reclamation has been linked with refuse disposal for many years. There is no doubt that all types of refuse – including building and demolition wastes – can be successfully used for the purpose, provided that very large quantities are not required in a short time. Moreover the introduction of refuse disposal plants would increase the scope of land reclamation considerably, for four reasons.

First, any kind of plant permits the final disposal site to be changed without disturbing the collection teams. Secondly, it permits the residue to be hauled more cheaply to the final site and so more distant sites can be used without serious extra expense. Thirdly, a larger number of local governments can all bring their plant residue to one site, so enabling it to be reclaimed much more rapidly. Finally, if the refuse is pulverized or incinerated, it is possible to use sites which would be impossible to reclaim with untreated refuse, owing to the nuisance caused.

However, to be properly referred to as reclamation, refuse disposal must finally achieve an improvement to the site. This means that the final treatment of the site will involve more expense than is necessarily demanded by the needs of hygienic refuse disposal alone. The interests of land reclamation are therefore not precisely those of refuse disposal, but continued cooperation between refuse disposal and land reclamation officials is certain to be beneficial to both services.

3   FINDING A THEORETICAL SOLUTION

In Section 2 it was demonstrated that the problems of refuse disposal can be reduced to the decision whether or not to install plants. Certain questions follow from this decision, such as: 'how many plants' and 'where?' The range of alternatives was described together with some of the social consequences of making a particular choice of plants.

The approach which operations research makes to the solution of the problems presented in the previous section is to develop a working model of the situation. In this case the model had to be a replica of all the important factors which go into a very extensive refuse collection and disposal operation, both present and future. With approximately one hundred existing collection rounds, a complicated distribution of population and many possible sites for plants, such a model is bound to be complex. Despite this, it must give simple answers. This could be achieved mathematically be using a computer to handle speedily the many calculations involved.

The objective of the computer model is to find answers to the questions: 'how many plants should serve the area?', 'where should they be installed?' and 'what type should they be?' The answers are given in terms of cost. But first there is the question: 'should plants be used at all?' The decision whether or not to use plants can be based on the difference in cost between continuing the present policy and installing a new system using plants. Proper allowances should be made for those factors that are not measurable in money values.

For this comparison to be made the costs of a hypothetical system using plants must be calculated. This is the purpose of the model. It is in fact a set of instructions asking a computer to imitate the operation of a refuse collection and disposal system in a geographical system representing the Tyneside/Wearside area. On being told how many plants of what type are to be considered, and where, the model works out the total weekly cost of that particular arrangement. In this way the cheaper arrangements could be found by a succession of trials.

In practice a second computer program is used which has the ability, on being told how many plants of what type, to work out automatically the best places to put the plants to obtain the cheapest arrangement. By using this model and the earlier one together it is possible to calculate the costs of systems using different numbers of properly located pulverizers, incinerators or controlled dumps. The number of plants having the least cost can then be selected.

By changing the preliminary information given to the computer, we can make it repeat these calculations for any date in the future, but the accuracy of its answers is only as good as the forecasts used to prepare the information and the assumptions inherent in the model. The results of these calculations are given in this section together with predictions of what will happen if plants are not used and estimates for a possible program of installations if they are.

Theoretical results
The calculations involving major plants are all in terms of incinerators or pulverizers. To obtain an estimate of the costs of composting or transfer with compaction simply read the results for incineration or pulverization respectively.

What will happen if plants are not installed? This question implies that the local governments in the area will continue to acquire and use sites for controlled dumping (without transfer) independently on a free-for-all, first-come-first-served basis until forced to cooperate by lack of sites. An individual government will use up its closest sites first and move steadily further afield. The overall effect is one of increasing haul distances. Curve A in Figure 10.1 shows the predicted costs per week for the area as a whole, when certain simple assumptions on the availability of disposal sites are fed into the model. The area as a whole includes, for the sake of completeness, the new town of Cramlington with Seaton Valley Urban District as well as the twenty-one local governments which formed the Northern Regional Planning Committee.

The sharp upward trend of curve A is a direct result of suitable disposal sites moving steadily farther afield. The actual increase in average haul distance for the area is from 3¼ miles in 1971 to 5 miles in 2000. The implication is that all local governments would still be using controlled dumping without transfer in the year 2000. But the use of an average haul distance hides the fact that individual governments might be faced with very serious difficulties long before that.

On this basis costs will almost treble by the end of the century and for four reasons this is a very conservative estimate. First, overhead charges are not allowed for in the total. Secondly, disposal sites are assumed to be equally available to all governments. At present this is untrue and certain local governments, especially near the coast, are already approaching a state of crisis. Thirdly, the costs are calculated on the basis of the most economic number of trips to the dump per day, in this case, two. And, finally, the effect of inflation is ignored.

The full part of curve B in Figure 10.1 is drawn through points

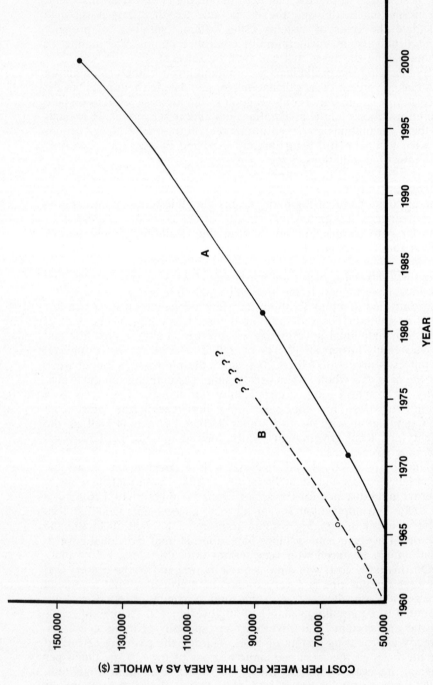

Figure 10.1   *The rising cost of the present system*

obtained directly from each government's *actual* costs for the years 1961/2, 1963/4 and 1965/6. The dotted portion is the projection of these costs approximately parallel to the predicted curve. The line ends in question marks because certain local governments, by then, would certainly have reached a state of crisis and would have taken unilateral action to install some sort of plant.

In the early years the margin between the conservative estimate and the projection of actual costs is about \$16,800 per week (approximately 16 percent) for the area as a whole. It must be emphasized that the dramatic increase in costs is almost entirely due to growth in what are usually known as collection costs. These are determined by the cost of manpower, the nature of the refuse and transportation costs. Actual disposal costs per ton (by controlled dumping) are assumed to be constant, *provided that disposal sites can be found and provided that controlled dumping continues to be feasible.* This, too, is a very conservative assumption.

Should plants be installed? This question is fundamental to the whole project. The case for installation of plants can be judged by making the assumption that plants will be installed and using the mathematical model to work out the consequences to find a favorable solution. All the following questions are subsidiary to this main one but must be answered first because of the need to make clear-cut comparisons.

Is the whole area suitable for plants? A preliminary series of trials using the model revealed that the best number of plants to serve the area as a whole was five. This was true whether the plants were incinerators or pulverizers. In addition, the calculated sites for the plants were unaffected by the type of plant.

These trials give an answer for the area as a whole but they do not justify the assumption that the area should be regarded as rigidly defined by the boundaries of the local governments which comprise it. One of the problems raised by this assumption is that by centralizing the refuse disposal function into five large plants some centrally located governments benefit at the expense of outlying jurisdictions who are faced with long haulage distances to the plants. An analysis of the preliminary trials showed that three areas, comprising in all six local governments, were in fact being penalized in this way. These areas are Seaton Valley Urban District including Cramlington New Town; Castle Ward Rural District and Ryton Urban District; Blaydon Urban District and Whickham Urban District. These areas are also those in which there are reserves of disposal site capacity so that to force them to use the central plant would be to make them send their refuse to the plant on one day only to receive it back the next. By allowing them to make separate arrangements, the expense of this backtracking can be avoided. For these governments controlled dumping is the cheapest method of disposal for the time being. As far as possible they should use disposal sites which are also being used by the major plants, thus avoiding duplication of dump machinery and men.

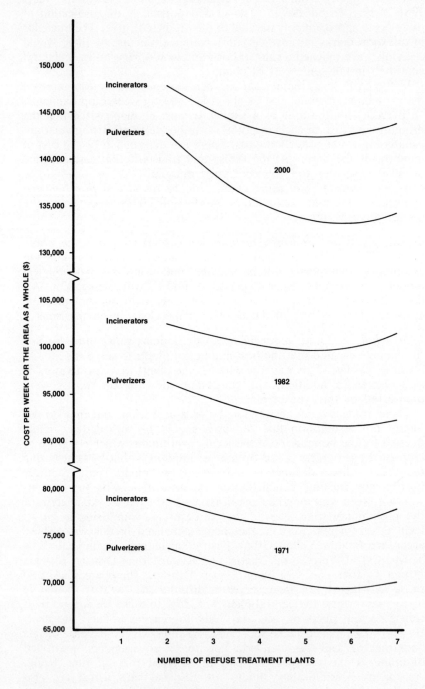

Figure 10.2 *Cost of refuse treatment plants*

In all later trials we used the computer model respectively to allocate the three areas specified above to controlled dumps at Low Steads dump; Prestwick Carr, or any equivalent site within the same range; and Ryton Greenside dump, or any equivalent site within the same range. With this arrangement, as opposed to the one in which all local governments use the plants, the area as a whole saves approximately $5,600 per week in the early years and rather more as time passes.

How many plants? With these adjustments, the trials for the best theoretical number of plants with optimum siting were repeated. Figure 10.2 shows the weekly cost to the area as a whole plotted against the number of plants (plus three controlled dumps) serving the area. The values given are for incinerators and pulverizers in the years 1971, 1982 and 2000.

As shown in the figure, the theoretical number of incinerators having the least cost is five, while the cheapest number of pulverizers is six.

What type of plant? Figure 10.3 shows how the costs of five incinerators or six pulverizers increase with time. For comparison both 'no-plants' lines from Figure 10.1 are also shown.

It can be seen that a system of six pulverizers (plus three controlled dumps) becomes the cheapest method of disposal after 1990 and remains so until the end of the century. But it is important to note that the gap in costs between six pulverizers and five incinerators at the end of the century is only $9,200 per week in a net weekly expenditure of $133,300, that is 6.9 percent of the total. The difference in cost, per ton of refuse collected, is only $0.70 per ton. This presents a difficult situation. Because of the uncertain nature of the forecasts used in the model, the calculated difference in costs cannot be absolutely reliable. Furthermore, the valuation of the benefits of land reclamation, dump hygiene, public amenity and, above all, conservation of disposal site capacity, although previously ignored, now become important.

In fact, incineration scores over pulverization on every one of the factors above with the possible exception of land reclamation. This emphasizes the deep conflict between the two goals of refuse disposal: cheapness and amenity. But how much is amenity worth? We do not believe it is our place to offer a definite recommendation on the slim margin of difference between pulverization and incineration. The choice must be left to those with first-hand and local experience of the issues involved.

On the question of the use of disposal site capacity, the use of pulverizers between 1971 and 2000 will require approximately 16 million cubic yards of site capacity – twice as much as the use of incinerators. The three scheduled controlled dumps will need a further 2½ million cubic yards.

Should plants be installed? The recommendation in this case is clear-cut. Plants should be installed as soon as possible after 1971 in view of

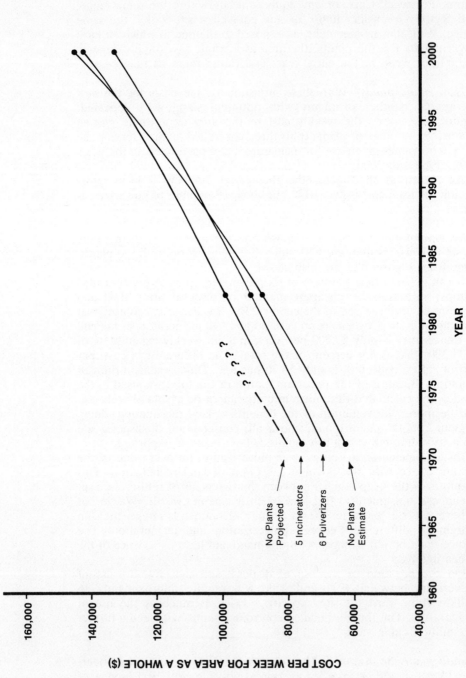

Figure 10.3 Cost of alternative systems

the discrepancy between the estimated and projected costs of not using plants. On an economic basis alone any system using plants must be fully operational before the end of the century.

Phased installation. Knowledge of the availability of possible future disposal sites is neither precise nor comprehensive. In consequence it is not possible to lay down a rigid, economic policy of phased installation of plants. The five plants, in effect, form five natural subregions, each one virtually independent of the others. Within these subregions the installations of the plant is only a question of timing not of phasing.

The most realistic policy for timing is one which takes account of local needs as they arise. Usually this will mean exhaustion of disposal space within a radius of about five miles. This again is a question for on-the-spot decisions, but it does seem clear that the coastal plants, that is, Tynemouth and South Shields, should have priority because of lack of sites for controlled dumping in these areas. Sunderland may need similar priority after clarification of the present situation. Gateshead has a reserve of disposal capacity for controlled dumping and Newcastle has its existing transfer facilities.

It is clear that a continuous review of the availability and restrictions on disposal space is highly desirable. This schedule could be used at any time in conjunction with the computer programs to evaluate relative priorities.

Summary of theoretical results
Costs. The weekly costs of the three alternatives analyzed in this section are summarized in Table 10.1.

Table 10.1 *Estimated minimum costs for alternative refuse disposal systems*

System	Weekly cost ($) of system in year		
	1971	*1982*	*2000*
All controlled dumps	62,284	87,421	143,169
Six pulverizers + three controlled dumps	69,420	91,543	133,313
Five incinerators + three controlled dumps	75,880	99,587	142,482

Plant positions. The calculated theoretical positions of the six pulverizers are given in Table 10.2.

Table 10.2   *Optimum locations for six pulverizers*

Plant number	Plant name	Ordnance survey map reference east	Ordnance survey map reference north
1	Gateshead	27.03	60.89
2	Newcastle East	27.47	66.48
3	Newcastle West	21.69	66.34
4	South Shields	35.87	64.32
5	Sunderland	38.32	56.34
6	Tynemouth	34.48	69.15

For five incinerators the calculated theoretical positions are given in Table 10.3.

Table 10.3   *Optimum locations for five incinerators*

Plant number	Plant name	Ordnance survey map reference east	Ordnance survey map reference north
1	Gateshead	27.03	60.89
2	Newcastle Central	24.58	66.21
3	South Shields	35.87	64.32
4	Sunderland	38.32	56.34
5	Tynemouth	34.23	69.44

The locations shown in Tables 10.2 and 10.3 need not be regarded as rigid. In practice an allowance of up to one mile may be made to meet planning needs without significantly changing the total costs. The positions of the sites are not affected by the type of plant so that if, for any reason, six incinerators were chosen, they would be installed at the places given for six pulverizers.

Despite changes in population the plant locations do not change appreciably between 1971 and the end of the century. Furthermore, both systems have the advantage that no refuse collection vehicle is forced to use the Tyne Bridge or Tunnel.

4   PROPOSED POSSIBLE SITES

Following the identification of the optimum sites for plants the possibility of actually erecting plants on the sites was examined by the steering committee for this study, composed of representatives from local governments in the Tyneside/Wearside area. For a variety of reasons all the theoretical sites were found to be impracticable.

The steering committee then undertook to supply a list of possible sites as near to the best sites as practical considerations would allow and entirely without prejudice to the ultimate use of the sites. In particular, Newcastle was asked for three hypothetical sites, a pair of

sites (Newcastle East and Newcastle West) for the six-plant arrangement and a single site (Newcastle Central) for the five-plant arrangement. Preliminary calculations revealed that the site of Newcastle
Central was sufficiently far removed from the best site to make a five-
incinerator system for the whole area more expensive than a six-
incinerator system using the Newcastle East and Newcastle West sites.
The situation in relation to six pulverizers was unchanged. Consequently, the use of the proposed possible sites implies that six plants,
irrespective of whether they are incinerators or pulverizers should be
used to serve the area.

Two further amendments to the theoretical solution were requested
by the steering committee. First, in view of the fact that significant
growth of population is expected in Whickham, this jurisdiction should
use the nearest plant (Gateshead) rather than continue controlled
dumping. Secondly, to maintain the balance of South Tyneside, the
northern half of Chester-le-Street Rural District should be included in
the area.

With these adjustments and using the proposed possible sites, the
calculations were repeated. The revised cost estimates are given in
Table 10.4.

Table 10.4 *Estimated costs using available sites*

System	Weekly cost ($) of system in year		
	1971	1982	2000
Six pulverizers + three controlled dumps	71,490	94,046	137,044
Six incinerators + three controlled dumps	78,360	102,707	146,666

The costs in Table 10.4 compare very favorably with those of the
optimum system, bearing in mind that they include the extra refuse
from Chester-le-Street Rural District. Table 10.5 gives the amount of
capacity in tons per day that will be needed to treat refuse at the
proposed sites, assuming the plants are operated for two eight-hour
shifts each day.

Table 10.5 *Capacity requirements needed at proposed sites*

Plant name	Daily capacity (in tons) in		
	1971	1982	2000
Gateshead	299	387	449
Newcastle East	192	251	287
Newcastle West	253	320	370
South Shields	200	260	297
Sunderland	291	374	432
Tynemouth	191	251	287

The local governments served by each plant are listed below.

- The Gateshead plant serves Gateshead, Felling, Washington New Town, Whickham and Chester-le-Street Rural District;

- the Newcastle East plant serves Newcastle (east of route A1) and Longbenton including Killingworth New Town;

- the Newcastle West plant serves Newcastle (west of route A1), Gosforth and Newburn;

- the South Shields plant serves South Shields, Hebburn and Jarrow;

- the Sunderland plant serves Sunderland (including Sunderland Rural district) and Boldon;

- the Tynemouth plant serves Tynemouth, Whitley Bay and Wallsend.

In addition, Seaton Valley, including Cramlington New Town, uses Low Steads for controlled dumping; Castle Ward uses Prestwick Carr *or any equivalent site* for controlled dumping; and Ryton and Blaydon use Ryton Greenside/Woodside for controlled dumping.

In most cases one plant serves three local governments and, in general, this defines the level at which cooperation is most beneficial.

Design of plants

The calculated capacities of plants given in the previous tables meet the daily requirements of their service areas exactly. In practice these capacities should be rounded off upwards to the nearest fifty tons.

The best policy is to round off the 1982 capacities to give the actual design capacities of the plants. The results are shown in Table 10.6. The reason for choosing 1982 rather than 2000 is that the through-put of no plant in 2000 exceeds its capacity in 1982 by more than 50 percent. Thus, the entire growth between 1982 and 2000 can be dealt with by changing from two-shift working to three-shift working as the need arises. By doing this the actual weekly costs in 2000 are very slightly reduced and the error caused by rounding off is compensated.

Table 10.6 *Plant capacities needed when rounded off to 1982 requirements*

Plant name	Rounded off capacity for design purposes (tons/day)
Gateshead	400
Newcastle East	300
Newcastle West	350
South Shields	300
Sunderland	400
Tynemouth	300

Rounding off to 300 tons per day of the Newcastle East plant and the Tynemouth plant, both of which have calculated capacities of 251 tons per day, leaves a very useful reserve of capacity in the area should future circumstances ever require Seaton Valley, including Cramlington, to use the plants.

Capital outlay on plants
The initial costs for each type of plant at each location, assuming the plants will be constructed in 1966, is given in Table 10.7. It must be emphasized that the costs shown in the table are for plants built to specifications requiring basic-essential standards only. An ideal site for the construction of the plant is assumed. It is also assumed that service facilities will be added whatever type of plant is chosen. Every $100,000 added to the capital cost of a plant adds $160 to the weekly costs after discounting.

Table 10.7 *Capital costs for constructing incinerator and pulverizer plants at the proposed sites*

Plant name	Capital cost (1966 prices)	
	Pulverizers	Incinerators
Gateshead	530,000	2,230,000
Newcastle East	450,000	1,790,000
Newcastle West	500,000	1,980,000
South Shields	450,000	1,790,000
Sunderland	530,000	2,230,000
Tynemouth	450,000	1,790,000

Compromise policies
In this report the installation of plants is dealt with in terms of either six pulverizers or five or six incinerators. All plants in the same system are of the same type. Of course a large number of mixed systems are possible. In fact for five plants there are thirty-two combinations of incinerators and pulverizers and for six plants, sixty-four combinations. To avoid confusion the costs of these systems are not given here but in

general the cost of a mixed system can be found by using the model.

It is hoped that this report will provide a general basis for the formulation of refuse disposal policy. If a compromise system of incinerators and pulverizers is agreed on we will be happy to carry out the appropriate calculations.

11
Discussion

Chapter 7 describes the evaluation of five alternative bypass routes that had been proposed to reroute traffic around a small town on a major road in order to reduce the congestion, noise and pollution from traffic through the center of the town. The study considered road construction costs, the benefits to road users and the environmental impacts of each proposal. The bypass that was built is a combination of two of the alternatives studied, incorporating the best aspects of each. Environmental issues played a major role in the selection of the bypass, which has since been built, and we believe this study is of particular interest because of the way the qualitative environmental impacts, as well as the quantitative ones, are identified, analyzed and presented in the final report.

An extensive study of bus operations in a city of approximately 144,000 is summarized in Chapter 8. The study was in three phases. The first involved collecting data on transportation needs in the study area and how well the bus system was serving these needs. This information was used to construct, calibrate and verify a set of computer models of bus operations, used during the second phase of the study to examine alternative short-term improvements in the system. As a result short-term improvements were recommended that were expected to reduce annual expenditures by 6 percent, while maintaining the present level of service to bus users. These savings amounted to approximately one-half of the public subsidy received by the bus system at the time of the study. The final phase of the study examined the options available to the city to cope with medium-term changes as a result of national economic trends and local housing and development. No specific recommendations were made as a result of this phase of the study, but a number of potential problems were identified and possible solutions suggested.

A severe flood in 1969 and flooding again in 1970 prompted a small town to commission the evaluation of a proposed flood relief scheme, presented in Chapter 9. The project was to involve widening and straightening two brooks, lining one with concrete where it passed through the town, and raising several bridges and was estimated to cost $2/3$ million. Against this, the economic benefits the project would provide to property-owners and to community services over a sixty-year period were found to be approximately $36,000. Based on these results the flood relief scheme could not be justified. However, the study recognized the existence of a number of non-quantifiable benefits of the project, such as relieving fears associated with flooding. It helped to identify and clarify the issues concerning flood relief for the town and the local government decided to go ahead with the project despite the economic case against it.

Chapter 10 presents the results of a study to help twenty-one local governments solve the problems caused by a severe shortage of refuse disposal sites in their region. The study found that treating refuse by either pulverization or incineration would be the most economic long-term solution to the region's problems and determined the best number and location of treatment plants that would minimize the total cost of refuse collection and disposal. Six plants were recommended, but it was suggested that these should be erected progressively as the needs of the region developed. In the event the local governments decided to construct five incinerators. The first four were built within six years and were located at the sites recommended. By the time the fifth incinerator was to be constructed it was found that the existing four could handle the refuse treatment needs of the region and a reclamation plant was built on the site earmarked for the fifth incinerator. The study demonstrated to the local governments involved that regional cooperation in the sharing of refuse treatment facilities would be approximately 10 percent cheaper than for each local government to act independently.

DESCRIPTION OF METHODS

In this section we briefly describe the mathematical models and methods used by the four studies included in Part Two. For a more complete description of these methods the reader is referred to published articles or books on these subjects.

Cost-benefit analysis
Which By Pass for Faringdon? (Chapter 7) and *Evaluating Flood Relief in Towcester* (Chapter 9) both employ cost-benefit analysis to assess capital improvement projects. Chapter 7 illustrates two criteria for evaluating such projects while Chapter 9 illustrates a third. In addition, the study in Chapter 7 analyzes the quantitative and qualitative environmental benefits and disadvantages of each of the alternatives examined. These, however, are not put in monetary units but are used to rank the alternatives on the basis of their environmental impacts. Nonquantitative benefits were also identified in Chapter 9 and in both studies the benefits that were not included in the cost-benefit analysis model played a significant role in the final decision.

The total cost savings to road users are the benefits calculated for each of the alternative bypass routes in Chapter 7. These savings result from reductions in vehicle operating expenses, accidents, and passenger travel time, all of which were expressed in monetary units. The first criterion used to compare the bypasses is their economic rate of return. This was found by dividing the total road-user benefits for the first year of operation of an alternative bypass by the capital cost of constructing that alternative. This is similar to the way many commercial organizations calculate their return on investment.

The second criterion used in Chapter 7 involved determining the construction and maintenance costs of each alternative and their road-user benefits over an assumed thirty-year life for the project. These costs and benefits were discounted to present value and a ratio was formed by dividing the net present value (NPV) of the total benefits for each alternative by the construction cost of that project. The NPV was defined as the difference between the total present value of user benefits and the total present value of construction and maintenance costs for each project. By this criterion a negative ratio means that the project cannot be justified economically; a ratio of zero represents a project in which discounted user benefits are equal to the sum of discounted construction and maintenance costs; and a ratio greater than zero means that the discounted user benefits are greater than the discounted construction and maintenance costs and the project can be justified on economic grounds. These ratios, as well as the economic rate of return, were used to rank the five alternative bypass routes.

In Chapter 9 the benefits were calculated by determining the reduction in losses to property-owners and to community services that would result if the proposed flood relief project were built. To do this it was necessary to weight these estimated losses by the probability that floods of different severity would occur in the future. The effects on land development in the area were also considered in determining the benefits of the project. All the benefits were discounted to present value, assuming the flood relief project would have a life of sixty years. The criterion used to evaluate the project was to form the ratio of the present value of all future benefits to the cost of constructing the project. The interpretation of this ratio is different from that found in Chapter 7, however, because total benefits rather than net benefits are used. Here, the benefit-cost ratio needed to be greater than one for the project to be deemed economically justifiable.

Forming a benefit-cost ratio as was done in Chapter 9 is the most commonly used criterion in cost-benefit analyses and is considered quite appropriate when only one project is being evaluated. However, in comparing two or more alternative projects which have different construction costs, as was done in Chapter 7, the NPV approach is better. This method avoids the possibility that projects with low construction costs might produce high benefit-cost ratios, although their total net benefits might be smaller than the net benefits of a more costly project. For a comparison of the various criteria used in cost-benefit analysis, see the work by Sassone and Schaffer (1978, pp. 13–29). There are a number of sources of information on cost-benefit analysis. Wolfe (1973) provides a collection of papers on the subject, including three applications. Frost (1971) describes how to use cost-benefit analysis in project appraisal and Wood and Campbell (1970) have compiled an annotated bibliography of the subject.

Shortest path and modal split models

A computer-based model known as TRANSEPT was used to evaluate short-term changes in the bus network in the *Huddersfield Bus Study* (Chapter 8). TRANSEPT is really a complex set of models. Rather than attempt to describe all its elements, we limit ourselves in this discussion to two of its components: a shortest path algorithm and a modal split model. The basic input to TRANSEPT is the bus network that is to be evaluated. Given this network, which consists of a number of nodes (bus stops), the various elements of a bus journey, such as the time it takes to walk to a bus stop, waiting time, travel time between nodes and the fare paid, are weighted and reduced to one measure – the generalized cost of a journey.

The shortest path algorithm is used to minimize the generalized cost of traveling from one node to another. The minimum generalized cost is also found for other modes of travel such as walking and private car. These costs are the data used to predict the proportion of trips that will be made by each mode of transportation available to the traveler. An n–dimensional logit model is used to carry out this prediction. Having determined the proportion of travelers who will use buses, and given the number of trips that are expected to be made during a period of time, TRANSEPT then assigns passengers to buses and evaluates the network in terms of its benefits to travelers, its cost to operate and its reve;'ues. Last and Leak (1976) provide a more detailed description of TRANSEPT.

Nonlinear programming

Two mathematical models were used in tandem in the study *Refuse Disposal in the Tyneside/Wearside Area* (Chapter 10). The first, a nonlinear programming model, found the locations for a given number and type of refuse treatment plant that minimized the distance traveled by refuse collection vehicles and the trucks used to dispose of treated refuse. The region was divided into small areas (collection rounds) and the location of these areas, an estimate of the amount of refuse generated by each one and the locations where treated refuse could be dumped were the other inputs. The output from this nonlinear programming model – the locations of treatment plants that minimized the total distance traveled using a given number and type of treatment plant – was used in the second model to calculate the total cost of the given system.

These models were first used to answer the question whether refuse treatment plants should be installed. Having established that treatment plants were needed, the models were then used successively to find the total cost per week of installing one, two, three and so on plants of a given type. In this way the best number of plants, their location and the areas they should serve were determined for each of the major methods of refuse treatment – pulverization and incineration. This information, along with estimates of other benefits such as land reclamation, health and safety and public amenity, was used by the local governments involved to decide on the best long-term refuse disposal policies for the region. The methods employed in this study are similar to those used by the meals-on-wheels study (Chapter 3). Both studies used a method developed by Powell (1964) to solve the nonlinear programming problem.

ANALYSIS OF PROBLEMS

There are several parallels among the studies in Part Two and we conclude this chapter with a discussion of two of them: the dilemma public officials commonly face when trying to solve transportation problems in which there are significant environmental issues; and the need to take into account qualitative as well as quantitative factors in reaching a final decision.

The transportation/environmental dilemma is best illustrated in Chapters 7 and 8. In deciding which alternative route was best for bypassing a small town (Chapter 7), the routes that could be justified by the cost-benefit analysis were not the most satisfactory in improving the deteriorating environment of the town. On the other hand, those alternatives which required more motorists to go farther out of their way to bypass the town and thus most contributed to improving the local environment were found to have construction costs that exceeded the benefits derived by road users. None of the proposed bypasses had positive benefits for *both* road users and local residents.

In Chapter 8 the study team investigated short-term improvements in a bus system from two different points of view. First, changes were recommended which provided the best service for no additional public subsidy. Secondly, changes were recommended that minimized the cost of operating the system, thus minimizing the public subsidy while maintaining the current level of service. The choice between the two approaches illustrates well the transportation/environmental dilemma. On the one hand, economic and environmental conditions are now such that local governments and private citizens are viewing public transportation as a way to overcome congestion, pollution and fuel shortages, as well as providing a means of inexpensive transportation for people with low or fixed incomes. These factors tend to support greater public subsidy of public transportation. On the other hand, the decision to increase public transportation subsidies is politically an unattractive alternative, especially at a time when public officials are facing growing demands for reduced public expenditure. Once again, the solution that helps to overcome environmental problems is not the solution that is cheapest or easiest for a local government to implement.

The qualitative aspects of the problem contributed to the final decision in all four studies. It is of course important to recognize and consider the qualitative as well as the quantitative factors of a problem. Just because qualitative factors are not built into a mathematical model and thus do not influence the solution derived from that model is not a reason to ignore such factors when making a decision.

The qualitative environmental impacts of the proposed alternative bypasses were a very important consideration in deciding which alternative to implement (Chapter 7). Some of the impacts considered were the type of land needed for the new road (farmland and National Trust property were involved); effects on local industries, such as improving access, and on farmers during the period of construction; destruction of sites of geological interest; effects on planned development; potential changes in the town's character; and potential for providing vehicle free shopping areas. Although it is impossible to say exactly how these factors influenced the final decision, they were brought out during the course of the study, summarized in the report along with the quantifiable environmental impacts and undoubtedly had an influence at public meetings devoted to discussing the proposed alternative bypasses.

In the evaluation of the proposed flood relief project (Chapter 9), it was found that the costs of the project far exceeded the future quantifiable benefits it would provide. Although the project could not be justified in cost-benefit terms, it was pointed out at the conclusion of the analysis that there were a number of qualitative results of flood relief, such as reducing the fear of drowning. When it came to making a decision, it was these qualitative features of flood relief, rather than the results of the benefit-cost ratio, which were used to justify the decision to go ahead with the project.

In the study in Chapter 10 the research team did not make a recommendation on the type of refuse treatment plant that should be built, believing that this decision involved nonquantifiable considerations, particularly the effect on local amenity, which should be made by the twenty-one local governments which had commissioned the study. The choice was between pulverizers and incinerators, which were estimated to cost approximately $400,000 more per year but which offered greater advantages in terms of health and safety, public amenity and conservation of disposal site capacity. In the event these were considered the deciding factors by the local governments involved, leading to a decision in favor of the more expensive incineration scheme.

In each of these studies the qualitative factors played an important role in the final decision, and it is interesting to note that in each case the solution that was implemented was the one which most improved the quality of life of local residents. It is also important to point out that some seemingly qualitative features of a problem can, in fact, be modeled quantitatively. This was done in constructing the model of bus operations presented in Chapter 8, where behavioral aspects of traveling, such as deciding which mode of travel would be used by local residents, were built into the mathematical model.

We conclude this chapter by listing a selection of other applications of operations research to transportation and environmental problems. No attempt has been made to provide an exhaustive collection of references. We hope the ones that follow will serve as a start for further investigation.

Air and water pollution problems are developing areas of operations research applications. Singpurwalla (1975) gives a general description of the air pollution problem and discusses some models for evaluating, monitoring and controlling air quality. Marks (1975) summarizes recent developments in using models to study water allocation problems and the improvement of water quality. Topics covered include pollution control, regional waste management and the design of local water distribution systems. Thrall *et al.* (1976) have put together a collection of papers on the development and application of models to a variety of water-related issues, including water allocation for food production, water treatment, recreation and water quality improvement. At the local government level there have been studies on routing and scheduling refuse collection vehicles and street cleaning equipment, determining crew sizes and locating transfer facilities used in refuse disposal. A method for minimizing refuse collection costs is presented by Martin (1974) and a number of models which have been developed to solve problems in the area of solid waste management are reviewed by Liebman (1975).

In the area of transportation Edie (1967) discussed operations research uses by the New York Port Authority, including studies of toll lane usage, the design of loading platforms at a commuter bus terminal, a telephone information service, a rapid transit system and tunnel congestion. A number of models used in urban, inter-urban and national transportation planning are reviewed by Webb *et al.* (1975), and Ferreira (1972) presents some driver accident models and discusses their use in evaluating policies concerning driver licensing and traffic safety. Two professional journals, *Transportation Science*, the publication of the transportation science section of the Operations Research Society of America, and *Transportation Research*, are sources for a number of models and methods dealing with a wide range of transportation problems, from the design of roads to strategies for operating bus systems.

Transportation is often a major issue in resource allocation problems. This is demonstrated by three of the studies presented in Part One which concern finding the number and location of emergency ambulances (Chapter 2), the number and location of kitchens for a social service program (Chapter 3) and the routes for vans used to transport inter-library loans (Chapter 5). There has also been much work on vehicle management problems – vehicle replacement and buy/lease decisions, operating policies for repair and maintenance facilities and determining the number of back-up vehicles that are needed to support a fleet of vehicles used to provide a public service. Many of these topics fall under the heading of administrative services and are discussed in Part Three of this book, which includes a simulation study of a vehicle repair facility (Chapter 14).

Part Three

Planning and Administrative Services

INTRODUCTION

Planning and administrative services cover a range of activities that may at one time or another be required by all departments of a government but are not usually directly associated with the functional responsibilities of the department concerned. Under administration, for example, services such as building maintenance, duplicating and printing, computer services and vehicle repair and maintenance are examples of routine activities that cut across departmental lines. And planning is a broad term that can equally well apply to determining future trends in land use, housing needs, education, transportation and population distribution. Sometimes referred to as management services, planning and administrative services can be performed either by a separate, self-contained department or by specialized staff units within each main department.

With the growth in government-provided services of all kinds and with the increasing sophistication of methods of analysis for tackling the problems of government, there has been a corresponding growth in the size and range of responsibilities of these specialist services. They offer a wealth of questions that are ideally suited to the application of operations research methods.

This part presents four studies directed at four very different problems of planning and administration. Chapter 12, 'Evaluating Alternative Strategies for Land Use Planning', is concerned with preparing a plan for long-term growth in an area, taking into account considerations of landscape, housing need and access to jobs and services. Chapter 13, 'Cost-effective Invoice Checking', presents a study which recommends the most cost-effective balance between the expense of checking invoices and the risk of losses through error or fraud if checking were not carried out. Chapter 14, 'Simulation of a New Service Facility', describes a study that helped a local authority evaluate its plan for a new vehicle repair and maintenance facility. Chapter 15, 'Local Government Reorganization and Relocation', illustrates a special project designed to help determine the office accommodation needs for a new administration recently created from the amalgamation of three former local governments.

Each chapter begins with a discussion of how the results of the study were used and the final chapter (Chapter 16) summarizes the studies and shows how they illustrate some of the common themes of operations research problems and methods of solution. In particular, it is shown how the four studies presented in Part Three illustrate a variety of decision problems. References to other applications in planning and administration are provided for further reading.

12

Evaluating Alternative Strategies for Land Use Planning

The population of Northamptonshire was forecast to increase from 500,000 in 1974 to 800,000 in 1991. In preparation for this growth the planning department of the county council undertook, in 1974, a study aimed at providing a general plan for the long-term development of the area. It was anticipated that this study would serve as a framework for more detailed studies to follow. The purpose of the general plan was to recommend in broad terms suitable locations for the houses and jobs that would be needed; to show that these sites could be economically provided with roads, schools and other essential services; and to ensure that as far as possible the natural resources and generally attractive landscape of the area would be preserved.

There are, of course, many different ways to satisfy these objectives. Before drawing up a final plan, therefore, the council wanted to investigate the alternatives open to them. Consequently a study was commissioned which evaluated the five basic alternative strategies that had been identified to find those that best met the overall requirements of the area. The study was conducted by Stewart N. H. Mackie, whose final report, *Evaluation Tests for Northamptonshire*, was submitted to the county council in mid-1974.

Mackie carried out the evaluation of the five strategies in three stages. First, the performance of each strategy was measured in terms of how well it satisfied each of six objectives. Secondly, weights were attached to the importance of achieving each of the objectives. The weights were obtained from a questionnaire survey of members of the public and a survey of staff in the county planning department. Finally, the results of the first two stages were used to calculate an overall score for the performance of each alternative strategy, thus enabling the strategies to be ranked.

The second part of the study tested the ranking of the strategies in terms of its sensitivity to uncertainties about the data used to obtain the overall scores and about possible future changes in this data. From these tests Mackie concluded that the three best strategies were not very sensitive relative to the worst two. Large shifts in the weights attached to the objectives and in the scores that the worst two alternatives achieved were needed in order for their overall scores to be equal to those of the top three strategies. Therefore he recommended that the council discard the two worst strategies and focus attention on the top three alternatives in determining which of these strategies should form the basis for the general plan.

When *Evaluation Tests for Northamptonshire* was commissioned Northamptonshire was more or less locked into the planning-for-growth syndrome of the late 1960s and early 1970s. As a result, the county council accepted, almost without question, the population forecasts that were the basis for the alternative strategies of the general plan – the strategies that were subsequently evaluated by Mackie. However, by the end of 1974 (after Mackie's evaluation study was completed), it became increasingly obvious that projections that the population would increase from 500,000 to 800,000 between 1974 and 1991 were not going to materialize. Consequently the forecasts were radically revised downwards to 600,000 by 1991. This meant that large areas no longer needed to be set aside for new development. The more gradual growth now anticipated could be absorbed in areas of Northampton and Corby that had already been designated as growth areas.

Five years after the study was completed we spoke with the county planning department to learn how *Evaluation Tests for Northamptonshire* had been used. The purpose of the study was to help Northamptonshire decide on a planning strategy for the development of residential areas, public services and access of jobs, under the assumption that the administration would experience a considerable increase in its population. Thus it was no surprise to learn that the council had made little use of the study and the strategies that were evaluated once it realized that growth would not be taking place at the projected rate. Northamptonshire did not reject the study because the methods were thought to be wrong, but because the results became inappropriate to the changing circumstances. However, the results of the survey of the public did serve to force a reevaluation of some of the assumptions previously accepted by the planning department, notably that growth was necessary and desirable. Since the study was completed the county council has produced a general plan far less ambitious than originally envisioned in terms of the amount of land set aside for new development.

The report, *Evaluation Tests for Northamptonshire*, follows. It illustrates some useful methods, even though in the event its results were not implemented. Of particular interest are the tests of how sensitive the ranking of the alternative strategies is to changes in some of the raw data and in the weights on which this ranking is based. One of the results of such tests is to eliminate from further consideration alternative courses of action. By narrowing the field of alternatives, resources can be more effectively concentrated in examining which alternative – in this case, which planning strategy – should be further investigated.

With hindsight, it is clear that such an evaluation should also have been performed on the effect of changes in population forecasts on the selection of the alternative planning strategies. If such a sensitivity analysis had been performed it is likely that strategies which provided for much less growth would have been more fully evaluated. In most operations research studies it is necessary to make assumptions in order to develop or simplify a model of a real situation and to estimate some of the parameters of the model. Occasionally one or more assumptions can be so wide of the mark that a situation arises where the results of a study prove to be invalid. Usually the assumptions will not prove to be so wide of the mark as was the case in selecting the alternative strategies to be evaluated for Northamptonshire.

The study is divided into three sections. The first describes the objectives for the general plan and outlines the three-stage process for evaluating alternative strategies. The results of this process are presented in Section 2. As a part of the evaluation process several tests were performed to assess the sensitivity of the evaluation to possible future changes in the performance of the strategies or in the public's valuation of the plan's objectives. Section 3 is devoted to a description of the results of this sensitivity analysis.

Evaluation Tests for Northamptonshire

STEWART N. H. MACKIE

1   PLAN EVALUATION PROCESS

The generation and evaluation of the alternative strategies for the Northamptonshire general plan (also known as the structure plan) began with an investigation of the factors that are known to affect an area's potential for development. This investigation produced forty-two different maps showing the overall potential for growth in different parts of the county. These were then combined to produce four clearly different basic alternative plans, each of which met all the essential objectives of the general plan. A fifth alternative strategy was then added, based on past trends in the location of buildings in the study area.

These five alternatives were then examined in much more detail and evaluated against a set of discriminatory objectives for the general plan. Eight broad objectives were originally identified. These objectives, defined in Table 12.1, relate to the provision of services and a good residential environment, losses in agricultural land and good landscape, accessibility to shops, houses, jobs and labor, costs and benefits of the transportation system and flexibility in the plan to adapt to future changes. Of these, the flexibility objective is considered outside the main framework of this study and the transportation objective cannot be included because data from a transportation study for the area is not yet available

The evaluation of the five alternative plans was carried out in three stages.

(1) *Measuring the objective-achievement scores.* The performance of the five alternatives was measured against each of the six objectives that could be measured, and expressed as raw scores in units of area, cost, and so on, in a 'plan evaluation matrix'. The scores on each

objective were then transformed into common units expressing the relative effectiveness of each alternative.

(2) *Weighting the objective-achievement scores.* The relative importance of achieving each of the six objectives was also estimated by asking members of the public, through a questionnaire survey, to rank the achievement of each of the objectives in order of importance. The rankings expressed by all respondents were then used to produce three different sets of weights on the objectives. These sets were obtained by placing a varying degree of emphasis on first preferences, second preferences, and so on. A fourth set of weights was produced from a survey of staff in the planning department.

(3) *Calculating the overall performance scores.* Finally, the sets of weights were used in conjunction with each plan evaluation matrix to calculate overall measures of the performance of each alternative strategy. This was done by first multiplying each objective-achievement score by the weight attached to the achievement of that objective and then summing the resulting products over all the objectives for each strategy.

Table 12.1   *Objectives of the general plan*

Objective	*Description*
(a) minimize service costs	Locate new development so that the costs of new utility services, communications and land development generally are kept to a minimum.
(b) preserve farmland	Locate new development so that the loss of good-quality farmland and valuable mineral resources are kept to a minimum.
(c) preserve good landscape	Locate new development so that the loss of good quality landscaped areas is kept to a minimum.
(d) provide good residential areas	Locate new residential areas in an attractive environment.
(e) maximize access to homes and shops	Locate new residential areas and new shopping areas to give a wide choice of sites.
(f) maximize access to jobs and labor	Locate new residential areas and new employment areas to give a wide choice of labor supply and employment locations.
(g) provide good transportation conditions	Locate new roads to give maximum benefit to road users and public transport undertakings.
(h) maintain flexibility of action	Be able to adapt to change within a foreseeable range of departures from the most likely forecasts, and retain some flexibility in strategy development in case variations in economic and social circumstances generate the need for strategic change.

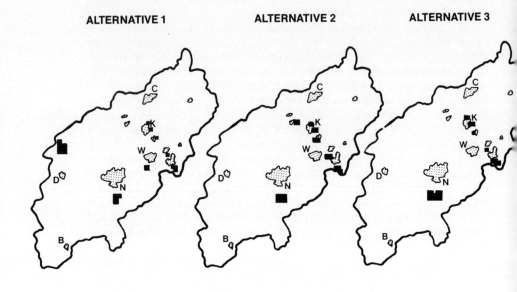

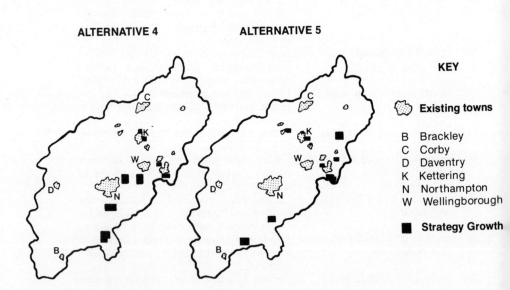

Figure 12.1 *Alternative strategies*

2 RESULTS OF THE EVALUATION

This section describes the results of the three-stage evaluation of each of the strategies.

Measurement of objective-achievement scores
The five alternatives for the general plan are similar in the total levels of population, employment and other activities they will accommodate. The major differences between them are the locations of some areas designated for growth over the twenty-year period of the plan. The remaining growth areas, which have already been decided, are common to all alternatives.

Figure 12.1 shows the choice of growth areas in each strategy in relation to existing towns. Table 12.2 gives an appraisal of the performance of each strategy against each of the objectives in Table 12.1. The objective-achievement scores given in this appraisal are rescaled raw scores which were originally in units of area, cost, and so on. For a given objective, the rescaled score is determined by assigning a score of 10 to the strategy out of all the alternatives that has done most to achieve the objective, and giving a score of 0 to the one that has done least. The scores for the remaining strategies are scaled proportionately. For example, alternative 2 is assessed to be most effective in preserving farmland, while alternative 4 is least effective. Hence these alternatives are given scores of 10 and 0 respectively. The score for alternative 1 is found by linearly rescaling the raw descriptive data which represents the effectiveness of this strategy in terms of the raw data for alternatives 2 and 4 and their scores of 10 and 0. The rescaled score is 7. Similarly, the rescaled scores for alternatives 3 and 5 are found to be 8 and 9 respectively. The results are as follows.

Alternative 1 was designed to emphasize accessibility, the preservation of good-quality landscape and farmland and the provision of a good residential environment. The detailed evaluation of the strategy shows it to be relatively successful in giving good access to jobs and labor, in preserving farmland and providing a good residential environment. However, in terms of the objectives of preservation of good landscape and accessibility to homes and shops, it is the least successful of all the alternatives.

In the generation of alternative 2 most weight was placed on high accessibility to jobs and labor, followed by a good residential environment and the preservation of good landscape. However, the evaluation of this alternative shows that it does not perform well on any of these objectives, yet scores highest of all five alternatives on minimizing service costs and preserving farmland.

In the case of alternative 3 the factors which affect an area's potential for development were weighted so as to place a strong emphasis on job and labor access together with the preservation of good-quality farmland. The results show that these two objectives do score highest, but that alternative 3 performs badly on the other objectives.

Table 12.2 *Performance of each strategy in achieving each objective*

Scores of alternative 1	Objective		Score
	(a)	minimize service costs	0
	(b)	preserve farmland	7
	(c)	preserve good landscape	0
	(d)	provide good residential areas	6
	(e)	maximize access to homes and shops	0
	(f)	maximize access to jobs and labor	6

Scores of alternative 2	Objective		Score
	(a)	minimize service costs	10
	(b)	preserve farmland	10
	(c)	preserve good landscape	4
	(d)	provide good residential areas	2
	(e)	maximize access to homes and shops	9
	(f)	maximize access to jobs and labor	4

Scores of alternative 3	Objective		Score
	(a)	minimize service costs	2
	(b)	preserve farmland	8
	(c)	preserve good landscape	1
	(d)	provide good residential areas	0
	(e)	maximize access to homes and shops	0
	(f)	maximize access to jobs and labor	5

Scores of alternative 4	Objective		Score
	(a)	minimize service costs	3
	(b)	preserve farmland	0
	(c)	preserve good landscape	7
	(d)	provide good residential areas	10
	(e)	maximize access to homes and shops	10
	(f)	maximize access to jobs and labor	10

Scores of alternative 5	Objective		Score
	(a)	minimize service costs	10
	(b)	preserve farmland	9
	(c)	preserve good landscape	10
	(d)	provide good residential areas	8
	(e)	maximize access to homes and shops	8
	(f)	maximize access to jobs and labor	0

Alternative 4 was based on maximizing accessibility and providing a good residential environment. In fact the strategy performs very well on both these criteria, giving better access to homes, shops, jobs and labor than any other alternative and providing the best environment for residential areas.

Alternative 5 was not generated from maps indicating the potential of particular areas for development, but by projecting present building trends. Nevertheless, this strategy scores well on five of the six objectives and only in its provision for easy access to jobs and labor does it perform badly.

The scores of the alternatives listed in Table 12.2 thus reflect their relative performance in achieving any particular stated objective of the general plan. However, the community considers the achivement of some objectives to be more important than others. The scores on each objective must therefore be weighted according to the importance of that objective so that the scores of a strategy on different objectives can be compared directly.

Weighting of objective-achievement scores
In Northamptonshire four different sets of weights were calculated, three from a questionnaire survey of the public and a fourth from a survey of the county planners. In the public survey individuals were asked to rank the objectives according to the importance they attached to their achievement. Then three different methods, A, B, and C, were employed to convert these preference rankings into a set of weights:

A   The total number of individuals giving each objective first preference was counted. These totals were used to calculate the weights.
B   Each first preference for an objective was given 8 points, each second preference 7 points, each third preference 6 points, and so on. The points for each objective were then summed and the totals used to calculate the weights.
C   Each first preference for an objective was given 1 point, each second preference ½ point, each third preference ⅓ point, and so on. The points for each objective were again summed and the totals used to calculate the weights.

Thus method A takes into account only first preferences, whereas method B and, to a lesser extent, method C attach some importance to the lower preferences. The sets of raw weights derived by these methods were then rescaled so that they summed to 100. In the planning department survey individuals were asked to give a weight to the achievement of each objective. These weights were then simply averaged over all respondents and rescaled to sum to 100 so as to be comparable with the other sets of weights.

Table 12.3 shows the four sets of weights for comparison. Clearly the estimate of the relative importance of each objective depends to a considerable extent on the method used to make the estimate. It is important to test whether or not the final overall ranking of the strategies is affected by the choice of method. This type of test, called a sensitivity test, is described in the next section.

The results of the public survey indicate that greatest weight should be attached to the preservation of good-quality landscape. Considerable weight should also be placed on the preservation of good-quality farmland and the provision of a pleasant residential environment. Comparatively little importance is attached to accessibility or to the costs of services.

However, these weights should be viewed with suspicion, as the reliability of the results of the public survey is open to doubt. The objectives of the general plan were described on the questionnaire form in very broad qualitative terms and at a scale that the individual might find hard to grasp. The respondent was asked only to rank the objectives and not to weight them. Further, the survey forms were completed by a sample of only about 0.1 per cent of the population of the county and this sample does not appear to have been representative of the views of the county's residents as a whole. For these reasons considerable uncertainty must be attached to the estimates of the public's weights. The possible effects of this uncertainty on the overall evaluation of each strategy are examined in the sensitivity tests described in the next section.

The survey of the planning department staff indicates that county planners attach more equal weights to all the objectives than do the public. In fact, they give greatest emphasis to maximum accessibility and minimum service costs for the new residents, the very objectives that the public survey indicates are of least importance to the existing community.

Table 12.3 *Weights attached to achievement of the objectives*

Objectives	Public's weights – method: A	B	C	County planners' weights
(a) minimize service costs	8	13	12	18
(b) preserve farmland	24	20	21	15
(c) preserve good landscape	40	20	26	15
(d) provide good residential areas	17	18	17	14
(e) maximize access to homes and shops	4	14	11	19
(f) maximize access to jobs and labor	7	15	13	19
Total	100	100	100	100

Calculation of overall performance scores
The plan evaluation matrix in Table 12.4 summarizes the scores (given
in Table 12.2) of each alternative strategy on each of the objectives.
These scores represent the effectiveness of each strategy in achieving a
particular objective. They have been transformed from raw descriptive
data by rescaling the data so that the worst alternative scores 0, the best
scores 10 and the rest are scaled proportionately.

Table 12.4   *Unweighted scores of all alternatives*

	Objective	Score of alternative				
		1	*2*	*3*	*4*	*5*
(a)	minimize service costs	0	10	2	3	10
(b)	preserve farmland	7	10	8	0	9
(c)	preserve good landscape	0	4	1	7	10
(d)	provide good residential areas	6	2	0	10	8
(e)	maximize access to homes and shops	0	9	0	10	8
(f)	maximize access to jobs and labor	6	4	5	10	0

Each row of scores in the plan evaluation matrix is then multiplied by
the weight on that row's objective derived in the previous section. There
are in fact four sets of weights and therefore four different matrices of
weighted scores, as shown in Table 12.5. Each column of these matrices
contains the weighted scores of a particular alternative. These can now
be added together to give an overall score for that alternative, which is a
measure of its performance relative to the other strategies.

Table 12.5   *Weighted scores of all alternatives*

(1)   *Weighted scores using the public's weights derived by method A*

		Score of alternative				
		1	*2*	*3*	*4*	*5*
(a)	minimize service costs	0	80	16	24	80
(b)	preserve farmland	168	240	192	0	216
(c)	preserve good landscape	0	160	40	280	400
(d)	provide good residential areas	102	34	0	170	136
(e)	maximize access to homes and shops	0	36	0	40	32
(f)	maximize access to jobs and labor	42	28	35	70	0
	Overall score	312	578	283	584	864

(Table 12.5 continued over)

(Table 12.5 continued)

(2) *Weighted scores using the public's weights derived by method B*

				Score of alternative			
	Objective	*1*	*2*	*3*	*4*	*5*
(a)	minimize service costs	0	130	26	39	130
(b)	preserve farmland	140	200	160	0	180
(c)	preserve good landscape	0	80	20	140	200
(d)	provide good residential areas	108	36	0	180	144
(e)	maximize access to homes and shops	0	126	0	140	112
(f)	maximize access to jobs and labor	90	60	75	150	0
	Overall score	338	632	281	649	766

(3) *Weighted scores using the public's weights derived by method C*

				Score of alternative			
	Objective	*1*	*2*	*3*	*4*	*5*
(a)	minimize service costs	0	120	24	36	120
(b)	preserve farmland	147	210	168	0	189
(c)	preserve good landscape	0	104	26	182	260
(d)	provide good residential areas	102	34	0	170	136
(e)	maximize access to homes and shops	0	99	0	110	88
(f)	maximize access to jobs and labor	78	52	65	130	0
	Overall score	327	619	283	628	793

(4) *Weighted scores using the county planner's weights*

				Score of alternative			
	Objective	*1*	*2*	*3*	*4*	*5*
(a)	minimize service costs	0	180	36	54	180
(b)	preserve farmland	105	150	120	0	135
(c)	preserve good landscape	0	60	15	105	150
(d)	provide good residential areas	84	28	0	140	112
(e)	maximize access to homes and shops	0	171	0	190	152
(f)	maximize access to jobs and labor	114	76	95	190	0
	Overall score	303	665	266	679	729

Finally, Table 12.6 shows these overall scores for all the alternatives, which have been ranked according to their scores. The trend strategy (alternative 5) always comes out on top, whichever set of weights are employed. Alternatives 2 and 4 always rank second with very similar scores, and alternatives 1 and 3 score lowest with all sets of weights. Clearly, the ranking of the strategies is not dependent on the method used to estimate the weights.

Table 12.6   *Overall scores of all alternatives*

Alternative strategy	*Overall scores using: Public's weights – method:*			*County planners' weights*
	A	*B*	*C*	
5	864	766	793	729
4	584	649	628	679
2	578	632	619	665
1	312	338	327	303
3	283	281	283	266

3   SENSITIVITY ANALYSIS

In evaluating the alternative strategies being considered for a general plan, it is important not only to rank the strategies according to their overall scores but also to test the ranking in terms of its sensitivity to uncertainties about the scores. Uncertainties exist about the accurate estimation of the overall scores at present and about possible changes in the overall scores in the future. These uncertainties in the overall scores depend in turn on uncertainties in the measurement and prediction of the individual objective-achievement scores and the weights on the objectives. Such uncertainty may be reduced, although never completely eliminated, by making more accurate measurements, for example, by carrying out more extensive surveys and by using more powerful predictive models.

What matters, however, is not the degree of uncertainty surrounding a particular score or weight, but the extent to which this lack of knowledge may affect the correct choice of strategy for adoption as the general plan. Tests have therefore been carried out to measure how much the weights and scores calculated in Section 2 may change before they affect the ranking of the strategies according to their overall scores. These sensitivity tests do not show how much any individual score or weight must change on its own, but how large a change is required in a combination of scores or weights. Clearly there are many different sets of values that would change the ranking. The sensitivity analysis finds the set that only just reverses the ranking and for which the measures of sensitivity are as small as possible. These measures are called 'the minimum distance' scores or weights.

The results of these tests will enable planners in Northamptonshire to: (1) estimate the reliability that can be placed on the original

ranking of the alternatives and decide whether or not the lower
ranking strategies are worth retaining for a more detailed evaluation;
and (2) determine which, if any, of the objective scores or weights are
likely to change to the extent of affecting the ranking of the strategies.
The uncertainty surrounding those scores or weights that are critical to
the evaluation may then be reduced, where possible, by making more
accurate measurements or predictions. Some general conclusions can
be drawn about the reliability of the ranking of the five alternative
strategies. This ranking is based on the overall scores of the alternatives that were calculated using the weights and scores on the individual objectives described in Section 2.

Alternative 5 scored highest with any of the four sets of weights
described in Section 2. This strategy is based on the continuation of
existing trends in dispersed growth across the county. Alternatives 2
and 4, based on growth in the towns along route A6 and to the south
of Northampton, have approximately equal overall scores, which are
between 10 and 30 percent lower than that of alternative 5. Alternative
1 and alternative 3, with extensive growth to the south of
Northampton, perform worst, with overall scores generally less than
half those of the other three strategies. Furthermore the ranking of the
top three strategies is not very sensitive relative to these worst two, as
a large shift of at least 20 percent is required in each of the individual
weights and scores of alternatives 1 and 3 to give them overall scores
equal to the top three strategies. It is recommended therefore that
alternatives 1 and 3 should be discarded in the final examination of the
strategies. Attention can then be focused on a detailed study of the
merits and disadvantages of the other three strategies.

The strength of the trend strategy (alternative 5) with respect to
either of the two remaining alternatives depends on which set of
weights is applied to the scores on the general plan's objectives. The
views of the existing residents as expressed in the public questionnaire
survey suggest that greatest weight should be given to preserving good-
quality farmland and attractive landscape. The county planners on the
other hand give roughly equal weight to those objectives likely to be
more important to new residents in the growth areas, namely accessibility to jobs, homes, shops and labor.

If the views of existing residents predominate, the trend strategy
scores considerably better than the other two and is likely to continue
doing so even if their weights shift on average by as much as 10
percent. This is mainly because alternative 4 performs badly on the
'preservation of farmland' objective and alternative 2 on the 'preservation of landscape' objective. The position of the trend strategy above
alternatives 2 and 4 is most sensitive to the weights on the 'service
costs', 'farmland' and 'access to jobs and labor' objectives. These
weights should therefore be examined more closely than the others in
the final stage of the evaluation. The overall score of the trend strategy
is also particularly sensitive to its score on the 'preservation of good
landscape' objective because of the emphasis placed on this objective,
especially with the weights derived from the public's first preferences

(method A in Section 2). The scores of the alternatives on this objective should therefore be measured most carefully.

If the wishes of both existing and new residents are to be taken into account through the weights of the county planners there is not much to choose between the three alternatives. In fact only a small shift in several of the individual weights or scores would be required to affect their ranking. The scores of the alternatives on all the objectives should therefore be measured most carefully.

Whichever set of weights is used, the overall scores of alternatives 2 and 4 are very close, even though they each perform well on different objectives. In addition, their minimum distance measures are small, indicating that only a small shift in their scores or the weights is needed to place alternative 2 above alternative 4.

We recommend that the three higher scoring strategies (2, 4 and 5) should be examined in greater detail in the next stage of the general planning process. Particular attention should be paid to the uncertainty surrounding the estimates of the weights and scores on the objectives. From the best elements of these three alternatives it should then be possible to synthesize a plan that will best satisfy as many as possible of the community's objectives.

13

Cost-Effective Invoice Checking

The supplies department of the city of Stonebridge serves as the purchasing agent for all the goods used by the rest of the city's departments. Although the department handles the purchasing and then processes the suppliers' invoices (bills) for payment, most of the items purchased are delivered directly to the department requesting them. Such direct purchases accounted for over 150,000 invoices during a twelve-month period in 1961/2. These invoices are sent by suppliers to the supplies department, where they are approved and then sent to the treasurer's department for payment.

The procedure used by the supplies department to approve invoices for payment involved ensuring that the goods were received, that the prices on the invoice were as quoted when the purchase was negotiated, and that the invoices were arithmetically correct. These checks of delivery, price and arithmetic entailed considerable clerical costs, and the supplies department was having difficulty finding qualified staff to perform this work. Therefore, in 1962 the department commissioned a study to investigate ways of reducing invoice-checking costs and the number of staff needed.

This chapter presents the report of this study, adapted from an original report by Ray A. Ward. (To protect the city from possible fraud, Stonebridge is not its real name.) In his investigation of the invoice-checking function, Ward found that it was costing the department more in clerical costs to verify the delivery of items purchased and to check invoice prices and arithmetic than the losses that would have resulted if the errors found had not been detected. He estimated the department would save about $17,500 a year in operating expenses if it reduced the amount of checking of delivery, price and arithmetic. These savings took into account the possible losses, estimated at $2,300 a year in 1962, from not performing a thorough check of all the invoices for direct purchases by the department. Ward established 'selective' checking rules for the supplies department, based upon the most cost-effective level of checking invoices. He recommended that the department verify delivery and check price and arithmetic only on invoices with a total value greater than $200. This represented approximately 10 percent of all the invoices received by the department. To control the process, he further recommended that a random sample of 3 percent of all the other invoices be checked in full.

When Ward's report was submitted in 1962 the management of the supplies department was satisfied with the results and recommended that the city council accept the recommendations of the study.

However, the treasurer opposed using selective checking methods for the approval of invoices for payment. To resolve this conflict, an independent local government financial auditing organization, the District Audit, was asked to advise on whether to implement the study's recommendations. In their assessment of the study, the District Audit officials overwhelmingly supported selective checking of invoices for delivery, price and arithmetic. The only question they raised concerned the checking level of $200. They suggested that the treasurer and the supplied department consider setting this level at $300. With this endorsement from the District Audit, the treasurer agreed to allow the supplies department to implement selective checking of invoices, but insisted upon a more conservative set of decision rules – a $150 checking level (all invoices over $150 were to be checked in full) and a 5 percent (rather than a 3 percent) random sample.

When we visited Stonebridge in 1978 we found that the number of invoices had increased from 150,000 a year in 1962 to 240,000, representing direct purchases of some $44 million a year. (The magnitude of annual purchases is accounted for by the fact that the supplies department now purchases for a number of smaller local governments in the region and that Stonebridge and some of these other governments run education and social service departments, which are large purchasers.) We found that the selective checking system was still in operation, and that it had been successfully updated to meet changing demands. For example:

- To keep pace with inflation, the checking level (the 10 percent of highest value invoices) has been progressively increased and in 1978 stood at $600. However, the random sample rate has been held at or close to 5 percent.
- Several changes have been introduced into the clerical procedures involved, in particular a process to speed up the notification that goods that are being checked for delivery have in fact been received.
- The allocation of staff to the various tasks has been changed. Before the introduction of selective checking, different staff carried out each of the three checks of delivery, price and arithmetic. Now, any invoice that is selected for checking is handled throughout by a single clerk.

Moreover, modification of the system continues. Consideration is currently being given, for example, to establishing different checking levels for different types of commodities. Already minor claims for shortages of goods issued from the warehouse are satisfied without checking, although random checks are performed as a control measure.

The aim of the study was to reduce clerical costs, and thus reduce the service charge the supplies department makes on its customer departments. As a result of implementing selective invoice-checking procedures, management estimates that the clerical staff has been reduced by ten positions, and that this has had a major impact on their ability to keep costs down. However, the study has had a benefit that overshadows the very sizable reductions made in clerical costs. Because the receipt of goods is checked on only 10 percent of the invoices, and because the delivery reports on these goods have been speeded up, the supplies department is able to take advantage of discounts for the quick payment of invoices (twenty-eight days are usually allowed) which was virtually impossible before the implementation of selective invoice checking. In 1977 these discounts amounted to over $\$^2/_3$ million.

Thus this study is a particularly good example of the application of cost-effectiveness analysis (more fully explained in Chapter 17) to government problems. The new checking system has been in use for over eighteen years and the results have been extremely rewarding. In addition this work also provides excellent examples of two key aspects of an operations research study: testing the results of a study and incorporating management control in the implementation of the results.

By testing the sensitivity of his results to changes in some of his input data, Ward was able to overcome potential concern about possible inaccuracies in the estimates of some of the data he used, thus preempting arguments against implementing his results. He showed that his estimates of the percentage of goods that are not delivered and the percentage of price and arithmetic errors, under various levels of selective checking, could be considerably at variance with the actual values and yet the consequences would still be small.

Concern about the estimate of losses the city would be exposed to if selective checking were implemented was further reduced by instituting a random check of all invoices. Even more important, random sampling provided management with an excellent and relatively inexpensive means of controlling this new invoice-checking system. It is desirable in any study to set up a management control system as part of the implementation process in order to be certain that the results that are predicted actually do materialize. It was especially important to have such a control system in this study, where the treasurer was reluctant to accept the new methods. The random sample provided the control needed to prevent systematic abuse of the new system. It also helped to determine when the decision rules – the level of checking – needed to be revised to take account of inflation and changes in the types or quantities of goods purchased.

The report that follows, originally entitled *The Checking of Invoices*, begins with an introduction that sets out the size of the study. The body of the report consists of three sections that describe and analyze the individual processes of checking the delivery, price and arithmetic of invoices for direct purchases and suggest ways of cutting clerical costs almost 60 percent by selectively performing these checks. All costs have been expressed in dollars at 1962 prices. The average exchange rate in 1962 was 0.3561 pounds sterling per dollar.

The Checking of Invoices

RAY A. WARD

INTRODUCTION

The city of Stonebridge has a large supplies department which is responsible for purchasing goods for all the city's departments. This system of centralized purchasing enables the city to buy goods used by a number of departments in large enough quantities so that quantity discounts can be obtained. It also means that each department does not need to employ specialist staff to deal with purchasing.

The administrative offices of the supplies department are located at the department's Hillside Warehouse, where it employs staff devoted to purchasing goods, maintaining records, approving invoices from its suppliers for payment by the treasurer's department and billing its customers – the various other departments that order goods through the supplies department. Goods ranging from office supplies to refuse collection trucks are purchased by the supplies department. Although some high-volume items such as stationery and cleaning supplies are stored at the Hillside Warehouse, most of the items purchased are delivered directly by the supplier to the department requesting them. Such 'direct purchases' accounted for over 150,000 invoices during a twelve-month period in 1961/2 and the total value of these purchases was approximately $8,400,000. It is the direct purchases, rather than the goods stocked at the warehouse, that are the concern of this report. The number of invoices for stocked goods is considerably less than the number of direct purchases, amounting to less than 11,000 during the same twelve-month period.

In order to make centralized purchasing worthwhile for the user departments it is imperative that the supplies department keep its operating expenses and overhead costs to a minimum. Otherwise each of the user departments might find it cheaper to do its own purchasing. This report presents the results of a study concerned with helping the supplies department to reduce one of its administrative expenses – the checking of suppliers' invoices before approving them for payment by the treasurer's department.

At present the department approves an invoice for payment after careful scrutiny to ensure that the goods have been received, the prices are correct and the invoice sums are arithmetically correct. These checking procedures involve a lot of time and hence a lot of administrative expense. The cost of these checks must be balanced against the risk of losses due to error or fraud to which the city council might be exposed if these precautions were reduced or removed. The aim of this study is:

(1)   to estimate the extent of the possible losses if different invoice-checking procedures were adopted;
(2)   to relate these possible losses to the cost of making the checks;
(3)   to suggest control procedures that would enable the combined cost of the possible losses and of clerical checking of invoices to be held at a minimum.

It is convenient to study the subject under three headings which reflect the existing clerical procedures employed at the Hillside Warehouse. Upon receiving a requisition for goods from a department the purchasing section of the supplies department prepares a purchase order. The purchase order form consists of an original and three copies. The original is sent to the supplier of the goods and the first copy, called the 'advice note', is used to notify the department which made the requisition that the goods have been ordered. When the goods are shipped the supplier sends an invoice to the supplies department, where the checks on delivery, price and arithmetic are carried out before approval is given to the city treasurer's department to pay the invoice. Upon receipt of the goods by the department which requested them, the advice note is returned to the supplies department and serves as a verification that the goods were delivered. It now becomes a delivery report and any exceptional information about the delivery, such as incorrect quantities or damaged goods, are noted on the advice note before it is returned. An advice note with such comments is referred to as an 'altered' advice note. As part of the process of approving an invoice for payment the prices of the goods ordered and the total charges are matched with the second copy of the purchase order, known as the 'charge note'. The charge note is then sent to the department that requested the goods to let it know what it will be billed. The third copy of the purchase order remains as a file copy at the supplies department.

The various checks carried out are, in the order they occur, checks for delivery, price and arithmetic, described locally as 'batching up', 'marking off' and 'extending'.

1   DELIVERY (BATCHING UP)

The checking operations made at the stage of delivery consist of the four comparisons listed below:

(1)   comparing the order number on the invoice with the file copy of the purchase order;
(2)   comparing the descriptions of items on the invoice with those on the file copy of the purchase order;
(3)   comparing the quantities of each item on the invoice with the quantities on the file copy of the purchase order;
(4)   comparing the quantities of each item on the invoice with those on the advice note – the note from the department verifying that the goods were received.

Each of these checks can lead to two or three different results, so that several dozen logically different situations can arise. Some of these possibilities differ in such a trivial manner that the list of distinctly different results can be reduced to the nine types listed in Table 13.1.

If any or all the comparisons above were discontinued, then the ability to distinguish between the various situations would be greatly reduced. Types 1 and 6 are correct invoices, but the staff must identify them in order to take the appropriate action. The remaining types of invoices defined in Table 13.1, that is, types 2, 3, 4, 5, 7, 8 and 9, call for corrective action, and in general such invoices would have to be altered in value if they were to be approved for payment immediately. If the alterations were not made and the invoices were paid unchanged, the city council would expose itself to financial loss (or gain). The extent of the loss, however, would depend on a number of subsequent events which will be discussed later. Estimates of the number of times each particular type of alteration can be expected are given in the third column of Table 13.1.

Table 13.1 *Distinct types of invoices which the present practice of batching up identifies*

Type	Definition	Number and % of invoices for direct purchases	
1	All goods have been delivered as ordered and the correct quantity invoiced.	148,975	(98.9%)
2	The invoice agrees with the order but the delivery is missing wholly or in part.	890	(0.591%)
3	The invoice agrees with the order but the delivery is unsatisfactory because of damage, quality or timing.	304	(0.202%)
4	Delivery of more than the ordered quantity has occurred although the invoice does not charge for these additional goods.	35	(0.023%)
5	The invoice is for more than the ordered quantity and these additional items have not been delivered.	190	(0.125%)
6	The invoice is for more than the ordered quantity and this additional amount has been delivered and is acceptable.	8	(0.005%)
7	More than the ordered quantity has been delivered and invoiced. The extra goods are not wanted (for example, duplicate delivery).	75	(0.050%)
8	Order and delivery agrees but the invoice is for a smaller quantity of goods.	31	(0.020%)
9	The invoice is for goods not ordered by the department (for example, copy invoice).	126	(0.084%)
	Total invoices October 1961 – September 1962	150,634	(100%)

The fact that approximately 1 percent of all invoices are of a type which calls for modification does not of course mean that the city council is exposed to a 1 percent loss of the value of direct purchases. In order to establish the extent of this loss, three further aspects of the subject must be considered. It is necessary to ask:

- the number of incorrect invoices, as listed in Table 13.1, that would be found and put right under various checking conditions;
- the relationship between the number of invoices which are in error and the direction (for or against the council) and size of the cash mistake which they carry;
- the extent to which invoices needing alteration, but which are approved for payment, will be put right by the supplier.

It is possible to consider a very wide range of different checking procedures. At one extreme these might consist of the payment of invoices without any attempt to verify that the goods were delivered, that is, without making any of the comparisons above. The supplies department might, for example, approve invoices for payment having satisfied themselves that a 'realistic' order number has been quoted by the supplier and make no further checks. In this case some type 9 invoice errors would be identified but none of the others would be apparent. However, in this report only the following procedural change has been analyzed.

Checking delivery by exception
Suppose that the batching-up procedure described earlier was modified to operate on the following basis:

(1)   comparing the order number on the invoice with the file copy of the purchase order;
(2)   comparing the descriptions of items on the invoice with those on the file copy of the purchase order;
(3)   comparing the quantities of each item on the invoice with the quantities on the file copy of the purchase order;
(4)   matching only altered advice notes, that is, those which show that there was a problem with the goods delivered, to the invoice and to the file copy of the purchase order, and acting upon those alterations.

Such a process removes very little significant information from the system and the bulk of the errors already listed will continue to be identified.

Provided that advice notes bearing alterations are returned within some finite period after receipt of the invoice, and before it is paid, the city council will not be exposed to any increased risk of loss. Subject to human error, all such incorrect invoices will be identified and adjusted. On the other hand, if an advice note which needs alteration is *not returned*, then two explanations may hold: either (a) the customer who received or was to receive the goods knows that the delivery or its failure calls for comment on the advice note, but has failed to make one, or (b) the customer knows nothing about any delivery and is continuing to await its arrival.

In the first case there is a possibility of loss only if invoice types 2 or 3 (from Table 13.1) occur. Note, however, that such a situation arises from wilful neglect on the part of the department that ordered the goods to tell the supplies department there is something wrong. Losses arising from this cause have not been taken into account in the calculations that follow.

The second case can occur only when the invoice agrees with the order, but the delivery is missing wholly or in part (type 2, Table 13.1). Here the customer might know nothing about the delivery because the goods were either missing in total or thought to be missing in total. It is in this situation that the supplies department runs the risk of loss if it removes from its clerical checking procedures all unaltered advice notes.

The risk of loss
The best estimate of the number of type 2 invoices is 0.591 percent of the total invoices received (see Table 13.1), based on 1961/2 data. But some of these invoices were for part deliveries, which implies the customer had the necessary information to notify the supplies department of his dissatisfaction. Others were for goods thought to be missing which were found to have been delivered. When these two types of invoices are removed from the type 2 total we find that a small proportion of all invoices (0.234 percent) were for goods actually missing or not dispatched. Such discrepancies can be remedied only if the supplies department and the supplier are made aware that the goods have gone astray. Under the existing checking system this information is deliberately sought because no invoice is approved for payment without notification by the customer (on the advice note) that the goods have been received, but the effort to do this is equivalent to employing two clerks full time.

Under the system being considered the supplies department would automatically approve the payment of an invoice unless it had received from the customer an advice note indicating some problem with the goods. However, invoices for goods missing or not dispatched would probably be paid before the discrepancy was discovered and this is the risk the city council would take, that is, a risk confined to an element of premature payment of 0.234 percent of the total number of invoices received for goods ordered. If the customers did eventually inform the supplies department that goods had not been received, we are told that the department's commercial relationship with its suppliers is such that the fact that the money had been paid would not substantially affect the prospects of recovery.

The real risk, therefore, is with that fraction of the 0.234 percent of the total number of invoices where the customer would completely fail to report nondelivery and would subsequently accept without comment a charge from the supplies department for goods that had not arrived. It is impossible to say how often customers would behave in this way. The head of the supplies department estimates it may happen in 20 percent of cases of nondelivery. If this estimate is accepted then the ultimate risk is confined to 20 percent of 0.234 percent (0.047 percent) of the total number of invoices received. Thus if there is absolutely no checking on the delivery of goods for which an advice note is not received before an invoice is paid the maximum financial loss to the city of Stonebridge, based on the figures for 1961/2, would be $3,948 out of total purchases of $8,400,000. This estimate is at best a crude one, but it does serve to indicate an order of magnitude of the losses at risk.

Controlling the losses (selective checking)
Two possibilities now face the supplies department. First, it must be asked what processes can be used to cream off the largest of the errors that might occur as a result of nondelivery or nondispatch of goods. Secondly, if some level of loss is accepted on grounds of overall economy, how can the department be sure that such losses are in fact being satisfactorily estimated, particularly as the introduction of such a system might leave the organization open to abuse.

One obvious means by which high-value losses can be avoided is deliberately to seek an advice note for all goods above some specified value. That is, to bring into the batching-up process all advice notes associated with invoices above, say, $200, in this case the top 10 percent. The preferred choice of level can in fact be determined mathematically by procedures not discussed here (see Chapter 17). Operating a selective checking scheme at the $200 level would cost the supplies department $1,700 a year, which is approximately $11,600 a year less than the cost of their present (100 percent) checking scheme. Moreover it is possible to examine the practical importance of the assumptions used to obtain this result. The relative crudeness of the estimate that the supplies department would expose itself to a 0.047 percent loss, if all unchanged advice notes were removed from the system makes it necessary to consider the consequences of that value being seriously in error. Suppose, for example, that this figure proved to be wrong by a factor of two, that is, the risk of loss was twice as great at all levels than the calculated figure. Analysis shows that for the best performance the department should check about 20 percent of all invoices. It is important to stress, however, that the consequences of checking only 10 percent, if errors are twice as serious as supposed, is only to add about $400 to the department's operating cost. In this case, that is, the cost of too little checking is $400.

Controlling the losses (random sampling)
Finally, in order to maintain control and thus be able to adjust checking procedures in the event of changes in the pattern of errors, the supplies department must be able to estimate all the factors that have gone into the analysis. For this purpose a nonselective sampling procedure must

be introduced at, say, the 3 percent level. The purpose of this sample will be quite different from that of the 10 percent selective sample. Its function will not be to put right the errors of delivery and dispatch, but to act as a monitor on the system. In this way management will be kept informed of the level of undetected errors that are passing through the unchecked part of the system.

Random sampling control can be achieved in the following way. A proportion of all orders must be marked in a way which holds no significance for anyone but the supplies department. For example, to achieve a 3 percent random sample, order numbers that end in 33, 66 and 99 might be taken as the sample. (The fact that the orders are written at random ensures that the process is not selective.) The department must then monitor these orders through the organization, recording what happens to the invoices that are received, but doing this in a way that treats this random selection exactly as though they were not under special scrutiny. For example, the types of errors listed in Table 13.1 should be noted as a routine procedure. If the advice note is not returned then the fact should be noted but the invoice paid. Only after sufficient time has elapsed to ensure that all likely actions on the part of the customer and the supplier have occurred should the actual story be followed up and recorded.

In this way the department will build up a dossier of factual information about the risks to which it is exposed by adopting any system of incomplete checking, and from the changing pattern of this record will be able to identify all relevant external changes. The introduction of a random sampling procedure will call for extensive and detailed discussion about the exact clerical methods to be used and will also involve a period of training and experiment so that control by sampling becomes as familiar as the comprehensive methods adopted at present.

Summary
The present cost of verifying the delivery of all direct purchases is just under $13,300 per year. It is recommended that confirmation of delivery should only be sought on invoices above $200 in value. This represents 10 percent of the total number of invoices currently received per year. This level provides the best compromise between excessive checking and risk of loss. It would save $11,600 per year in clerical costs and expose the city to an average loss of $1,500 per year, a net saving of $10,100. To control this operation, a further 3 percent random sample of all invoices should be checked, the cost of which has been allowed for in the above figures.

2   PRICE (MARKING OFF)

Marking off serves two purposes: to provide an information service for client departments and to check the accuracy of the price charged for goods. In order to achieve the first aim, the third copy of the purchase order is held in the supplies department. When an invoice is being approved for payment, details of the total price and reference numbers are entered on this copy. Staff of the supplies department are therefore able to notify client departments whether an invoice has been approved for payment or whether the account is still outstanding. Clearly it is important to ask how much this information service is used and to relate the answer to the cost of providing it. This question was not within the scope of this study, however, and attention has been directed solely to the activity of comparing the expected price with that actually charged on the invoice.

Calculations based on a six-day sample of the work of the marking-off section indicated that approximately 5.5 percent of all invoices were returned to the purchasing section with price queries, while others were returned to the purchasing section because they were in excess of a nominal figure of $150 and for this reason required additional authority before they could be approved for payment. Despite the fact that 5.5 percent of all invoices appear to have some discrepancy in the price charged, only a small fraction of these ever reach the point of provoking correspondence with the suppliers. Table 13.2 shows the percentage of invoices for direct purchases which led to a change in the price charged.

Table 13.2 *Occurrence of price errors*

Type of error	Percentage of invoices in error	Average error as a percentage of total value of invoice	Percentage of value in error for all invoices
Overcharge	0.235	13.3	0.031
Undercharge	0.057	9.9	0.006

Approximately a quarter of the incorrect prices arise because the supplier has charged tax incorrectly, failed to provide an agreed trade discount, or has included a charge for delivery or postage which did not agree with previously negotiated arrangements. Wrong price should therefore be taken to include these errors.

Two points must now be considered:

(1) What forms of price checking could be introduced as an alternative to the present practice and what would be the consequence of such changes?
(2) What cash value is represented by this mixture of positive and negative price errors?

The marking-off procedures involve a comparison between the expected price and that actually charged and lead to three distinct types of invoices: correct, overcharge and undercharge. Suppose that this comparison was eliminated and no attempt made to check the price charged on any invoice. Unlike the loss of goods through nondelivery, the city would not be exposed to loss of the total value of the invoice. Wrong price in so far as it implies overcharge will in general be less than the full value of the invoice. Taken over a large number of errors, however, mistakes of price against the city tend to have an average value of 13.3 percent of the invoice, while errors in favor of the city average approximately 9.9 percent of the total value of the invoice. The payment of invoices regardless of price errors would therefore lead to a gross loss on direct purchases of 0.031 percent (0.235 percent of 13.3 percent) of the value of all direct invoices. Errors in the city's favor amount to 0.006 percent (0.057 percent of 9.9 percent) of all direct invoices. These figures are for conditions of zero checking and also assume that the payment of an incorrectly priced invoice will pass unheeded by the supplier. In practice, staff of the supplies department estimate that some 85 percent of all errors of price would remain unchanged if invoices were not checked.

Therefore, if no invoices were checked for price prior to payment, we estimate that overcharges (losses) would amount to about $2,200 per year and that undercharges (gains) would amount to about $430. This gives a net loss of $1,770. Because the value of price errors tends to be proportional to the total value of the invoice on which it occurs it can be assumed that over a period of a year errors on invoices of specified prices will be a constant fraction of that price. Also, price errors were found to occur at approximately the same rate regardless of the value of the invoice. These facts make it possible to calculate a desired level of selective checking for price errors in the same way as for delivery errors, discussed in Section 1.

Controlling price errors (selective checking)
The cost of making the present 100 percent check and of the activities included in marking off has been estimated at $10,400 per year, although only a portion is attributable to the checking of prices. By means of two experiments it has been possible to estimate the effect of reducing the checking process while leaving the information service in its present form. Checking 100 percent of the invoices was found to occupy about 33 percent of the clerical time. If all price checking were removed then the remaining operation would cost $7,000. Checking documents for price errors also places a small burden on the purchasing section, estimated at approximately $2,100 per year.

If a check of price were performed on approximately 10 percent of the highest value invoices, this would involve scrutiny of all invoices over $200. Adopting such a procedure would reduce the operating costs for marking off by approximately $4,000 per year. We carried out several mathematical checks to ensure that this 10 percent level would not incur heavy losses for the city if the assumptions used in arriving at it were wrong. The results showed that the selection of the level of checking for price errors is not a critical decision, providing the city does not underestimate the extent of price errors by a factor of more than two or three times.

Controlling price errors (random sampling)
To ensure that selective checking is being maintained at the best level

and to protect against abuse of the system, a random sampling procedure must be added to the selective sampling already described. The insensitivity of the checking system is important, as it means that the control that management must achieve over the checking procedures can be based on small samples, for example, a 3 percent level of random checking as suggested in connection with delivery errors.

Further analysis is required to establish that the level of 3 percent random sampling is in fact the most suitable level. We would suggest that the supplies department set up a monitoring system to check the results of the scheme and if necessary take corrective steps.

Summary

This check forms part of a wider clerical activity known as 'marking off'. The check itself costs nearly $5,500 per year and protects the city against overcharges averaging $1,770 per year. It is recommended that price checking should only be carried out on invoices above $200 – equivalent to a 10 percent check. The net effect of this change would be to reduce clerical costs by approximately $4,000 per year. The procedure also requires a further 3 percent random check to provide management control and reduce the risk of fraud.

3   ARITHMETIC (EXTENDING)

The third clerical activity performed on invoices before they are approved for payment serves several purposes beyond that of checking the arithmetic accuracy of the invoice. Some suppliers offer the city a discount for quick payment of invoices, which must be calculated. In addition the total invoice value is entered on the charge note and the advice note for accounting purposes. In the special case of the purchase of materials for the housing department, itemized rates and values are also entered on these notes as an aid to the department's internal costing procedures. Thus, checking the arithmetic accuracy of the invoice is only a part of the extending operation, and the various processes are carried out concurrently in a manner that makes it difficult to separate them in practice.

A study of the value of arithmetic errors indicated that on average those against the city were the same as those in its favor. It is clear that in the long run arithmetic errors will tend to cancel each other out. In any one year, however, there can arise an imbalance in the number and value of these errors which may cause the city financial loss. In the particular year studied the errors were on balance against the city and amounted to nearly $1,800. The two largest errors both happened by chance to be against the city and together accounted for $1,200 of the $1,800. The financial significance of these high-value errors suggests a practical justification for setting up a limited check on invoices where high-value errors can occur.

Because of the interaction of positive and negative errors the arithmetic check is not suitable for analysis by the methods adopted for delivery and price. Instead we adopted a solution based on consideration of the practical problems of implementation. The previous sections have shown that a 10 percent check on receipt of goods should be adopted together with a 10 percent check on the accuracy of price. In practice, it is obviously economic to set a general level of checking throughout. This is particularly true in cases where the organization of a supplies department is not subdivided into 'batching up', 'marking off', and 'extending'. We therefore suggest a 10 percent check of arithmetic on high-value invoices.

The value of reducing arithmetic checks
In order to estimate the time spent checking the arithmetic accuracy of invoices as distinct from other clerical operations performed by the same staff, a series of spot checks was made of the various activities. At each observation the particular activity being performed was recorded. The results (see Table 13.3) showed that only about one-sixth of the working day was occupied by checking the arithmetic accuracy of invoices, the remainder being used to aid the costing procedures of the supplies department, to evaluate discounts, and to carry out the physical task of handling the documents. The last activity accounted for about a third of the time.

Table 13.3   *Proportion of time on various extending activities*

Activity	Percentage of time observed performing activity
Collecting invoices	2.5
Separating documents	15.0
Checking accuracy of arithmetic	13.5
Entering details of invoice on advice and charge notes (including checking the addition)	24.0
Calculating discounts	7.0
Sorting into contract and official invoices	1.0
Completing certification stamp	10.0
Returning invoices	2.0
Counting number of invoices handled	7.5
All other activities	17.5
	100.0%

From Table 13.3 it is clear that economies of operation in extending are unlikely to be dramatic if selective checking of arithmetic is instituted. Considering the number of staff, their salaries, and the amount of time spent on checking invoices for arithmetic errors, we estimate that this check is costing the city $3,500 per year. If the level of checking were reduced to 10 percent, the work of checking for arithmetic errors should cost about $800, an annual saving of $2,700. If selective checking of price and delivery were adopted, then most invoices would pass through this section without an advice note attached. This would introduce additional economies of effort in handling documents and allied activities, and would result in a further saving of about $700 per year. In total, therefore, the possible economies to be achieved by a reduction of the arithmetic checking to 10 percent of direct purchase invoices cannot be expected to exceed about $3,400 per year.

Finally, there is a risk that fraudulent advantage might be taken of any reduction of checking. To protect against this and to ensure that the supplies department maintains control over their financial activities, some form of random sampling check must also be introduced. We would suggest a 3 percent level of random checking to correspond to the random check also being undertaken for price and delivery, and subject to the same control procedures.

Summary

In the long run arithmetic mistakes on invoices tend to cancel themselves out. In any financial year, however, the city might experience a net loss. In the year studied a net loss amounting to $1,800 was avoided by clerical checks which cost about $3,500. Checking invoices above $200 would have been adequate to eliminate all the significant errors and would have reduced clerical costs by $3,400.

CONCLUSIONS

The supplies department of Stonebridge should adopt a 10 percent selective check on all invoices for direct purchases processed at the Hillside Warehouse. Only invoices in excess of $200 should be checked. This check should apply to receipt of goods, price charged and arithmetic accuracy. At the same time a random scrutiny of 3 percent of all invoices should be carried out regardless of invoice value (1) to ensure that changes in the pattern of errors are not occurring which would necessitate a different level of selective checking, and (2) to set limits on the losses which could arise from fraudulent abuse of the system of selective checking. Management control records should be maintained on the 3 percent sample indicating the level at which various errors are occurring, the reaction of the city's departments, and the reaction of suppliers in the face of these errors.

The adoption of these methods can be expected to lead to a net reduction in the clerical costs at the Hillside Warehouse of about $17,500 a year. This figure allows for possible financial losses amounting on average to $2,300 a year.

In addition, the study has disclosed the existence of other clerical activities that appear to warrant study by similar methods. In particular, we would suggest investigating the possibility of further reductions in the checking procedures in the batching-up process, the possibility of not marking the third copy of the purchase order, and the scope for reducing the costing activities and discount calculation on individual invoices.

14

Simulation of a New Service Facility

In 1971 the London Borough of Ealing found that its vehicle maintenance and repair garages were inadequate to maintain its fleet to the required standards. This situation had resulted from considerable expansion in recent years in the size of the fleet, without a corresponding increase in the service facilities, and the introduction of stricter statutory requirements for vehicle maintenance. To alleviate this situation, the borough's technical services group drew up a plan for a new vehicle maintenance facility.

Like most local governments, the borough must maintain a large number of different types of vehicles and equipment. Its fleet includes ambulances and cars, buses and refuse disposal vehicles and specialized road maintenance and repair equipment such as road sweepers and rollers. In all there were nineteen different types of vehicles in the borough's fleet in 1971 and it was estimated that the new service facility would need to be able to maintain a future fleet consisting of approximately 440 vehicles. Before implementing the plan for the new maintenance facility, the borough council commissioned a study to investigate the ability of the proposed facility to handle the repair and maintenance requirements of the future fleet and to recommend any amendments that might be necessary. The study, conducted by Barry Pilgrim, involved the use of a computer model which simulated the arrivals to, repairs in and departures from the various workshops of the facility over many weeks. While concentrating on the proposed design the study also assessed the performance of many possible alternatives.

The purpose of the study was to help the borough assess the resources that should be allocated to the major functions of the new facility – monthly servicing, repairs, bodywork and painting. By simulating the operation of the shops that would perform these functions it was possible to estimate how well service staff and facility space would be utilized, as well as measure the availability of facilities for a vehicle in need of repair or maintenance. For example, it was intended to give all vehicles an inspection and primary service once a month in the new maintenance facility. To accomplish this the proposed facility was to include four hoists in its monthly servicing workshop. Pilgrim examined the effects of changing the number of service hoists used for monthly servicing. In comparing the use of four hoists in the proposed facility to a facility with three and then two hoists, he found that the average utilization of hoists and mechanics in the four-hoist facility was 59 percent, compared to 78 percent for a three-hoist facility and 99 percent for a two-hoist facility. But two hoists were not quite enough to provide a monthly servicing to all the vehicles in the fleet, whereas three or four hoists could easily handle the entire fleet. Therefore, as a result of delays in performing monthly servicing under a two-hoist system, it was estimated that there would be twenty more vehicle breakdowns per month under such a system as compared to using three or four hoists.

In another comparison, this time of the repair shop, Pilgrim simulated the operation of the proposed shop, which was to include fourteen vehicle spaces, and compared it to a shop with eighteen spaces. In so doing he found that the facility with fourteen spaces had one or more vacant spaces 65 percent of the time, compared to 92 percent for the shop with eighteen spaces. But the simulations also showed that there would be times when both the fourteen-space and the eighteen-space repair shops were filled and vehicles had to wait for repairs. In the case of the repair shop with fourteen spaces, one or more vehicles waited for a repair space 26 percent of the time, while waiting occurred only 4 percent of the time under an eighteen-space repair shop.

Numerous other results on resource utilization and availability were found by simulating the operation of the proposed maintenance facility and various alternatives to it. The results were presented in Pilgrim's final report, *Simulation of the New Vehicle Workshop in the London Borough of Ealing*. This report was submitted to the borough council at the end of 1971. In it Pilgrim summarized the simulation results and predicted what would happen if the size and staffing of the various shops in the proposed facility were changed. In addition, he suggested possible changes in the alignment of various shops within the facility in order to improve the utilization of resources. One such suggestion was to arrange the hoists for monthly servicing next to the repair shop in order to take advantage of the repair shop facilities during periods of peak demand in the monthly servicing shop.

The borough council authorized construction of the new maintenance facility in 1972 and construction began that summer. It took almost two years to construct and equip the new facility and it has been in operation since March 1974. The design of the facility is virtually the same as the one originally proposed by the technical services group. Although it incorporated a few modifications in the allocation of space it did not vary significantly from the original design.

The simulation model was quite accurate in terms of the estimates it used of the number and types of vehicles that would comprise the future fleet. In 1979 the new service facility maintained a total of 475 vehicles or pieces of equipment (Pilgrim used 438 in his simulation). There have been a few changes in the types of vehicles serviced, for example, small (half-ton) vans have replaced most of the cars and six large trucks have been added to the fleet, but generally it appears that the simulation results accurately reflected the present fleet. We spoke with Mr Eric Wagg, assistant chief executive at Ealing, about the borough's use of the simulation study. He said that the study's results were thought to be quite plausible by the borough's staff and it was felt that the study tended to confirm that the proposed plan was a good one.

On discussing the report it became clear, however, that the greatest value of the study lay not in its final results but in the way it forced careful definition of some of the underlying issues. For example, the simulation model depended heavily for its accuracy on the precise specification of the work of the various maintenance shops, which affected the time and flexibility available, and on the rules governing such determinants as maintenance intervals, replacement policies and number of reserve vehicles. In the course of the study many, although not all, of these points were clarified. The process continued after presentation of the final report.

It is not unusual for an operations research study to be used to clarify issues involved. Often studies are undertaken with full knowledge that in order to obtain results based upon scientific analysis it will be necessary to clarify a procedure or decide how a particular operation will be run. We believe that *Simulation of the New Vehicle Workshop in the London Borough of Ealing* illustrates a situation in which the issues that were raised and subsequently resolved during the course of the study were more important than the final results.

Simulation is a very useful technique for studying complex service systems. It is used to compare and assess alternative systems in terms of their utilization and the level of service provided. It provides an efficient way of trying out ideas concerning the operation of a complex system without necessarily resorting to changing an existing system or building a new system. This study presents a good general introduction to the types of questions that can be investigated and the types of results that can be expected from a computer simulation model.

The final report of the study follows. The first section provides the framework within which the simulation operated. In particular, it gives the design of the proposed service facility and the vehicle maintenance policies under which it would operate. Section 2 presents the results of using the simulation model to examine the size of the proposed facility. Section 3 discusses other factors, not considered in depth by the study, which might affect the design of the new maintenance facility.

Simulation of the New Vehicle Workshop in the London Borough of Ealing

BARRY PILGRIM

1   INTRODUCTION

The London Borough of Ealing inherited its present vehicle maintenance garages from the Middlesex Borough in 1965. These are now inadequate to maintain its fleet to the required standard. Consequently it is extremely difficult, if not impossible, for the borough to discharge its responsibilities without putting work out to contract. This is particularly true for inspection and routine maintenance work where the borough is short of the necessary hoists or repair pits.

To alleviate this situation, the technical services group have drawn up a plan for a new maintenance facility to be built at Greenford. The new facility is designed to repair and maintain the whole of the borough's fleet and has six main sections: vehicle servicing, vehicle inspection, general repairs, bodywork, painting and unit repairs.

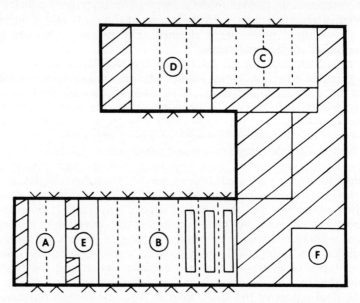

Figure 14.1   *Plan for proposed maintenance facility showing principal repair shops*

The proposed facility
Figure 14.1 shows a plan of the proposed maintenance facility. The U-shaped design with doors along each side allows easy access to the workshops. The six main sections and their sizes are as follows:

A   vehicle servicing: four hoists for monthly service and inspection
B   general repair shop: eight bays and six pits for mechanical and electrical repairs and extended maintenance
C   body repair shop: three bays for vehicles and 1 bay for equipment
D   paint shop: six bays
E   vehicle testing: two bays
F   unit repair shop: for repairs of parts removed from vehicles.

The number of mechanics required obviously depends not only on the level of utilization, but also on the opening hours of the new facility. It is intended that these will be the same as at present. This means an eight-hour working day, Monday to Friday, plus two hours of overtime, which will be worked by up to 70 percent of the mechanics if work is available. On Saturday up to eight hours of overtime will be available for the same number of men, but normally five hours will be worked. On Sunday the facility is not expected to be open.

Fleet policies
The workload imposed on the new facility depends on two basic policies relating to the vehicles which had to be defined before we could perform the simulations. These are the size of fleet to be maintained and the policies on vehicle replacement.

Size of the vehicle fleet. Because the new facility must be capable of maintaining Ealing's vehicles and plant for many years we asked the transport managers for estimates of the future fleet size. These estimates are shown in the third column of Table 14.1. Some estimates were necessarily speculative, but the inaccuracy in the overall fleet size is not large enough to affect our results. The estimated fleet size shows an increase over the present numbers. This expansion arises in two ways: extra vehicles to cater for increases in the services provided and additional vehicles to act as reserves while others are being repaired. The policy of holding reserves is considered in Section 3 of this report.

Table 14.1 *Estimated future fleet for vehicle types included in the simulation*

Type number	Vehicle type	Number of vehicles	Critical number	Number of vehicles fitting into 60 feet
1	Ambulances	12	1	2
2	Bulk gritters	7	1	2
3	Highway repair trucks	31	4	3
4	Library vehicles	5	1	3
5	Simon tower	11	2	2
6	Sewer and gully cleansers	12	2	2
7	Main drainage vehicles	2	1	3
8	Pakamatics and side loaders (refuse collection)	64	12	2
9	Bin lift (refuse collection)	9	1	2
10	Meals-on-wheels and school meals vans	38	2	4
11	Health and welfare cars	26	2	4
12	School buses	12	1	2
13	Refuse collection vehicles	16	2	3
14	Road sweepers	16	2	4
15	½- to 1-ton vans	50	4	4
16	Small vans and cars	104	8	4
17	Mechanical shovels	5	1	3
18	Road rollers	8	1	3
19	Compressors	10	1	4
	Total	438		

Replacement policies. Because the repair and maintenance required depends critically on a vehicle's age, we had to define a vehicle replacement policy to be used in the simulations. We used the borough's present policies, which are: refuse vehicles, ten years; heavy trucks, seven years; and cars, vans and ambulances, five years. By using the present replacement policies in simulating the operation of the proposed facility we were also able to use the borough's data on breakdown rates and repair times which were collected under and are based on these replacement policies. The relationship between vehicle replacement policies and the size of the facility is considered in more detail in Section 3.

2   TESTING THE PROPOSED FACILITY SIZE

In this part of the report we consider each section of the proposed facility separately, then the facility as a whole. For each section we aim to show two things: how well the section is utilized and how often vehicles have to wait for repair. For the facility as a whole we offer a general comment on its design and give details of the vehicle availability achieved.

Monthly servicing hoists

In the new facility it is intended to give all vehicles an inspection and primary service once a month and four hoists have been specially reserved for this purpose (section A in Figure 14.1). Each hoist will have two mechanics who will take an average of one hour for each vehicle serviced. If faults are found by the inspection the vehicle will be passed to the repair shop for repair.

To operate this full servicing policy successfully will require an adequate number of reserve vehicles and hoists. We found that there were sufficient reserves in the fleet to achieve full servicing. Reserve vehicles are necessary because, although vehicles are called in for servicing at a predetermined time, when the time arrives so many other vehicles may have broken down that to go ahead with the servicing may seriously disrupt the borough's work. In this case the vehicle will continue on the road but be on call, so that it will come into the shop as soon as either a replacement vehicle is available or its tasks are less urgent. In column 4 of Table 14.1 we give the maximum number of vehicles of each type that can be off the road before other vehicles of the same type have to be put on call. We call this maximum number the *critical number*.

We measured the effects of having two, three or four servicing hoists: with four, six and eight mechanics respectively. We were aiming to find the size of the servicing section that gave a high utilization of the hoists and mechanics without incurring too many missed services. As well as estimating directly the number of missed services we found the number of breakdowns that occurred. The number that involved vehicles on call was extracted to estimate the faults that would have been found by routine inspection had it been possible. The results are shown in Table 14.2. As can be seen, three hoists provide as good a service as four, with each hoist and mechanic being used for an extra 17 percent of the time. With either three or four hoists full servicing is achieved. This involves 430 vehicles per month which is slightly less than the number in the fleet (438) because there are vehicles in the shop for lengthy repairs or maintenance which do not require their monthly service.

Table 14.2 *Effects of changing the number of service hoists*

No. of hoists	No. of mechanics	Average utilization of each mechanic and hoist (%)	No. of services per month	No. of services per month per hoist	No. of breakdowns per month	No. of breakdowns of vehicles on call per month
2	4	99	390	195	210	36
3	6	76	430	143	190	4
4	8	59	430	108	190	4

Decreasing the number of hoists to two makes maximum use of both hoists, with nearly two hundred services per month on each. But about fifty vehicles miss a service each month under this arrangement which means that each vehicle misses, on average, one monthly service every nine months. This results in a sharp increase in the number of breakdowns of vehicles on call. Also, the full amount of overtime is required to fulfill the high utilization of the hoists. These facts must be weighed against the economies of reducing the number of hoists.

Repair shop
The repair shop (section B in Figure 14.1) will handle four main types of repair and maintenance: preparation of vehicles for inspection, extended maintenance, breakdown repairs and repairs of faults found by the monthly service.

Preparation for inspection. Preparing vehicles for inspection will involve cars and vans once a year after they are three years old and other vehicles each year of their lives. For cars and vans, preparation for inspection requires approximately eight hours of work in the repair shop; for trucks and other large vehicles it can require as much as thirty-two hours.

Extended maintenance. This is designed to prevent major breakdowns and involves all vehicles and plants when they are three years old and every third year thereafter. The repair times associated with extended maintenance range from 56 hours to 136 hours, depending on the type of vehicles.

Breakdown repairs. In order to simulate breakdown repairs (including accidents) we needed to know how often vehicles break down and how long it takes to repair them. The necessary information was found from data relating to Ealing's present fleet. This was collected by the borough's management services section and involved on-the-spot recording at the present Greenford shop over a period of three weeks and investigation of past records. The average breakdown interval varies widely for different types of vehicles. For example, the average number of days between breakdowns of refuse collection vehicles was found to be thirty-one days, while for cars it was seventy-one days.

Since the length of time between consecutive breakdowns varies we used statistical distributions to enable us to reproduce the variations when simulating the operation of the shop. Thus for each vehicle type we had data not only on the average breakdown interval but also on the probability that the breakdown interval would be a given number of days. We also allowed for the fact that the number of breakdowns will be reduced once regular servicing is introduced, thus increasing the average length of time between breakdowns. For example, for refuse collection vehicles the increase was from thirty-one to forty-three days and for vans from forty-five to eighty days.

Repair of faults found by monthly service. To estimate how many faults are likely to be found by monthly servicing and how long they will take to repair, we examined data from another London borough that already has the facilities for regular servicing. This investigation showed that when a fault was found its repair time was insignificantly different from the time it would have taken if the vehicle had broken down. We were thus able to use the same repair times as those for breakdowns.

The planned repair shop is designed to hold seven lines of vehicles side by side. Three of these lines will be equipped with pit facilities, as shown in Figure 14.2.

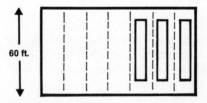

Figure 14.2   *Plan for the repair shop*

To run the simulations it was assumed that, in general, each line would hold two vehicles. We therefore defined the repair shop as having fourteen 'spaces'; that is, eight bays and six pits. In practice, when the repair shop is busy more than one of the smaller types of vehicle can be repaired in the same bay or pit at the same time. We allowed for this in the simulations. In column 5 of Table 14.1 we give, for each type of vehicle, the number that can be repaired simultaneously in a sixty-foot line.

We simulated different sizes of repair shop to find out how the number of vehicles under repair was affected by size and how many spaces these occupied. We did not examine how the repairs were affected by different numbers of mechanics, but included sufficient mechanics – calculated separately for each size of repair shop – to ensure that no vehicle ever had to wait for a man. Although this produced low utilization of the men we believe that they will be well occupied when other work (particularly repairs on the road) is also taken into account.

We found that, if the repair shop were large enough to prevent a queue of vehicles waiting for space, the number of times when more than eighteen vehicles were under repair at any one time was negligible. With the mix of sizes in the fleet these eighteen could be repaired in fourteen spaces, which means that any size of repair shop greater than or equal to fourteen spaces (the proposed size) would enable the vehicles to be repaired as soon as possible. A maximum of twenty mechanics was necessary to achieve this level of service.

Maximum vehicle availability is thus achieved with the planned repair shop. However, this is at the expense of having vacant bays for much of the time in order to cater for peak workloads. We also found that, with the proposed design, considerable work was done in the pits that would normally have been done in the bays if these had been available. We therefore examined the results of two changes: changing the overall size of the repair shop and changing the number of pits.

Changing the size of the repair shop. We examined repair shops which were (1) smaller and (2) larger than the proposed design. We found that less than ten spaces results in an ever-increasing backlog of work, whereas with more than eighteen spaces the extra room was never used. There is very little difference between the vehicle availability achieved with each of these sizes. Even with only ten spaces the vehicle availability is only 1.5 percent less than the maximum possible – measured by the average time that each vehicle is off the road. The final decision on the size of repair shop must therefore be taken on the basis of how well the available spaces are utilized.

The workload in the repair shop varied considerably. For some of the time there are few vehicles needing repair and there are vacant spaces. On other occasions it is necessary to put more than one vehicle in each bay. We looked at these two aspects – underutilization and double use of bays – for the different sizes of repair shops tested.

The percentage of time for which there were vacant spaces is shown in Table 14.3 for each size of repair shop. It can be seen that for the planned repair shop (fourteen spaces) there is one or more vacant space for 65 percent of the time and as many as five for 22 percent of the time. Removing four bays reduces these numbers to 25 percent and adding four increases them to 92 percent and 66 percent.

Table 14.3 *Percentage of time that spaces in the repair shop are vacant*

		Spaces in repair shop				
		10	12	14	16	18
	5 or more	2	6	22	40	66
Vacant	4 or more	5	10	31	52	74
spaces	3 or more	9	17	42	63	82
	2 or more	16	27	55	72	87
	1 or more	25	38	65	82	92

All the repair shops tested have high utilization of the spaces. Even for the largest, each space is in use (that is, one or more vehicles are being repaired in it) for 78 percent of the time. This increases to 85 percent for the planned design and to 94 percent for a repair shop with ten spaces. When there are more vehicles requiring repair than spaces in which to repair them, the smaller vehicles are repaired more than one in a bay. The frequency with which this occurs is shown by Table 14.4.

Table 14.4 *Percentage of time with more vehicles than spaces in the repair shop*

		Spaces in repair shop				
		10	12	14	16	18
Number	at least 1	65	50	26	12	4
of vehicles	at least 2	53	39	19	7	1
greater	at least 3	40	27	13	3	0
than	at least 4	22	16	8	1	0
number of	at least 5	*	*	4	0	0
spaces						

*No results are shown for repair shops with ten and twelve spaces since there was no room to park five extra vehicles and vehicles had to wait.

This gives the percentage of the time when there were more vehicles than spaces in the simulated repair shop. With sixteen or eighteen spaces the repair shop is never completely full, provided more than two vehicles occupy some bays. With the planned design it is full for 6 percent of the time and reducing the size to twelve and ten bays increases this figure to 22 percent and 41 percent respectively.

The smaller repair shops require fewer mechanics to prevent any

Table 14.5 *Maximum number of mechanics needed for different size repair shops*

Spaces in repair shop	10	12	14	16	18
Number of mechanics	15	17	18	20	20

vehicle waiting for a man since the maximum number of vehicles that can be accommodated is reduced. The maximum number of mechanics required is shown in Table 14.5. The total workload is, of course, the same for all sizes of repair shop and is equivalent to eleven and a half mechanics. Thus with twelve mechanics or more, there will be manpower available for work other than in the repair shop.

These results exclude two factors. They do not include space required for vehicles and plant excluded from the simulation and they do not include space that could be required for waiting vehicles. We believe that the total extra space required for the excluded items is not greater than two bays. The space used by these items will obviously vary from day to day. However, this variation need not be considered; only the average space requirements need to be determined. It can be shown statistically that virtually all the variations in the number of excluded items can be considered as already included in the results for the rest of the fleet. Thus, to determine the right size of repair shop the manager must first choose the preferred size for the simulated fleet from an examination of our results, and then add to this the average space required for the additional items.

Waiting vehicles are those requiring spare parts or space. If these wait inside the repair shop the results given in Tables 14.3 and 14.4 change to those shown in Tables 14.6 and 14.7 respectively.

Table 14.6 *Percentage of time that spaces in the repair shop are vacant – vehicles waiting inside*

		Spaces in repair shop				
		10	12	14	16	18
	5 or more	0	0	2	5	23
Vacant	4 or more	0	0	4	10	33
	3 or more	0	1	8	17	45
spaces	2 or more	0	3	14	27	54
	1 or more	2	6	22	40	66

Table 14.7 *Percentage of time with more vehicles than spaces in the repair shop – vehicles waiting inside*

		Spaces in repair shop				
		10	12	14	16	18
Number	at least 1	95	90	69	48	26
of vehicles	at least 2	91	83	58	37	18
greater	at least 3	84	73	45	28	13
than	at least 4	75	62	35	18	8
number of	at least 5	*	*	26	12	4
spaces						

*No results are shown for repair shops with ten and twelve spaces since there was no room to park five extra vehicles and vehicles had to wait.

With waiting vehicles parked inside the repair shop, the percentage of time that the shop is completely full increases. The results are shown in Table 14.8.

Table 14.8 *Percentage of time repair shop completely full – vehicles waiting inside*

Spaces in repair shop	10	12	14	16	18
Completely full (%)	80	67	30	12	4

Changing the number of pits. For all but the largest repair shop (eighteen spaces) some bay work was performed in pits because bays were not available. The extent of this is shown in Table 14.9 where we give the man-hours per week of bay work done in pits for the various

Table 14.9 *Bay work done in pits*

Spaces in repair shop	Man-hours of bay work done in pits per week
10	109
12	74
14	28
16	5
18	0

repair shop sizes. We examined the use of the pits for pit work under two methods of working: first, for a situation where more than one of the smaller types of vehicles can be repaired in the same pit at the same time; and secondly, where each pit can take only one vehicle at a time. The results are given in Table 14.10. Under the first method of working the pits 5 and 6 are hardly used and the work can easily be done on four pits without any appreciable waiting by vehicles. These

Table 14.10 *Percentage utilization of pits in the repair shop*

	With more than one vehicle per pit	With no more than one vehicle per pit
1st pit	95	95
2nd pit	78	88
3rd pit	50	72
4th pit	24	50
5th pit	6	30
6th pit	1	14

two pits are used appreciably more for the second system of working, although their workload could still be done on the other pits if some vehicles wait for space. We were not able to simulate this situation to show the extent of waiting but we do not believe it would have a significant effect on vehicle availability.

Body shop

The body shop in the proposed service facility (section C of Figure 14.1) will handle all body repairs. At present some of these repairs are done at Greenford and some by outside contractors. We examined the effect of running the body shop with three men and then investigated the effects of reducing this to two and one.

Three men. With three men the body repairs kept each man occupied for only 20 percent of their time. The number of vehicles requiring repairs (either under repair or waiting) was as follows:

> 1 or more vehicles 40 percent of the time
> 2 or more vehicles 10 percent of the time
> 3 or more vehicles 3 percent of the time
> 4 or more vehicles never.

Thus the planned shop with three bays for body repairs is large enough to cater for all vehicles requiring repairs and moreover the second and third man are only occasionally occupied. These figures make no allowance for trailer repairs, which will be done in the body shop. With three men there is the equivalent of over two men available for these.

Two men. Two men were each utilized on vehicle repairs for 31 percent of the time, leaving the equivalent of 1.4 men for trailer repairs. The space required was as follows:

> 1 or more vehicles 55 percent of the time
> 2 or more vehicles 20 percent of the time
> 3 or more vehicles 10 percent of the time
> 4 or more vehicles 3 percent of the time
> 5 or more vehicles never.

The planned body shop caters for all the vehicles for 97 percent of the time and still only requires more than one bay for 20 percent of the time.

One man. One man was occupied on the vehicles for 60 percent of his time, leaving only 40 percent for trailer repairs. The space requirements were:

> 1 or more vehicles 60 percent of the time
> 2 or more vehicles 35 percent of the time

3 or more vehicles 20 percent of the time
4 or more vehicles 10 percent of the time
5 or more vehicles 5 percent of the time
6 or more vehicles never.

For 10 percent of the time the planned body shop is too small to hold all the vehicles. With only one man the simulation showed that some vehicles had to wait for up to one week while a lengthy body job was being performed in the shop.

Paint shop
The paint shop will handle work of two kinds: painting after body repairs and planned repainting of vehicles. Touch-up painting is required after most body repairs. The shop manager estimated that the time needed for this work is 40 percent of the bodywork time. We therefore estimated the time required for this element of painting from the data on body jobs. To prevent deterioration of bodywork all vehicles and plant will be repainted three years after purchase and every three years thereafter. The time required to carry out repainting depends on the vehicle type, with estimates ranging from 24 to 112 hours.

We examined the effect of running the paint shop with different numbers of men. The simulation results are given in Table 14.11. On

Table 14.11   *Percentage utilization of various numbers of painters in paint shop*

		Number of painters			
		3	4	5	6
Number	1 or more	100	100	95	90
of	2 or more	95	80	75	70
vehicles	3 or more	80	50	50	50
in the	4 or more	70	40	30	30
paint	5 or more	60	20	15	15
shop	6 or more	40	10	5	5
	7 or more	30	3	2	1
Average utilization of each painter (%)		90	65	50	40

the basis of these figures the proportion of time for which there were more vehicles than painters were:

three men 70 percent
four men 20 percent
five men 5 percent
six men 1 per cent.

Four men give a good balance between the workload per man and the number of vehicles waiting. With more than four men only a marginal improvement is obtained in the waiting time of vehicles. With only three men each has a very heavy workload and vehicles are kept waiting for 70 percent of the time.

The amount of space required depends on whether an appreciable amount of the painting time involves rubbing down *outside* the paint shop. The figures shown above indicate that with four men, four bays are sufficient for 80 percent of the time, even with all the painting work done inside.

Other sections

We did not examine the other two main sections of the maintenance facility: the vehicle testing bays and the unit repair shop. Neither of these could be simulated because of the difficulty of collecting accurate data. The planned design has two bays for testing vehicles after they have been repaired. On average 160 vehicles per week leave the service facility after repairs or servicing (excluding bodywork and painting). If it can be estimated how many of these vehicles will require testing and how long the tests will take, the utilization of the bays can be calculated. The unit repair shop is designed to repair parts removed from the vehicles and does not involve standing vehicles. The size of this section is, therefore, determined by the necessary equipment and not the space required for parking vehicles. We did not investigate this equipment.

Maintenance facility as a whole

We now offer some general comments on aspects of the maintenance facility not directly related to the individual sections. In particular we consider the general design and summarize the vehicle availability achieved with different shop sizes.

Design features. In the course of the simulations it became clear that the number of vehicles in each section of the maintenance facility fluctuates considerably from day to day. Thus although most of the time there will be sufficient space inside each section for vehicles waiting for repair, on those occasions when the workload is abnormally heavy some vehicles will have to wait elsewhere. This will involve movement of vehicles which could be avoided, or at least reduced, if sections were combined.

For example, if the monthly service hoists were sited next to the pits then difficulties from abnormally high workloads in the pits might be alleviated by using the hoists. Under this arrangement the hoists could still be reserved for monthly servicing by giving top priority to this type of repair, but the shop manager is given greater flexibility in the use of space when emergencies arise. The same arguments apply to the body shop, which might be at one end of the repair shop.

We recognize that in making these observations we are applying a purely statistical measure and that other factors, such as the operational aspects of running the maintenance facility or the problem of fitting it

Table 14.12 *Vehicle availability achieved for the proposed maintenance facility*

Type of vehicle	Critical number	No. of reserves	% time this number of vehicles is off the road						
			None	1 or more	2 or more	3 or more	4 or more	5 or more	6 or more
Pakamatics and side loaders (refuse collection)	12	8	0	100	97	87	68	44	21
Bin lift (refuse collection)	2	2	46	54	8	0*			
Meals-on-wheels and school meals vans	2	2	18	82	37	4*			
Health and welfare cars	2	2	51	49	10	1*			
Small vans and cars	8	5	3	97	81	51	23	9	2*
Ambulances	1	—	36	64	13*	3			
Bulk gritters	1	—	60	40	3*				
Highway repair trucks	4	—	6	94	74	45	17	1*	
Library vehicles	1	—	82	18	0*				
Simon tower	2	—	46	54	16	0*			
Sewer and gully cleansers	2	—	31	69	31	2*			
Main drainage vehicles	1	—	91	9	0*				
School buses	1	—	42	58	9*				
Refuse collection vehicles	2	—	35	65	37	6*	1		
Road sweepers	2	—	38	62	26	3*			
½- to 1-ton vans	4	—	6	94	68	35	14	0*	
Mechanical shovels	1	—	78	22	0*				
Road rollers	1	—	68	32	2*				
Compressors	1	—	63	37	2*				

*These numbers show the percentage of time that more vehicles of a given type are off the road than the critical number for this type. Generally this occurs a very small percentage of the time, indicating that the maximum required availability is being virtually achieved.

on the proposed site, may deserve greater weight. However, we believe the possibilities of combining certain sections could profitably be considered before a final decision on the design is taken.

Vehicle availability. In comparing the availability of vehicles for the many different shop sizes we found that the differences in availability were very small over a wide range of sizes. The size of maintenance facility below which the vehicle availability decreases significantly is as follows:

> three service hoists
> six bays and four pits in the repair shop
> two men in the body shop
> three men in the paint shop.

Table 14.12 gives the vehicle availability for the planned design. Columns 4–10 show the percentage of the time when the simulation showed that various numbers of vehicles would be off the road. The column headed 'Critical number' shows the number of vehicles of each type which can be off the road without serious consequences. The results must be considered in relation to the number of reserve vehicles that will be included in the fleet. Some types have to have specific reserves. Reserves for other types are less specific; for example, a reserve truck can replace several types of vehicle. The number of reserves is shown in column 3 of the table and a fuller discussion of reserves is given in Section 3.

The vehicle availability which is achieved depends more on using the mechanics efficiently than on the size of a shop. These results on vehicle availability were obtained from simulation of shops where the mechanics were always used as efficiently as possible. This meant that if breakdowns caused changes in the priorities for repairing the vehicles, mechanics were shifted between vehicles immediately. In practice this may not be achieved so easily, particularly in the small shops where there is less flexibility in the use of the resources.

Conclusions

This section summarizes the conclusions found from the simulations.

(1) *Monthly servicing.* With a throughput of one vehicle per hoist per hour, three or more hoists achieve full servicing. To decide if two are sufficient the number of missed services must be weighed against the extra utilization of the hoists. Arranging the hoists next to the pits in the repair shop has advantages when peak workloads are encountered.

(2) *Repair shop.* The workload in the repair shop has large variations and its size must be determined by balancing the time that vacant space occurs against the time the shop is overloaded.

(3) *Body shop.* Two men can cope with bodywork if repairs on items not included in the simulated fleet are less than the equivalent of 1.4 men. Three bays are sufficient to handle the vehicles and plant for most of the time. Incorporating the body shop as a specified part of the repair shop has advantages when peak workloads occur.

(4) *Paint shop.* No more than four painters are required and three may be considered sufficient. The space needed depends on how much, if any, of the job can be done outside the paint shop. In any case no more than four bays are required to give space for the vehicles.

(5) *Vehicle availability.* Vehicle availability depends more upon the provision of reserve vehicles and the efficient use of the mechanics than on the size of the maintenance facility. In our simulations we used the mechanics as efficiently as possible.

3   GENERAL CONSIDERATIONS OF FACILITY SIZE

This section looks at two general factors which were not considered in depth by our study. However, they have a bearing on the provision of a suitable maintenance facility for Ealing and we present them as points for consideration before plans are made final. They involve two policies: the provision of reserve vehicles; and replacement ages for vehicles.

Reserve vehicles

The results given in Section 2 were based on meeting routine maintenance schedules. These schedules could be met because the estimated future fleet includes the provision of a sufficient number of reserve vehicles to take the place of vehicles that are off the road for routine maintenance. If less than an adequate number of substitute vehicles are available, either the planned schedules will not be met or the effective vehicle fleet on the road must be reduced. Experience indicates that the first alternative will occur, thus lowering the standard of maintenance achieved and in turn reducing the size of maintenance facility required. We would therefore emphasize that the provision of the necessary substitute vehicles is implicit in the decision to build a facility large enough to carry out the program of routine maintenance that is planned.

There are two possible means of providing substitute vehicles: by owning reserves or by leasing. In practice certain vehicle types are difficult, if not impossible, to lease. This applies particularly to the specialist types, such as refuse collection vehicles. Even with the less specialist vehicles careful comparison must be made of the service which firms that lease vehicles are able to offer and the costs involved before leasing is considered as the best method of providing substitute vehicles.

We made a preliminary analysis of the minimum number of reserve vehicles that would be needed to ensure the routine maintenance standards set by the borough. The results showed that, taking into account flexibility between some vehicle types, the number of reserves built into the simulation could be marginally reduced.

Vehicle replacement policies

In this section we consider in general terms how changes in the present vehicle replacement policies might affect the required size for the new maintenance facility. To do this we consider the two relevant aspects of the work in the facility: breakdown repairs and three-yearly maintenance (overhaul and repainting).

Repairs from breakdowns generally increase with a vehicle's age, even if general overhauls are performed regularly. This increase varies considerably from vehicle to vehicle, but we can take a 10 percent increase per year as a reasonable average estimate. On this basis a change of replacement policy such that each group of vehicles is replaced either a few years earlier or later has little effect on the total repair work required. Thus breakdown repairs have very little effect on the required shop size.

Three-yearly maintenance may have a more profound effect. The results of our simulations are based on the assumption that refuse collection vehicles would be given their three-yearly overhaul and repainting three times during their ten-year life; heavy trucks twice during seven years; and cars, vans and ambulances once during five years. In practice, however, it may not be worthwhile to undertake an overhaul and repainting if a vehicle is to be kept for only one more year. It may be more economic either to replace the vehicle one year earlier and avoid the maintenance, or to keep the vehicle for longer having done the overhaul. Either decision could have a significant effect on the maintenance facility, particularly the paint shop.

These comments look at only one aspect of the question of vehicle replacement: how much work is imposed on the maintenance facility. In practice the decision to replace vehicles must also be based on their value at time of disposal.

15

Local Government Reorganization and Relocation

In 1974 the city of Rochester, Chatham Municipal Borough and part of Strood Rural District merged to form a single government, to be called the Medway Borough Council after the River Medway on which each of the three communities stands. The new administration provides environmental, housing and recreational services to its inhabitants, over half of whom live in Rochester, a cathedral city, or in Chatham, a port and dockyard and the shopping center for the region.

Medway Borough Council was to inherit twelve buildings which were used as administrative offices by the governments of Rochester, Chatham and Strood. One of the first questions that would face the new government was whether to use the buildings it would inherit, which were scattered around the area, or to bring its entire staff together in one central location. And if the existing buildings were to be used, a decision had to be made on the allocation of the buildings to the various departments of the new government. These problems are addressed in *Office Reorganization in Medway*, a study conducted by David Cooper, Janet Rutherford and Robert Howell in 1974 for the governments of Rochester, Chatham and Strood just before their merger. The study involved estimating the office space requirements for the new government and evaluating the short-term and the long-term means of satisfying these requirements, taking into consideration ease of staff communications, effective use of space, convenience for the public and cost.

Two short-term solutions were considered. One was to rent office space in a large building known as the Pentagon which was under construction in Chatham. This alternative would enable all the staff to be brought together under one roof and would provide quick and easy communications for the staff, especially during the changeover period. The other solution was to use the twelve buildings to be inherited by the new government. This solution actually consisted of five alternatives, for it was found that the departments of the new government could be divided among these buildings in five different ways. A communications survey of all the staff employed by Rochester, Chatham and Strood prior to the merger of the three governments was an important part of the assessment of these alternatives. This survey identified the types, duration, and amount of interdepartmental as well as intradepartmental communications and enabled the study team to develop a communications disturbance index for assessing each of the five alternative ways to use the existing buildings.

On the strength of their evaluation of the short-term alternatives, Cooper, Rutherford and Howell recommended that the new Medway Borough Council should try to negotiate a short-term (five-year) lease on the Pentagon building and dispose of most of the buildings it inherited. Should these negotiations be unsuccessful, they recommended that the new government adopt the second of the five ways identified for using the existing buildings. This alternative, called Scheme II, put the chief executive and the administrative and legal department at Strood, the housing and finance departments in buildings at Rochester and all other departments in buildings at Chatham. It was shown that this alternative provided the most effective use of the existing buildings and would minimize communications disruption and inconvenience to the public.

In addition to considering the immediate needs of the new government, the study also investigated long-term solutions to providing office space for Medway's staff. Two alternatives were considered: obtaining a long-term (twenty-one-year) lease on the Pentagon; or building a new civic center on a ten-acre site in Rochester known as St Margaret's Banks. After comparing these two alternatives Cooper, Rutherford and Howell concluded that building the new civic center was the best way of satisfying the long-term office needs of the new government.

Four years after the amalgamation of Rochester, Chatham and Strood, we investigated the impact of the reorganization study presented in this chapter. We found that the decisions taken by the new government, Medway Borough Council, closely paralleled the recommendations made in the study, both immediately after reorganization in 1974 and in the longer term. The study had also had an important side effect on the staff of the new administration.

In 1974 the new council had to decide whether to make use of the buildings it had inherited or to rent office space in the newly constructed Pentagon building. For political reasons, we were told, the second option was not seriously considered. Because the council elected in 1974 had a Labour party majority, it was not inclined to consider the Pentagon, which was constructed with the support of the former Chatham Borough Council under Conservative control. A modified version of Scheme II, recommended by the study team, was therefore put into effect. This solution made use of existing buildings judged to be either 'good' or 'fair' for the purpose, and added to these a temporary building constructed behind Chatham Town Hall. By this device buildings judged to be 'poor' or 'not suitable for long-term use' could be left out of the final arrangements. The chief executive and administrative and legal services were located at the Strood council offices; recreation and environmental health were located in Rochester; and the finance, housing, technical services and planning and architecture departments were given offices in Chatham. In 1977 another temporary building was built in Chatham, which enabled the environmental health department to be relocated there from inadequate space in Rochester.

The Conservative party gained control of the Medway Borough Council in 1976. By this time the council had accumulated a reserve of funds and there was growing recognition that the decentralized location of its administrative staff had resulted in a number of inefficiencies. In addition, the staff had grown to 600 employees, which had further aggravated the problems of decentralization.

In 1978 we found that Medway was proceeding with plans to centralize its administrative staff in a new civic center. A major factor contributing to this change in thinking was the need for the new council to develop a recognizable identity, an 'image'. But decentralization had also proved to be more costly and inefficient than had originally been foreseen. For example, we were told that considerable difficulties had been caused to staff and to the public by an inadequate – and intractable – telephone system. It is possible that if the study team had identified the drawbacks of decentralization as successfully as they itemized the benefits of a central location, the case for a civic center could have been strengthened at the time the report was submitted.

The council has decided, in principle, to build the new civic center on the St Margaret's Banks site in Rochester and has authorized the preparation of preliminary plans for a building of some 6,500 square meters of office space to be completed by 1982. We learned that the comprehensive information contained in the study report (not all of it reproduced in the report that follows) about the space needs and desirable proximity of the various departments was of considerable value in the early discussions on the new building. Much of this information was still being used four years after the study was completed.

Finally, it is worth noting a less tangible but nevertheless important side effect of the study. In any major change the participation and active support of the people involved is necessary to achieve a successful transition. In Medway there were few problems in implementing the recommendations of the study, very largely because the communications survey had involved all the staff and had helped ensure that the reasoning behind the results was well understood. The factors determining the choices open to the council and their associated costs and benefits were made clear well in advance of final decisions being made. Looking back on this period Mr Philip Scarff, assistant to the chief executive, feels sure that the study itself played a large part in allaying the natural fears of many of the staff and in maintaining morale during the changeover period.

The report presented to the three governments and subsequently used by the Medway Borough Council follows. The first two sections consider the short-term needs of Medway. Office space likely to be needed in the immediate period after reorganization is identified, alternative ways of meeting these space needs are assessed and recommendations are made on the use of existing buildings. Section 3 considers the best long-term solution to the new government's office space problem and concludes by recommending that a new civic center be constructed to house the administrative staff. All costs have been expressed in dollars at 1974 prices. The average exchange rate in 1974 was 0.4273 pounds sterling per dollar.

Office Reorganization in Medway

DAVID COOPER, JANET RUTHERFORD and ROBERT HOWELL

INTRODUCTION

Following the reorganization of local government in England and Wales in 1974, the city of Rochester, Chatham Municipal Borough and part of Strood Rural District will merge to form the new Medway Borough. The new government will provide environmental, housing and recreational services for over 120,000 people. More than half of the population live in either Rochester or Chatham, while the remainder – some 55,000 at the 1971 census – live in a number of smaller settlements dispersed over a relatively extensive area north of the River Medway. The administrative staff of the three constituent councils of the new government are currently housed in a dozen separate buildings in their respective areas One of the many administrative problems raised by reorganizatio. is the question of office location: where should the staff of Medway be located? And, in the long-term, where is the best site for the new administrative headquarters?

Accordingly Rochester, Chatham and Strood have commissioned this study to determine the new government's office requirements immediately following reorganization and to make recommendations, in both the short-term and the long-term, for housing the new administration. A benefit-cost study was conducted; that is, the benefits and costs of each alternative solution were identified, analyzed and used to justify the recommendations. The purposes of the study were:

(1) to determine the best practical site for the new civic center for the Medway Borough Council;
(2) to evaluate alternative short-term office arrangements for the staff of the new government, with particular reference to the need for good communications between the departments;
(3) to make recommendations on the most appropriate use of existing buildings and temporary office space during the interim period.

For the immediate future the choice is inevitably constrained by the space that is currently available – or likely to become available in the next year or so. But choices do exist: buildings can be rented; departments can be grouped together in one building, or within a collection of neighboring buildings. In Section 2 of this report we present our analysis of the options open to Medway, together with our conclusions and recommendations for the immediate post-reorganization period. These recommendations are based on the overriding importance of providing for quick and easy communications between staff during the changeover period.

However, these arrangements which are based on a modified use of existing buildings can only be regarded as providing a temporary solution to the office needs of Medway Borough. There are two main reasons for this. First, the *internal* changes brought about by reorganization — changes in function, new committees, departmental restructuring under a chief executive and, of course, the wider administrative area – will inevitably modify both the way in which certain activities are carried out and, as a result, the pattern of communications necessary to sustain them. Until the new government has had a chance to settle in it will clearly be foolish to predict what these changed will be. The second main reason why existing buildings are likely to be inadequate springs from *external* changes. By this we mean the fact that many local personal services, such as health and social services, will be the responsibility of separate bodies. It seems reasonable to predict that cooperation between these bodies will be improved, and convenience to the public enhanced, if some provision is made for the joint use of facilities where appropriate.

Both these considerations suggest that the administration of local services in Medway would be more effective if housed in a single building, conveniently situated for the population as a whole. The selection of a site for such a building is the other major theme of this report. In Section 3 we examine two practical possibilities: the construction of a new building at a site on St Margaret's Bank, close to Rochester Station; or the renting of the Pentagon, a multistory office currently under construction in the center of Chatham.

1 PROVISION OF SPACE FOR 1974

In the immediate future the aim must be for the new government to ensure that the available office space is used in the most effective way. To do this the supply of space must be related to the demands that will be made on it. In this section we first assess the space that will be available, and then estimate the requirements of the new administration.

Buildings Available

Medway will inherit twelve buildings. Figure 15.1 shows the number of staff currently accommodated in each building, its general condition, and the scope for housing additional staff – either by modifying or extending the building. At present space is available for around 400 staff; extensions at Strood, Rochester (66/68 Maidstone Road) and Chatham (Engineer's and Surveyor's Building) could offer an additional 150 places. However, only about half the stock of offices is in good condition. Thus even if these buildings were expanded the office space suitable for long-term use would not provide for more than about 400 staff. The location of the buildings in relation to the road and rail network is shown in Figure 15.2. There is a train service between Strood, Rochester and Chatham, as well as a frequent bus service linking the main groups of offices.

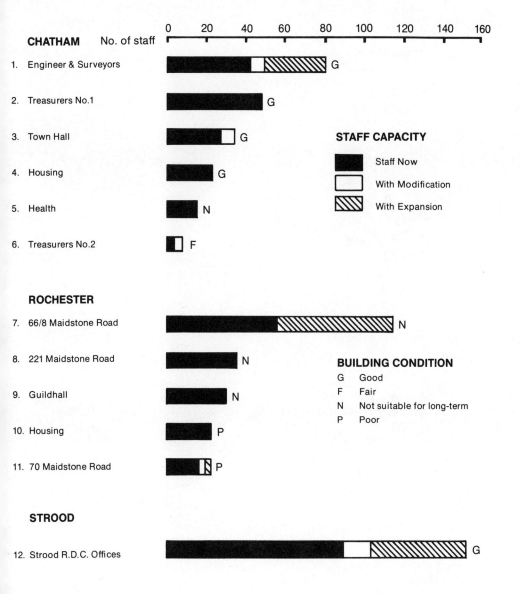

Figure 15.1   *Space available in present offices*

Source: Internal survey — 1973.

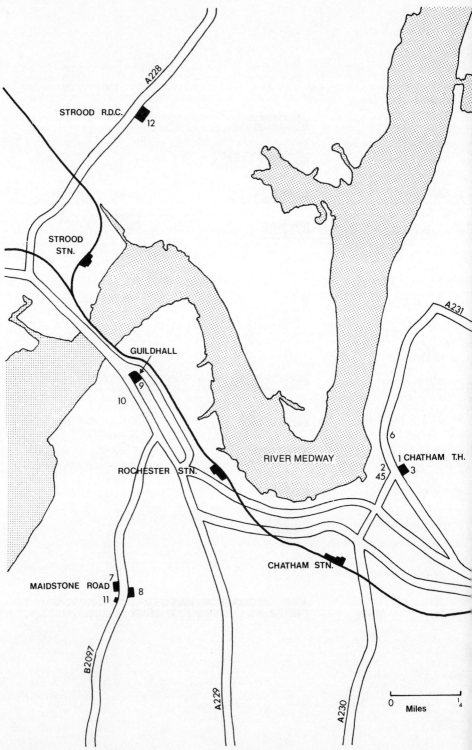

Figure 15.2 *Present location of Council offices in central Medway area*

In addition to the buildings currently occupied by the constituent councils of Medway Borough, another option is open. A large office building, the Pentagon, is nearing completion in central Chatham and the council has been offered a lease on it. This would provide sufficient office space for the entire administration and is thus an alternative solution to the short-term problem.

Space Required

Office space has two elements. The first is the floor area allocated to individual staff (or groups of staff) including space for personal storage and interviewing. This is called the net office area. The second is the additional space needed for storage, equipment and communal facilities. The total of this additional space and the net office area is called the usable area. The usable area needed by Medway can be estimated from: the proposed staffiing of the new government; personal space standards for different grades of staff; and an allowance for additional space likely to be needed. The proposed staffiing of the new government is shown in Table 15.1. The numbers have not yet been ratified but are realistic estimates of the sizes of the new departments.

Table 15.1 *Proposed staffiing of Medway Borough Council*

Department	Total staff	Headquarters staff*
Chief executive	17	17
Administrative and legal	69	69
Environmental services	35	32
Finance	108	107
Housing	99	48
Planning and architecture	69	64
Recreation	51	20
Technical services	121	57
All departments	569	414

*excludes field staff.

Using the office space standards suggested by the Department of the Environment, the net office area needed for a staff of 414 is about 3,700 square meters (1 square meter = 10.8 square feet). In terms of space per person, these figures correspond fairly closely with the average space per staff member at present in the three existing local governments. Using the existing buildings, it should therefore be possible – by making minor modifications to buildings and by regrouping staff where appropriate – to provide at least a temporary home for the new government.

However, the number of staff is not likely to remain at this level for long. In the past, local governments have taken on an increasing number of functions and, of necessity, have had to increase their staff to cope with the additional workload. The staff changes will vary

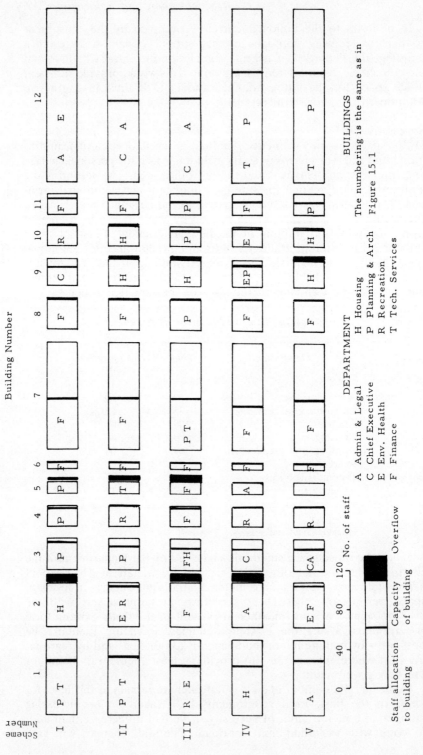

Figure 15.3 *Feasible short-term schemes*

between departments but if we assume that overall the staff will increase by about 3 percent per year, the number of staff to be accommodated will have increased to 480 by 1979. (In previous studies of the experience of London boroughs after reorganization we have found that annual staff increases have been between 3 and 5 percent.)

In addition Kent County Council will require offices in Medway Borough. Although it has sufficient space for the immediate post-reorganization period the county has expressed the view that it would like to work as closely as possible with its constituent councils and, where possible, to share the same buildings. The county currently occupies six premises in the district: two of these are leased and the remainder are on cramped sites with no room for extension. The estimated total net office area needed in Medway by the county in the foreseeable future amounts to some 1,000 square meters, which is about a quarter of Medway's current requirement.

2 ALTERNATIVE SHORT-TERM STRATEGIES

For the short term there are two options open to the Medway Borough Council: first, to use the existing offices to be inherited – within this category a number of arrangements are possible; or, secondly, to lease office space in the Pentagon.

Use Existing Buildings

With minor modifications the existing buildings could house just over 400 staff. Determining the best way of using these buildings is simplified because the number of practical alternative arrangements is quite small.

During the course of this study, we carried out a survey of communications in the three existing administrations. The conclusions that emerged provide a number of general guidelines for allocating departments. Briefly these are (1) that individual departments should be allocated to the same building or group of buildings; and (2) that departments with related functions should, wherever possible, be allocated to the same building or group of buildings. These departments fall into three main groups: chief executive and administrative/legal; technical services and planning; and housing and finance.

The opportunities for grouping departments in this way are strictly limited with the present buildings. As housing and finance cannot be fitted into the Strood offices, either technical services and planning, or chief executive and administrative/legal must go there. In either case the scope for locating the other departments in compliance with our guidelines – and the physical limitations of the buildings – is small. We have identified five basic feasible schemes that are broadly consistent with the guidelines. They are displayed in Figure 15.3. In evaluating the five schemes, the main priority has been to minimize the disruptive effect, on both the staff and the public, of running the authority from dispersed offices. We have therefore examined three features of each of the potential schemes:

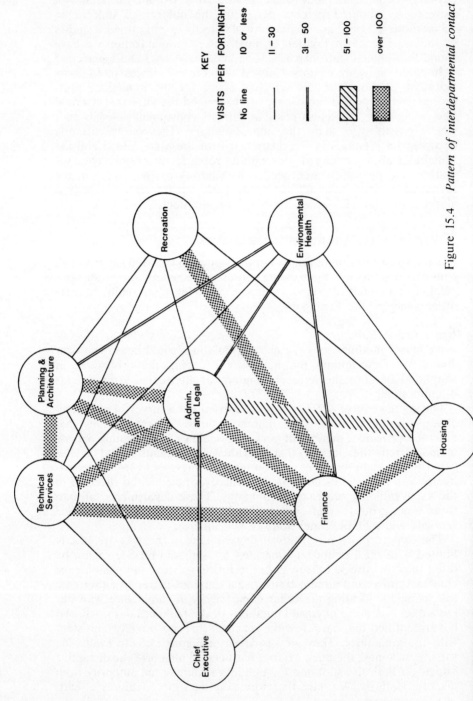

KEY

VISITS PER FORTNIGHT

No line   10 or less

——   11 – 30

══   31 – 50

▨   51 – 100

▦   over 100

Figure 15.4   *Pattern of interdepartmental contact*

- ease of communications for staff;
- effective use of space;
- convenience for the public.

Staff Communications. Local government staff in Rochester, Chatham and Strood were asked to complete a communications diary, listing details of their contacts – both face-to-face and by phone – over a period of two weeks. In following up this communications survey we had extensive discussions with section leaders in all departments. During these discussions we asked each section head to assess the priorities of his or her own section for face-to-face contact with other sections both inside and outside the department. We were thus able to build up a picture both of current contact patterns and of those likely to be necessary in the new government. The pattern of interdepartmental contact is illustrated in Figure 15.4. Using this information we were able to assess how effective each potential scheme was likely to be in satisfying communications needs.

The communications diaries, together with the subsequent interviews with each section head, enabled us to: estimate which contacts require face-to-face contact, that is, the high-priority contacts; obtain information about such contacts with regard to purpose, duration, location, prior arrangement and need for visual support material (such as maps, records and so on); and estimate the likely changes in the pattern of high-priority contacts as a result of reorganization. The main conclusions of this survey were as follows: in each department about 60–70 percent of all contacts are within the department. And, in each of the three governments, the pattern of interdepartmental contact is broadly similar. Most contacts are of short duration – rarely more than fifteen minutes – and visits are frequently made to consult records, plans or other documents.

The priorities that emerged from the survey were expressed in the form of a 'priority scale' – ranging from 5 (high priority – contact several times a day) to 1 (low priority – contact less than once in two weeks). It was then possible to calculate a communications 'disturbance index' for each of the five schemes for the short-term use of existing buildings. This index gives a broad measure of the degree of disruption involved in any particular arrangement. For each scheme the index was calculated by taking each pair of sections, multiplying the journey time between them by the priority of inter-section contact and adding the resulting figures over all contacts. The results for the five potential schemes are given in Table 15.2.

Table 15.2 *Disturbance index for the five alternative schemes using existing buildings.*

Scheme	Disturbance index
I	1.60
II	1.11
III	1.33
IV	1.50
V	1.50

When we compare the indices of different schemes it is clear that Scheme II, with the chief executive and the administrative and legal department at Strood, housing and finance at Rochester and all other departments in Chatham, is likely to provide the least disturbance of communications to the administration as a whole. There are two main reasons for this. First, because the Strood building is not large enough to take all the technical services and planning staff without further extensions of the building, this group of departments must be split by the river. This will result in extensive disruption to communications within the group. Secondly, unless the chief executive and administrative and legal departments are located at Strood there is no feasible way of keeping the financial and housing departments in reasonably close promiximity.

Use of Space. By comparing the number of staff in each building with the capacity of the building (determined by the Department of Environment office space standards), we obtain an overall view of the extent to which individual buildings are cramped or under utilized. Table 15.3 shows the results by building and scheme. It is apparent that whichever scheme is adopted the margin of over- or underutilization will be small – in most cases no more than the equivalent of five staff. Where a reasonable margin of excess capacity does exist – as in Strood in Schemes II and III and in Chatham Town Hall in Scheme IV – it is in the building allocated to the chief executive. However as the range and type of support services required by the chief executive has yet to be determined this is a sensible allocation of spare capacity.

From the point of view of space, the only disadvantage of Scheme II – which we have seen to be the one favorable to staff communication – is the fact that the Engineer's and Surveyor's Building at Chatham is cramped, with an excess of nine staff above its nominal capacity. However, this building is likely to be cramped in all schemes (see Table 15.3) and unless an extension is built significant reduction in overcrowding can only be effected either by splitting technical services and planning or at a high cost to the convenience of staff generally. We conclude therefore that Scheme II offers the best prospects for the short term though a minor extension may well be necessary at Chatham if growth in the number of staff over the next five years is to be accommodated.

Table 15.3 *Surplus or deficit of space by building and scheme*

Building	Scheme Surplus (+)/deficit (−)					Comments
	I	II	III	IV	V	
Chatham (Town Hall)	+2	+5	+3	+15	+3	Buildings with spare capacity in all schemes
Chatham (Housing)	+5	+1	+4	+1	+1	
Rochester (221 Maidstone Road)	+1	+1	+1	+1	0	
Rochester (Housing)	0	+1	+4	0	+1	
Rochester (70 Maidstone Road)	+1	+1	+3	+1	+2	
Strood (Rural District Offices)	+1	+13	+13	0	0	
Chatham (Engineer's and Surveyor's)	−5	−9	−1	−3	−8	Buildings with no spare capacity
Chatham (Treasurer's No. 2)	−2	−2	−2	−2	−2	
Chatham (Treasurer's No. 1)	−5	+2	−8	−10	+3	Others
Chatham (Health)	−3	−3	−5	0	+12	
Rochester (Guildhall)	+9	−6	−6	+1	−6	
Rochester (66/8 Maidstone Road)	+1	+1	−1	+1	−1	

Public Convenience. To ensure that the location of departments is convenient for the public two main factors should be considered. First, are the places where the public can obtain information and advice easily accessible from all parts of the district? Secondly, can such inquiries be satisfactorily answered within a single building – or, at worst, within the confines of a group of buildings?

As our recommendations for the short term involve retaining buildings at each of the existing locations, there should be no problem in meeting the first requirement, providing the public is given adequate information prior to changeover. The taxpayers will need to know where they can:

- pay their rent and taxes,
- inquire about rent and rebates,
- collect forms dealing with official matters,
- make inquiries about building regulations,
- discuss public health matters,
- receive advice on planning applications,
- obtain general information about the area.

The transition to the new Medway Borough will clearly be smoother if this kind of information is made available to the public as early as possible – either through leaflets sent to their homes or through announcements in the local press. There will, however, be more difficulty in meeting the second requirement. Although our recommended scheme is likely to reduce the inconvenience of referrals between buildings, it is unlikely that a split administration could ever overcome this problem completely. Evidence from other local governments operating from several premises suggests that clear and detailed guidance to the public on *how* and *where* to obtain information and advice can help to reduce the scale of the problem.

In conclusion, it is evident from our analysis that Scheme II provides the most effective use of the existing buildings. This scheme, by keeping departments together and by locating departments with frequent need for exchange of information and advice in close proximity, will minimize the disruption of running the new administration from these premises. It will also tend to reduce the inconvenience to the public when they are referred from one building to another.

Rent the Pentagon
The previous section has shown that although a workable arrangement is possible using the existing buildings any such scheme is far from satisfactory both for the staff and the public. These difficulties cannot be effectively overcome until the new government is housed under one roof. In Section 3 we look at two alternative long-term solutions – renting the Pentagon Building in Chatham, or building a new civic center. However, the prospect of using the existing buildings for five years or more until a purpose-built center is available indicates that it is worth considering the possibility of renting the Pentagon on a temporary basis. In this section we briefly summarize the costs and benefits of this course of action.

Costs. The main annual costs to be considered are:

Rent for 420 staff and a civic suite. About 5,600 square meters would be needed. Assuming $50 per square meter, the estimated cost is:	$280,000
Running costs, including cleaning, fuel, etc., estimated at:	$350,000
Furniture, partitioning, etc., estimated at:	$ 35,000
Total	$665,000

Against this total can be offset:

Running costs of present buildings per year (excluding debt charges):	$165,000
Disposal value of buildings (annual interest @ 10 percent per year if the buildings were sold in 1974):	$ 50,000
Savings on inter-office travel (annual savings in travel costs plus reductions in travelling time):	$ 50,000
Total:	$265,000

On these considerations alone the net cost of renting the Pentagon over the period 1974–9 is about $400,000 per year. However, this calculation does not take into account the cost of modifying and extending the existing buildings over the five-year period, which would reduce the net cost of renting. On the other hand, the cost of renting may not fully reflect the additional premium that may be placed on a short-term lease. On balance, it seems unlikely that the net cost of the Pentagon would be less than $350,000 per year.

Benefits. Whether such a sum is worth paying depends on the benefits that use of the Pentagon would realize. The potential benefits of a new building include:

- better working conditions for staff;
- easier office communications;
- advantages to public callers;
- benefits of centralization, including better use of staff and equipment.

Few of these benefits will show up in the new government's accounts, including the major impact: that staff will be able to use their time more effectively and thus improve the level of service provided. The only significant savings will appear under the last heading, benefits of centralization, but it is unlikely that these will amount to more than 5 percent of the administrative cost, or about $175,000 per year.

Thus the argument for renting the Pentagon *as a short-term option* depends largely on the extent to which the benefits – especially the intangible benefits – of a single center can be attained in a short time. Evidence from local government reorganization in London suggests that it would be unwise to expect tangible savings in the early years of the new administration. However, the intangible benefits are real enough: Medway would have a single focal point for its administration, and thus have an ideal opportunity to establish a corporate identity in the early years of its life.

Recommendations
We therefore conclude that efforts should be made to negotiate a short-term lease on the Pentagon, for a period of five years. If such an arrangement is made, the Strood building could be sold; in this event it would be sensible to retain a local information and advice point in the building. Failing a successful outcome of these negotiations, we recommend that Medway adopt Scheme II for using its existing buildings.

3 THE LONG TERM

At the end of the last section we discussed some of the potential benefits that could be realized if the new government were located in a single civic center. There are two feasible sites for such a center: the Pentagon Building in Chatham and a new building at St Margaret's Banks in Rochester. In this section we determine which of these two sites is likely to offer the best long-term solution to Medway's office space problem.

Alternative Sites
The Pentagon. With 414 staff in 1974 and an average growth rate of 3 percent per year, the total number of staff to be accommodated in 1979 will be about 480. Allowing 600 square meters for a civic suite, a total usable floor area of about 6,300 square meters will be needed. If in addition Kent County's need for about 1,400 square meters is to be met, the total requirement is 7,700 square meters.

The Pentagon Building, which forms part of the comprehensive development scheme currently under construction in Chatham town center, offers 8,500 square meters of floor space. This includes 1,260 square meters on the third level and 7,100 meters on levels five to twelve. At level two, 1,180 square meters of the space has a depth that would be suitable for use as a council chamber or as a computer center.

The developers propose a twenty-one year lease with rent reviews every five years, but this arrangement is subject to negotiation. The latest available information is that the building will be ready for occupancy by May or June 1974.

From the point of view of public access the building is ideally situated. Previous studies indicate that many visits to local government offices are made on shopping visits. As the Pentagon lies in the center of a major shopping area for the new district and beyond, its convenience for the public as a whole is unquestionable.

St Margaret's Bank. St Margaret's Bank is a ten-acre site, half of which is currently owned by Rochester City Council. The site offers ample scope for the construction of a building of the required size. It is also large enough to provide for further extensions to the building, if required, as part of a phased building program.

The site is conveniently situated close to Rochester Station, though not as obviously central as the Pentagon. The accessibility of the site, especially for pedestrians, depends on the general improvement in traffic conditions in the vicinity.

Cost Comparison
In comparing the costs of the two sites, the only items that need to be considered are those that differ in the two schemes, that is, rent, construction and land costs. The major items – runnings costs of the building and savings in travel time – can be taken to be broadly similar which-

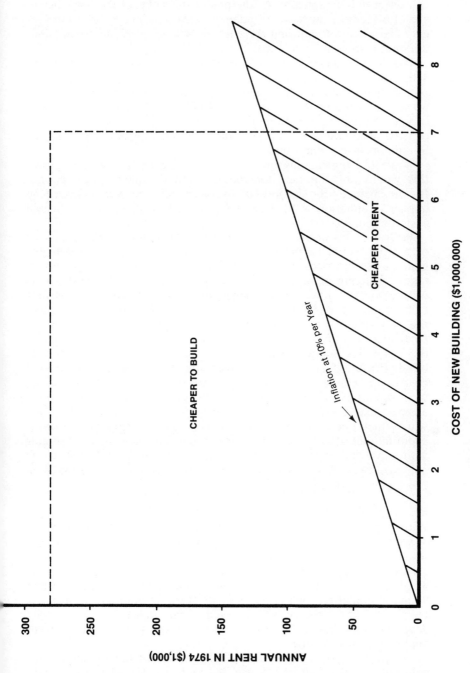

Figure 15.5 *Cost of building or renting a civic center over 80 years*

ever building is chosen. Location - related costs, such as travel costs, will differ only marginally. As the potential benefits of the two schemes are also identical in terms of administrative efficiency, the decision is essentially one of choosing the cheaper way of financing a new office building – to rent or to buy.

The estimated capital cost of a new building, at 1974 prices, to house 480 staff is about $4.35 million. Adding approximate estimates for site preparation, professional fees and salaries and provision of car parking, we arrive at the figure of about $6.45 million. The cost of raising this capital will depend on the method of finance – either direct borrowing or leaseback – but the net cost to the government is unlikely to exceed $7 million in current values.

While the repayments on a loan would be fixed in money terms, this would only be true for renting until the next review period. If we assume the proposed five-year rent review period, the impact of inflation is likely to have a marked effect on the overall costs of renting.

With inflation at around 10 percent per year, for example, the cost of renting would be prohibitive if rent increases keep pace with the general rise in prices. Figure 15.5 illustrates the overwhelming advantages of buying in such a situation. The estimated capital cost is read off the horizontal axis and the negotiated annual rent for 1974 (assumed to be around $280,000) is read off the vertical axis. If the point where the two values intersect lies above the diagonal line drawn for this particular rate of inflation, then it is cheaper to build them to rent. If the point lies below the inflation line, it is cheaper to rent than to build. If a building were rented under these circumstances the overall cost to the council would be high – the net cost over thirty to forty years would exceed $11.7 million. However, if inflation is contained at a lower level – say 5 percent per year – then renting at around $44 per square meter could be comparable in cost to purchasing. Whatever the eventual rate of inflation, it is clear that the financial benefits of renting with a low rate (say 3 percent) would be small – about $1.75 million – in comparison with the costs that would be incurred if inflation is at the higher level.

Recommendations

With an estimated population in Medway of around 175,000 in 1991 – of whom 100,000 will reside south of the river – it is clear that either site would be well located for the population as a whole. But it is evident that the slight locational advantages of the Pentagon are outweighed by the heavy risks involved in committing the council to renting its accommodation for twenty years or more. In addition, it does not seem sensible for the council to occupy prime space in a commercial development which could bring income and jobs to the area if it were taken by a private firm.

The St Margaret's Banks area is a large, central site eminently suitable not only for staff of Medway Borough, but for other bodies with responsibilities in the area, including Kent County Council and the area health authority. Some expenditure will be incurred in acquiring the part of the site not owned by Rochester city, but this is likely to be fairly small in relation to the other costs of the development. We conclude therefore that constructing a new building at St Margaret's Banks will be the best way of meeting the long-term office space needs of the new administration.

16
Discussion

SUMMARY OF RESULTS

The study presented in Chapter 12 evaluated five alternative strategies for future land development. Shortly after the study was completed it became evident that the population of the area was not going to grow as large or as rapidly as had been assumed. Consequently, none of the five strategies assessed by the study could be used as the basis for future planning. Although its results were not used, this study does provide a good illustration of the 'solution-testing' stage of problem-solving, as defined in Chapter 1. In this case, the solution was a ranking of the alternative strategies based upon how well they satisfied a weighted set of planning objectives. The final ranking was tested to determine how sensitive it was to changes in the scores achieved by the strategies in satisfying the planning objectives and how sensitive it was to the weights applied to the objectives. As a result of these tests it was found that the two worst strategies were unlikely ever to be one of the best strategies, even if their scores or the weights of the objectives were to change dramatically.

Chapter 13 presented a study concerned with reducing the clerical cost of processing invoices received for goods purchased by the supplies department of a large city. The study found that the total cost of the system, including the clerical cost of checking and the losses that could be expected to result from not checking some invoices, would be minimized if a selective checking process were introduced. By implementing selective invoice checking, the study anticipated the supplies department would save approximately $17,500 per year (in 1962 prices). Moreover, when we visited the supplies department in 1978 we found the city was saving over $\frac{2}{3}$ million per year in discounts by paying invoices quickly. This study is an excellent example of the entire operations research problem-solving process and we use it in Chapter 17 to illustrate the stages of that process.

The results of using a computer simulation model to evaluate the plan for a new vehicle maintenance and repair facility were presented in Chapter 14. The computer model simulated arrivals to, repairs in, and departures from the various workshops of the proposed facility and a number of alternative designs. The results of the simulation were then used to compare the various alternatives. The process involved in constructing the computer simulation model appears to have been the major benefit of the study. Constructing the model required careful definition of the rules under which the new facility would operate, which forced management to clarify a number of issues that would affect vehicle availability and utilization of repair staff. The study is a good illustration of the types of questions that can be investigated and the types of results that can be produced by a computer simulation model.

The final study in this part, presented in Chapter 15, was concerned with satisfying the immediate and long-term office space needs of three local governments which were to be reorganized into a single government. The study identified and classified the office space that would become available as a result of the reorganization and estimated the office space needs and likely communications patterns of the new local government. This information was used to evaluate a range of alternative schemes for relocating the staff involved. When it came into existence the new government implemented a modified version of the study recommendations for immediate relocation of staff. Four years later, when enough reserve funds had been accumulated, it was decided to build a new civic center and the information gathered by the study was still found to be of use in working with architects on the plans for the new building. The close involvement of the staff in this study seems to have helped reduce rumors and maintained staff morale during the changeover period.

Even from the limited number of studies presented in this part it is clear that planning and administrative services share some common problems. Local and regional planning departments are primarily concerned with the economic, environmental and social problems associated with population changes and land use, as well as enforcing existing planning policies. Glasson (1978, p. 19) describes planning as 'a sequence of actions which are designed to solve problems in the future'. Such problems vary in terms of time horizon (short, intermediate, or long-range), the level of government at which they are attacked and the type of problem. Glasson distinguishes between a number of types of regional planning, including physical planning, economic planning, and single- or multi-objective planning.

Planning is of course a general function of management and in this sense is of concern to all government departments. The last three studies in this part concern more than one department of a local government. They also deal with problems or services which directly affect how staff in a number of departments are able to do their work. For these reasons, these studies fall under the heading of administrative or staff services. The primary impact of implementing the results of these studies has been on the way local government staff do their work, with a secondary impact on the public served by this staff. In contrast the implementation of the results of most of the other studies in this book has had a direct impact on the public.

DESCRIPTION

In this section we briefly describe the methods used by the four studies included in Part Three and give references which provide a more detailed discussion of these methods.

'Plan Evaluation Matrix'

The method used in *Evaluation Tests for Northamptonshire* (Chapter 12) for ranking alternative planning strategies involved evaluating a given set of alternatives in terms of a set of criteria (objectives). The scores achieved by the strategies in satisfying a given objective were rescaled to provide a normalized measure of the performance of each strategy. Weights were then given to the objectives in order to distinguish their importance. These weights were applied to the scores to obtain a relative overall measure of performance (score) for each strategy. Although Mackie refers to the table of scores that each strategy achieves on each objective as a 'plan evaluation matrix', there is no general name given to this method of analysis.

This study illustrates the making of a decision under assumed certainty. This means that the initial ranking of the alternative planning strategies has been obtained by assuming that the scores they achieve in satisfying each objective and the relative weights of each objective are known with certainty. However, a major part of the study involved testing the importance of these assumptions. This was done by finding a 'robustness measure', a measure of the smallest changes in the combination of scores or weights just necessary to reverse the ranking of two strategies. The robustness measure is defined to be the Euclidean distance between the original scores or weights and the ones which just reverse the ranking. The booklet *Better Plan Evaluation* (LGORU, 1973) discusses the methods used in this study.

Cost-Effectiveness

In *The Checking of Invoices* (Chapter 13) it is assumed that some amount of the activity under study will be carried out. The purpose of the research is to determine the most cost-effective level of this activity, namely, the amount of checking of delivery, price and arithmetic that should take place. The level of activity ranges from checking none (0 percent) of the invoices to checking all (100 percent) of the invoices. Typically in such studies two or more costs compete, that is, at least one of the costs, like the clerical cost of checking invoices, increases as the level of activity increases, while at least one other cost, such as the losses which result from not checking invoices, decreases with the level of activity. The analysis finds the proper balance between the competing costs. This is the level of activity which minimizes the sum of the costs, in other words, the most cost-effective level of activity.

Some authors use the phrases 'cost-effectiveness' and 'cost-benefit analysis' interchangeably (see Laufer, 1979, p. 619). Others, like Anderson and Settle (1977), maintain that cost-effectiveness is a subset of cost-benefit analysis. They describe cost-benefit analysis as 'a tool for systematically developing useful information about the desirable and undesirable effects of public sector programs or projects' (p. 1). For example, cost-benefit analysis helps to decide whether to carry out a project, as was demonstrated by the flood relief study (Chapter 9), or which of several alternative projects is best, as was demonstrated by the study of alternative bypass routes (Chapter 7). Using cost-benefit analysis, alternatives with widely varying goals, costs and benefits can be studied and compared. On the other hand Anderson and Settle believe that:

> A cost-effectiveness analysis is appropriate if it has already been determined that a certain project of a certain size is worth doing, and the only concern is to undertake the project as inexpensively as possible. (pp. 16–17).

In the next chapter we use *The Checking of Invoices* to illustrate the seven steps of the problem-solving process defined in Chapter 1. This will include a thorough discussion of the methods used to determine the best level of checking invoices, including how the mathematical model was constructed and how the solution was derived from it.

Simulation
As the title of the report suggests, *Simulation of the New Vehicle Workshop in the London Borough of Ealing* (Chapter 14) employs the method of computer simulation. Simulation is used in many fields of research and training. For example, aerospace engineers use wind tunnels to simulate the conditions an aircraft will experience in flight. Small scale models of new types of aircraft are tested in the wind tunnel in order to select the best design for a plane. Other types of simulators are used to train students to operate equipment, such as automobiles. Such a simulator enables the student to experience and react to a variety of real driving situations in the classroom without exposing the student, other drivers or pedestrians to the dangers of training drivers on real roads.

In operations research, simulation is defined as:

> a numerical technique for conducting experiments on a digital computer, which involves certain types of mathematical and logical models that describe the behavior of a . . . system (or some component thereof) over extended periods of real time (Naylor *et al.*, 1966, p. 3).

The computer simulation model that was built to test the proposed vehicle repair and maintenance facility for Ealing consisted of a set of mathematical models which produced a sequence of times when vehicles would need routine servicing; generated random breakdowns of vehicles; generated the time it would take to perform repair and maintenance and the time waiting for parts; and described the size of the shop, the number of mechanics and the number of facilities. These models were used to generate by computer a flow of vehicles in and out of the proposed workshop over a long period of time. While this flow was taking place, records were maintained by the computer of the operation of the system, including the length of time each vehicle waited before being repaired, the number of vehicles of each type that were out of service at one time, how much time the mechanics were occupied and how often the facilities were used.

Using a high-speed digital computer, the arrivals to and departures from the workshop over a number of days could be generated in a very short time; and statistics on vehicle waiting times and mechanic and facility utilization could be quickly summarized to produce average values for the proposed design. Given the basic set of models it was a relatively simple task to alter the various parts of the models which described the design, such as the size of the workshop, number of mechanics, duration of the work day and number and type of facilities included in the shop. By making alterations in these factors and simulating the operation of the altered workshop, a new set of statistics on the length of time each vehicle waited to be served, and so on, could be generated and compared to the simulated operation of other designs. In this way the computer simulation model was used to test and compare a number of alternative designs for the proposed vehicle workshop. There are a number of books which describe how to carry out a computer simulation. See, for example, Naylor *et al.* (1966), Forrester (1969), Fishman (1978), and Gross and Harris (1974).

Cost-Benefit Analysis
Office Reorganization in Medway (Chapter 15) is a cost-benefit analysis of a number of short-term and two long-term alternatives for relocating the staff of a local government. The method of comparing the alternatives differs, however, from the two cost-benefit analyses presented in Part Two (see Chapters 7 and 9) which use ratios of benefits or net benefits to cost in order to select the best alternative. In this study there is no attempt to place monetary value on the various benefits of the alternatives – ease of staff communications, effective use of space and convenience for the public. Rather, in the study of the short-term alternatives these benefits are used to rank the alternatives and in particular to select the best alternative use of the twelve buildings to be inherited by the new government.

This alternative was then compared in cost with renting office space in a new building large enough to house the entire staff. In the discussion of the results of this evaluation it is made clear that housing the staff in a single building will have benefits in terms of staff communications, use of space and convenience for the public which would not exist if the twelve separate buildings were used. The comparison of the long-term solutions to the problem, renting space in a large building or constructing a new civic center, was made strictly on the basis of cost, since the benefits to staff and to the public are assumed to be the same under either alternative. See Chapter 11 for references on cost-benefit analysis.

ANALYSIS OF PROBLEMS

A variety of methods were applied in the studies presented in this book. Classifying problems by the methods employed to solve them might be a useful way for the analyst to distinguish problems, but it is not a particularly easy way for a public official to view a new problem.

Kraemer (1973, pp. 24–6) has divided local government decision problems into the following three categories: operational, programming (or management) and developmental (or planning). Byrd (1975, pp. 11–14), in talking about the levels of administrative decisions, uses essentially the same categories as Kraemer but calls his three levels operational decisions, strategic decisions and policy decisions. Both authors compare these three types of decision problems in terms of a number of dimensions, including the type and number of objectives a problem might have and how well the objectives are defined, the measures of effectiveness, the models and techniques used for deriving solutions and the time frame of the problem (short, intermediate, or long-range). The decision problems investigated by the studies presented in Part Three provide an illustration of each of the categories defined by Kraemer and Byrd.

Deciding which invoices should be checked (Chapter 13) is a good example of an *operational* problem. Kraemer defines such problems as having a single, well-defined objective and many well-defined alternatives. In this case the objective was to minimize the total cost of the system, and there were a large number of alternative solutions, although they varied only in terms of the percentage of invoices checked. In addition the criteria used to judge alternative solutions to an operational problem are usually easy to select and measure. Standard mathematical, statistical or economic models can often be used for such problems and it is usually possible to derive analytically a single best solution.

Both the simulation study presented in Chapter 14 and the reorganization study in Chapter 15 were concerned with problems which fit the *programming* (or management) category. Such decision problems are characterized by having multiple and possibly conflicting objectives. It can often be difficult to define the objectives to these problems or to achieve agreement on their definition. Although mathematical models are used to solve this category of problem there are usually important nonquantifiable factors which help to determine the eventual solution.

In the local government reorganization and relocation study both the alternatives for satisfying the short-term and the long-term office space needs of the new government were quite limited. The solution to both problems depended on satisfying two general objectives, which turned out to be conflicting in the short term. First, it was believed to be very important to minimize the disruptive effect of the reorganization. Therefore the short-term alternatives were evaluated in terms of ease of communication for staff, effective use of available space and convenience to the public. These factors tended to favor locating all the staff in a single building. The second objective was to minimize the cost of providing office space and it was found to be cheaper to use the twelve existing buildings, which were scattered around the new district, than to rent space in a large office building. It was thus not possible to identify a single best solution to the short-term problem.

The new vehicle service facility evaluated by the study presented in Chapter 14 could have been designed to satisfy a number of objectives, including maximizing the utilization of the facility's repair staff and maximizing the availability of vehicles for their normal duties – which are clearly conflicting objectives. Increasing the percentage of time the mechanics and repair facilities are utilized also increases the amount of time vehicles must wait for service, hence the utilization of those vehicles for their normal duties must decrease. Therefore instead of a single best solution being sought, the simulation model was used to evaluate the implications of the various alternatives:

> to characterize the range of alternatives in terms of the various measures of effectiveness but to leave the selection of the preferred alternative up to the administrator, who must impart his own value system to the conflicting objectives. (Byrd, 1975, p. 13)

The final category of decision problem, called *developmental* or planning problems by Kraemer, and policy level decisions by Byrd, is also characterized by multiple and conflicting objectives. But in this case there might be no general agreement on what should be included as an objective; and when objectives are agreed it is often difficult or impossible to find agreed quantitative criteria to measure them. In addition, alternative courses of action are not easy to identify or are not clear cut. Problems which are expected to exist in the future, and are being planned for now, fall into this category.

The planning problem presented in Chapter 12 had many of the characteristics of this category of decision problem. The five alternative strategies that were being evaluated as the basis for the county's general plan for land development were based on events that would take place over the next fifteen years. The result was that none of the alternatives proved to be usable since the population forecasts on which they were based were so greatly in error. A set of six objectives were used to evaluate and compare the five alternative land development strategies. The objectives were conflicting; for example, one was to locate new residential areas in an attractive environment while another was to preserve good-quality landscaped areas. Furthermore there was no general agreement between the public and the county planners on the importance that should be attached to each objective.

In recent years there has been considerable growth in the use of operations research methods in planning. Paelinck and Nijkamp (1975) and Isard (1975) discuss a number of quantitative methods for regional planning, including location theory, game theory, factor analysis, input-output analysis, gravity models, linear programming, transportation models and geometric programming. In *A Model of Metropolis* Lowry (1964) reports on the development of a computer model designed for evaluating the impact of public decisions in a metropolitan area and for predicting changes in the area over time due to changes in employment, transportation and population. This model was fitted to data from Pittsburgh, Pennsylvania. *Community Renewal Programming: A San Francisco Case Study* (Arthur D. Little, 1966) describes the use of a simulation model to analyze a city's long-range renewal needs. Chadwick (1978, ch. 9) describes a number of other operational models used in urban planning and their underlying theories and Harris (1968) discusses the role of quantitative models of urban development.

In addition there are studies in other parts of this book that would be of particular interest to urban and regional planners. For example, the studies presented in Chapters 3 and 10 are about the location of facilities. And since transportation is a major concern of planners the two studies in Chapters 7 and 8 would also be of special interest, as would Chapter 9, which is concerned with a proposed flood relief scheme.

There are many problems in the area of administrative services that can benefit from operations research, for example:

- How should building repair and maintenance be scheduled?
- How often should a building be painted?
- When should vehicles be replaced?
- What range of sizes of work clothing should be kept in stock?
- How big a warehouse should be built, where should it be located and what goods should it stock?

The methods for answering many of these questions are similar to those used to determine the best level of invoice checking (see Chapters 13 and 17). In addition Byrd (1975, ch. 11) describes the use of several models for determining when to replace government-owned equipment and buildings. He also gives an example of the use of simulation to analyze a maintenance schedule (pp. 170–4); and Ward (1964, ch. 4) discusses the use of operations research in building maintenance. Ward (1964, ch. 2, and 1967, pp. 18–28) also discussed a number of local government inventory problems, including whether to keep an item in stock or buy it as needed, when to place orders and how much to order. Most basic operations research textbooks devote a chapter to the study of inventory models.

Finally, readers interested in administrative services might find other studies in this book of particular interest, for example, the studies on facility location (Chapters 3 and 10), the study to determine the number of ambulances needed to satisfy a given level of service (Chapter 2) and the feasibility study of an inter-library loan transportation system (Chapter 5).

Part Four

The Art and Science of Operations Research

17
Summing Up

We have called this part 'The Art and Science of Operations Research'. By art we mean the skill necessary to achieve practical results using the scientific approach to problem-solving embodied in operations research.

The purpose of this book is to help those concerned with solving government problems to appreciate the value and wide variety of uses of operations research in the public sector. We selected particular studies because they can be read and understood by people with no prior background in operations research. The studies illustrate various types of applications in different functional areas of local or regional government. Included are some failures as well as success stories.

These studies also provide the reader with excellent examples of the various elements of the operations research problem-solving process. The following sections describe and illustrate the elements of a *typical* operations research study according to the outline presented in Chapter 1. In doing this we use one of the studies in the book to illustrate the entire process: the report from Chapter 13, *The Checking of Invoices*. We have chosen this study for three reasons. First, in order to illustrate the process a number of details are necessary, but the details of this study should not overwhelm the reader. Secondly, *The Checking of Invoices* nicely illustrates all the aspects of the process. Thirdly, the mathematical model used in this study can be given by a graph and the solution to the problem derived from an examination of the graph. This greatly simplifies the process and should aid the reader in more easily understanding two key stages in the process: constructing a mathematical model and deriving a solution from the model. However, since each of the studies presented in this book provides interesting examples of different applications of operations research we draw upon all the studies to illustrate the problem-solving process.

1 RECOGNIZE THAT A PROBLEM EXISTS

Public sector problems arise in a number of ways. To begin with, the allocation of limited public funds presents all sorts of problems. Satisfying public needs, overcoming complaints, or determining whether to expand, improve or cut back existing services are common problems faced by most local and regional governments. Some problems are obvious while others require extensive analysis before they are clearly recognized. In order to identify problems, many government departments conduct periodic evaluations for the purpose of determining whether their goals are being satisfied. This regular review represents a very important aspect of problem-solving and will be discussed in the section on evaluating results. Most public institutions are also faced with more problems than they can handle and have to decide which problems should be tackled first.

The Stonebridge Supplies Department (Chapter 13) wanted to reduce the clerical costs associated with the approval of suppliers' invoices for payment by the city treasurer. The department was also experiencing difficulty in finding staff to perform the necessary invoice checking. We spoke with eight other selective invoice-checking users and learned that although a variety of factors enabled these governments to recognize they had a problem, in all cases a selective invoice-checking system had been installed so that the government could speed up the passing and payment of invoices without having to increase the number of staff needed to check them. In most cases the government did not have the funds to support additional clerical positions and had to take alternative action. In a few cases the existence of a problem was quite clear – invoices were literally piled up to the ceiling.

Other studies in this book illustrate different ways of recognizing that a problem exists. In the studies of emergency ambulance services (Chapter 2) and office reorganization (Chapter 15) the problem resulted from a need to amalgamate under one authority services that had formerly been under separate jurisdictions. In locating new kitchens for a meals-on-wheels social services program (Chapter 3), selecting planning strategies for a county (Chapter 12) and designing a new vehicle maintenance facility (Chapter 14) the problem was planning for or providing for growth. The mounting evidence that ranking on a waiting list for city housing did not accurately reflect need for housing prompted the development of a new points scheme (Chapter 4). Three studies were about problems concerning serious physical or environmental issues: Faringdon (Chapter 7) faced congestion, noise and danger to pedestrians; Towcester (Chapter 9) had experienced recent flooding; and several of the twenty-one communities in the North East (Chapter 10) which banded together to solve their long-term refuse disposal problems were facing a severe shortage of places to dump refuse.

Cutting cost was a major issue in two studies: developing a trans-portation system for inter-library loans (Chapter 5); and the *Huddersfield Bus Study* (Chapter 8). Much of the effort in the bus study was devoted to identifying the problem. The study began with the collection and analysis of a considerable amount of local infor-mation which was initially used to identify problems with the current bus system. This detailed analysis identified where demand was not being met and where spare capacity existed. It also provided infor-mation that helped to develop alternative courses of action, thus enabling the study team to define clearly the short- and long-term problems of the Huddersfield bus system. This study illustrates well the importance of the problem identification phase of an operations research study. The careful collection and analysis of data during this initial stage forged the direction of the rest of the study. It not only provided data for defining the problems of the bus system but also provided the data base needed to construct, calibrate and verify the computer model used to represent that system.

2   DEFINE THE PROBLEM

Developing a formal problem definition requires an analysis of the situation and an understanding of the general background of the problem. It involves investigating the environment in which the problem exists, possibly gathering historical data, learning how a particular process works, and meeting with people who have firsthand knowledge of the problem. A problem definition is a written description of a problem. It generally begins with a statement on what motivated concern about the problem. Then it proceeds to describe the problem in terms of some if not all of the following elements:

- *problem statement* – the question or questions to be answered by solutions of the problem;
- *objectives* – the criterion or criteria for selecting one of a number of potential solutions to the problem;
- *measure of effectiveness* – the unit or units of measurement, the yardstick, for judging alternative solutions in light of the objective(s);
- *alternative solutions* – the alternative courses of action being considered;
- *constraints* – limitations or restrictions that help determine the courses of action that are feasible and the value of a particular solution, or that establish the time and money available to derive a solution;
- *decision-makers* – who they are and what special expertise they possess;
- *larger system* – interactions between this problem and other parts or activities of the organization, or system, within which the problem exists.

Problem statement

The problem statement should raise a specific question. In *The Checking of Invoices* three separate but related questions are studied. They concern the checking of invoices from suppliers to verify that (1) the goods have arrived, (2) the prices on the invoice are correct and (3) the arithmetic on the invoice is correct. In this chapter we focus on only one of these problems: which invoices should be checked for verification of delivery? Other studies examine such questions as: where should a town's bypass be located (Chapter 7)? How many mechanics are needed in a vehicle repair shop (Chapter 14)? How many points should be allocated to each of a set of needs factors when ranking applicants for housing (Chapter 4)?

Generally, the more specific a problem statement the easier it will be to follow through with the rest of the problem definition. Moreover if the problem statement is not precise at this point it will be very difficult to continue with the definition of the problem. Good or even acceptable solutions to a problem are seldom found if the problem is poorly defined, or if the wrong question has been asked.

The specific question being raised will not be immediately obvious in all the studies included in this book. Take, for example, the problem faced by the social services department of Worcestershire (Chapter 3). The social services department and the county council had set three goals for expanding the meals-on-wheels service:

(1)   to make the service available throughout the area,
(2)   to ensure each recipient received at least five meals a week,
(3)   to provide meals for all people who are in need.

With these goals in mind, it is tempting to say that the problem is: how can the council accomplish the goals of its meals-on-wheels program? Although there is nothing wrong with accepting this question as a very general statement of the problem, it is not specific enough to know how to proceed. The county's goals were made more specific by expanding them and setting specific target dates:

1973:   to give each present recipient four meals a week,
1974:   to give a four-meals a week service throughout the area,
1975:   to raise service to five meals a week.

By this refinement of the goals, a more concrete statement of the problem begins to emerge. It becomes clear that the fundamental problem must focus on what facilities and resources are needed to accomplish the target goals of the meals-on-wheels program. This leads to a more narrow and concise statement of the problem as follows: how many kitchens does Worcestershire need for its meals-on-wheels program, how large should they be, where should they be located and which area should they serve in order to achieve the goals of the program?

Objectives
After determining what questions to ask the next step is to set criteria for helping the decision-makers decide which of a number of answers to the questions that have been raised is the best answer for their problem. If a mathematical model is to be used it is necessary to put the objective in terms that can be quantified. For example, a precise statement of the objective of our invoice-checking problem is: find the answer to the problem (stated above) that minimizes the expected cost of the system, including the cost of checking and the expected losses resulting from not checking for the delivery of certain goods. Before giving examples of the objectives of other studies in the book, three points about setting objectives should be noted.

First, in many problems solved by operations research it is assumed that there is a single objective. This is not necessarily a limitation on the use of operations research methods, since in many problem situations there is only one quantifiable objective and in other cases one objective so clearly outweights the others in importance that viewing the problem in terms of this single objective produces valid answers.

Secondly, in setting objectives for solving problems in the public sector we invariably find that problem-solvers will either attempt to optimize the level of service of a program or minimize the cost of providing the service. Of course neither of these factors can be ignored, and the one that does not appear in the objective will usually show up as a constraint on obtaining a solution to the problem. We will return to this point at the end of this section.

Finally, most problems involve objectives that are difficult or perhaps impossible to quantify, as well as quantifiable objectives. Those objectives that cannot be quantified, sometimes called the subjective or intangible factors of a problem, should not be ignored. They should be identified and included in the problem definition for they could represent the criterion on which the solution to a problem is based. An example of the importance of a nonquantifiable objective can be seen in the study to determine whether to construct a flood relief project for a small town (Chapter 9). Based upon the quantifiable objective, the benefit-cost ratio, the answer was negative. But it was decided to build the scheme anyway because the nonquantifiable objective – reducing the fear of flooding – was in the event considered more important.

A variety of objectives are represented in this book. In the study to solve the refuse disposal problems for twenty-one local governments (Chapter 10), the objective was to minimize the refuse disposal cost per week. In finding the number and best locations of kitchens for a meals-on-wheels service (Chapter 3) the objective was to minimize the annual cost of operating the kitchens and delivering the meals. The short-term improvements in a local bus system (Chapter 8) were examined in two ways. One way of viewing the problem was to minimize the subsidy required to operate the system, while the other way was to maximize a measure of user benefit. A number of other studies involved multiple objectives, including those found in Chapters 7, 12, 14 and 15. In the work to determine the best location for the bypass of a small town (Chapter 7), for example, two economic criteria and several environmental criteria were employed. One economic criterion was to maximize the first-year rate of return. The other was to maximize the ratio of the total net economic benefits of each alternative route to the total construction costs. The environmental criteria included minimizing the amount of land needed for constructing the bypass, maximizing the reduction of traffic through the center of the town and minimizing the severance of existing roads and footpaths.

Measure of effectiveness
Once an objective has been selected, the measure of effectiveness is usually obvious. It is the unit or units of measurement, the yardstick, by which alternative solutions to the problem can be judged in light of the criteria established by the objective. For example, if the objective is to minimize the cost of providing a service, then the measure of

effectiveness will be in terms of money. In the case of the invoice-checking study the measure of effectiveness was in dollars per year and the solution that minimized the total annual cost of the system was judged the best solution to the problem.

Locating kitchens for the meals-on-wheels program (Chapter 3) and finding the office space that best satisfied the long-term needs of a newly reorganized local government (Chapter 15) also used annual cost as a measure of effectiveness. But in both studies future costs were discounted to present value, since capital expenditures were involved. The same was true in the refuse disposal study (Chapter 10), but in this case alternative solutions were compared in terms of their cost per week. Thus the period of time over which the cost of the service is measured or the way it is measured can vary.

The objective in several studies was to select a course of action that maximized a ratio. In these cases the measure of effectiveness for a given alternative is the ratio found by dividing the benefits of that alternative, measured in monetary units, by its cost. The study of alternative bypass routes for Faringdon (Chapter 7) used two such measures. One was formed by dividing the road-user benefits for the first year of the bypass by its total capital cost. The other was a ratio of the net discounted benefits to discounted construction costs. Other studies had as their objective improving the quality of life. For example, the evaluation of alternative land development strategies (Chapter 12) was based on a number of objectives, including providing good residential areas. Under this objective it was necessary to develop a measure for comparing alternative plans in terms of the environmental attractiveness of the new residential areas that they provided. An unusual environmental measure was found in the study of local government reorganization (Chapter 15), where one of the measures of effectiveness was a disturbance index based on the need for staff, who might be located in separate buildings, to communicate with each other.

If the objective is to find the alternative that provides the best level of service, then the way that level of service is measured becomes the measure of effectiveness. For example, short-term improvements in bus operations (Chapter 8) were first viewed with the objective of maximizing the user benefits provided by the system. These benefits were measured in units of cost per hour, but this measure incorporated an evaluation of such user benefits as reduced waiting time and reduced travel time. Alternative bus routes were then compared in terms of this measure of user benefit. The assessment of the design of a new vehicle maintenance facility (Chapter 14) and the study to develop a new housing points scheme (Chapter 4) were also concerned with providing the best level of service. In the former one of the measures of effectiveness used was the percentage of time vehicles were available for their normal work. In the latter study the measure of effectiveness was the degree to which alternative assignments of points to needs factors matched the subjective assessments of housing officials. A further example of a study that attempts to optimize a level of service is the one that determined the number and locations of ambulances for a regional health authority (Chapter 2). The measure of effectiveness for this study was the number of ambulances needed by the system and the implied objective was to minimize that number. This is not to say that the standard of service, in terms of the time needed to respond to an emergency, was ignored. It was a very important factor, but it served as one of the constraints on solving the problem rather than as the objective.

It is interesting to note that the measure of effectiveness used in this study, that is, number of ambulances needed by the system, served as a proxy measure for the cost of the system and that the real objective was to minimize this cost. Using proxy measures is fairly common in operations research and often overcomes difficult problems in obtaining data or in making certain types of measurements. In Chapter 3 the number of meals delivered was a measure of the benefit of the meals-on-wheels program and was therefore used in setting the goals of the program. The speed of service was made a constraint in the study to develop a national inter-library loan transportation system (Chapter 5) and also served as a proxy measure of the benefit of the inter-library loan service to the user. Furthermore the measure of effectiveness used on one of the problems examined by this study was the distance covered by the vans which delivered the books and this served as a proxy measure for the cost of the system.

Alternative solutions

The phrase 'alternative solutions' is a confusing one. We are brought up in mathematics to think that problems have only one solution and, in fact, many mathematical problems do have only one 'correct' solution. The key to understanding what is meant by alternative solutions is to recognize that it does not mean the correct, or best, solution, nor does it even mean a feasible solution. Alternative solutions are just the *possible* different courses of action for solving the problem. One of the alternatives considered might be the best solution to the problem, but it is entirely possible that none is even feasible. For example, purchasing office equipment to help staff check invoices is an alternative solution to our invoice-checking problem. It might not be a feasible solution because there might be no such equipment that can do the job, or it might not be the best solution because it does not satisfy the objective. But it is a possible alternative solution.

At this stage of problem-solving it is necessary to identify for investigation all the alternative solutions that are to be considered, whether or not they might be feasible. The analysis that follows cannot evaluate alternative solutions that have not been identified. In the invoice-checking problem the alternative solutions all involved changing clerical procedures and doing less checking. It was suggested that the amount of checking – and hence the clerical cost incurred – could be greatly reduced if some or all of the invoices were approved for payment without checking for delivery. Thus the alternative solutions to be investigated by the mathematical model ranged over the various possible levels of checking invoices, from a 100 percent level (the existing practice) to a 0 percent level. There are of course many alternative midway solutions, for example, checking only 30 percent of the invoices. It is difficult to know what other alternative courses of action were also considered and discarded at the time the study was conducted in 1962. However, in addition to purchasing equipment to aid the checking process, as suggested above, there are the following possibilities:

(1) placing fewer orders for goods,
(2) supplying more requests from stocks of goods kept at the warehouse,
(3) grouping purchases, that is, making larger purchases from fewer suppliers.

One alternative solution is common to all problems – the 'do nothing' solution. There are many valid reasons for doing nothing about a problem. There might be no feasible alternative solutions; there might be too many other more important problems to solve; or the problem might not have been recognized. Some problems known to exist have a low priority on an organization's problem-solving agenda, either because of lack of staff to deal with them, or for political reasons, or because no one cares enough. But even a problem that is tackled need not have a novel solution. The 'do nothing' solution should always be considered; it might well turn out to be the best solution after all.

In Chapter 9, the study to determine whether to build a flood relief project, only two alternatives were considered – to build the proposed flood relief scheme or to do nothing – and in this case the 'do nothing' alternative was recommended. (As it turned out, a third alternative, a more modest flood relief project not originally examined by the study, was eventually implemented.) The report of the study of a region's long-term refuse disposal problem (Chapter 10) clearly describes the alternative refuse disposal methods that were available. The alternative solutions in this case were the various numbers and locations of refuse treatment plants needed to implement each of the possible disposal methods. Several other studies also had as their alternative solutions various numbers and locations of facilities and staff, for example, ambulances (Chapter 2), kitchens (Chapter 3), and vehicle repair shop staff and facilities (Chapter 14). In Chapter 7, the study to determine the best location for a bypass of a small town, the five routes evaluated were the alternative solutions, while various bus routes and frequencies of bus operation were the alternatives in Chapter 8. In the development of a new points scheme for ranking applicants for housing (Chapter 4) the alternatives were the needs factors on which the applicants should be rated and the number of points that should be assigned to each factor.

Constraints
A number of factors place limitations or restrictions on a problem. It is

useful to divide these constraints into two categories: those that describe the environment surrounding the problem; and those that limit the approach to solving the problem. Both types of constraints serve to reduce the set of alternative solutions that need to be considered, that is, they help to identify those alternative courses of action that are feasible.

The first type of constraint results from efforts to model accurately the environment surrounding a problem. Here are some examples of this type of constraint.

(1) A recreation department needs to replace playground equipment but has limited funds for purchasing new equipment (a budget constraint).

(2) The emergency room of a county hospital is required to accept all patients regardless of their ability to pay for treatment (a service constraint).

(3) An adult education program wants to expand the number of courses offered at night but has run out of classrooms (a physical constraint).

In many cases constraints such as these can be expressed mathematically and built into the mathematical model, thus serving to make the model a better representation of the problem environment. Constraints not only reduce the number of alternative solutions that need to be evaluated but also help ensure that the solution derived from the model is feasible. The second type of constraint limits the way a problem is solved. Frequently the amount of time available to solve a problem and the personnel or money available to solve it place severe limitations on the problem-solving effort. All of the studies presented in this book were under some kind of limitation in terms of the amount of time and money that could be spent on solving the problem. The remainder of this section is devoted to examples and further discussions of the first type of constraint – the type that shapes the mathematical model.

In the last section we listed several hypothetical alternative solutions to the invoice-checking problem. These solutions were not mentioned in the report of the study, but they do represent the kinds of alternatives that might have been investigated. One constraint that could have eliminated these alternatives from further consideration was the fact that the supplies department has little control over the number of direct purchases that it places with suppliers or the amount of goods ordered. Each customer department acts independently when requesting goods from the supplies department. Thus it would not be possible for the department's purchasing agents to group orders or to place fewer orders with their suppliers. The alternative that remained was to reduce the amount of checking, that is, to verify only some of the invoices for delivery of goods. But this alternative includes a large number of possible solutions.

The primary constraint on the invoice-checking problem was the demand placed on the system in terms of the number and type of invoices that needed to be processed. The supplies department received over 150,000 invoices during a twelve-month period in 1961/2 and it was expected that the rate of demand for processing invoices would continue at this level or increase. In fact by 1977 the number of invoices received by the department had grown to 240,000 per year. The need to satisfy a certain amount of demand for a service is a common constraint in public sector problems and one found in most other studies in this book. Demand has been expressed as the expected number of calls for an ambulance from various parts of a health district at various times of day (Chapter 2), the number of meals that need to be served to satisfy the target goals of a meals-on-wheels service (Chapter 3), the number of applicants on a waiting list (Chapter 4), the expected number of bus riders from various parts of a city at various times of day (Chapter 8), population forecasts (Chapter 12) and the expected number of vehicle breakdowns (Chapter 14).

Numerous other types of constraints are also illustrated in the book. The locations of existing facilities and existing road networks placed restrictions on finding the best number and locations of ambulance stations (Chapter 2), kitchens (Chapter 3), vans for transporting inter-library loans (Chapter 5), bus routes (Chapter 8), refuse treatment plants (Chapter 10), land development (Chapter 12) and government offices (Chapter 15). Geographical conditions limited the placement of a town's bypass (Chapter 7) and the alternatives for providing flood relief (Chapter 9). Time was an important constraint in many of the studies. Meals could not take too long to travel from kitchen to recipient (Chapter 3), inter-library loans were to reach the requesting library within two days (Chapter 5), the probable time between floods was a major factor in evaluating a flood relief project (Chapter 9) and how often routine maintenance was to be performed dictated the number of mechanics and the size of a new vehicle service facility (Chapter 14). Achieving a given standard of service was the primary constraint in devising new bus routes (Chapter 8) and in deciding how many ambulances were needed to provide emergency services in a regional health authority (Chapter 2).

It is essential to identify all the relevant constraints on a problem and to state those constraints properly. If constraints are not identified, not included in the model, or are not accurate, then it is unlikely that the model is a good representation of the real system it is depicting; and the usefulness of the solutions derived from the model can be quite limited. At least two of the studies we have presented would have been more useful if an important constraint had not been left out of the definition of the problem, or had been stated properly.

In determining the number and location of kitchens for a meals-on-wheels service (Chapter 3), the solution derived would have been very different if a constraint on the availability of volunteers who delivery the meals had been included in the problem definition and in the subsequent mathematical model. In fact, obtaining volunteers has been the major constraint in limiting the growth of the service. If this limitation had been placed on the problem at the time, it would probably have been found that none of the alternative solutions being considered was feasible. This would have forced the decision-makers to consider other alternatives, or reduce the goals of the program. Evaluating alternative strategies for the planning of land development (Chapter 12) is a case where a constraint too narrowly defined the problem. In this study it was assumed that the population of the area would show much greater growth than actually occurred. The strategies that were evaluated were therefore virtually useless when it became apparent that the population was not increasing as fast as originally assumed. With the benefit of hindsight it is easy to identify the weaknesses in these two studies. At the time the studies were conducted, however, it was obviously not so clear that the basic assumptions would turn out so poorly.

Decision-maker
The person or group of people that decides whether the recommendations of a study will be implemented, or which of several good alternative solutions is the best solution for the problem, is called the decision-maker. The analyst is the person or group of people who carries out the process of problem-solving. Of course the decision-maker and the analyst may be the same person, although this was not the case in any of the studies we have presented. With government problems there is usually more than one person who serves as the decision-maker.

Decision-makers have several contributions to make to an operations research study. We have talked about intangible, nonquantifiable objectives as well as the quantifiable ones. It is usually the role of the decision-makers to synthesize the solution derived from the mathematical model, which is based on quantifiable objectives, and the more subjective criteria which relate to the problem to reach an overall decision. Decision-makers possess valuable information that can strongly shape the definition of a problem. For this reason the analyst should know who is going to use the results of the study and how these results might be used. In addition, decision-makers often determine the objective in the problem definition, provide some, if not all, of the alternative solutions and provide information that helps to identify constraints.

However, decision-makers can also act as a constraint on the implementation of a solution. For this reason it makes sense to understand the influences and pressures under which they make decisions. With this knowledge the analyst might be able to provide arguments for implementing a good solution that would otherwise not be implemented. Often recommendations resulting from a study are not implemented because the analyst has solved the wrong problem. Obtaining information from the decision-makers helps to ensure, but does not guarantee, that the analyst solves the right problem.

Larger system
Regardless of the size or detail of the model that is ultimately constructed, it is inevitably limited to describing a subsystem of the larger

system in which a problem exists. It is important to recognize early in the problem-solving effort that solutions to problems in one program or one service can affect the operation of other programs or services. The effect can be positive, but it can also be negative and can create more severe problems than the one solved. We therefore suggest that at an early stage the analyst and the decision-makers step back from the problem, broaden their view of the system within which the problem exists and try to identify how the approach being taken in the problem definition relates to the other parts of the larger system. Perhaps the types of system interrelationships identified at this point will change the elements of the problem definition that shape the model that is to be constructed; that is, it will change the problem statement, objectives, measures of effectiveness, alternatives or constraints. Or a better understanding of the larger system could influence the approach taken in testing or implementing solutions.

To illustrate this point, we examine some of the system interrelationships in the invoice-checking study. The problem is to find which invoices should be checked for delivery and the general solution that has been suggested is to check invoices selectively, that is, to check only some of the invoices. Suppose the solution were to check only 30 percent of the invoices. What impact would this have on the larger system? There are many possible ways to delineate the larger system. It could be the supplies department – all its goals, functions and staff. Or it could be the entire city – all its departments, functions and the people it serves.

In order to understand the system interrelationships it is necessary to ask specific questions about how implementing a solution to the problem might affect the rest of the invoice-checking process and the other departments which are served by the supplies department. Would information be lost that could cause a customer department more clerical effort than the savings resulting from implementing selective checking? Are there other elements of the invoice-checking process that would need to be changed? How will implementing selective checking of delivery affect the other checks of invoices that are performed? Are the other functions in the department so adversely affected as to make the alternative solutions identified thus far infeasible? In fact as the study progressed it was found that the check of arithmetic accuracy of an invoice would be affected in a positive way by implementing selective checking of delivery. Since advice notes would no longer be attached to many of the invoices, the work involved in handling documents would be reduced when the arithmetic check was performed. It was subsequently found that this would reduce clerical costs by about $700 a year.

To expand the meals-on-wheels service (Chapter 3), one of the alternatives considered was to increase the use of existing kitchens. In the larger system, some of these kitchens are used for other purposes, for example, school meals. How would this increased use affect the school meals program, run by another department of the county? The immediate road network of a small town was the primary concern in deciding where a bypass for the town should be placed (Chapter 7). The bypass would remove a severe bottleneck on a heavily used road, but would it cause congestion, noise and a bottleneck elsewhere? To overcome flooding a small town (Chapter 9), a flood relief project which involved straightening a meandering creek was considered. How would reducing the chances of flooding affect property downstream? Determining the office needs for a local government after a reorganization was the subject of Chapter 15. An important factor in this study was the relationship between the local government and the various county government departments which served the area. How would this relationship be affected by the various alternatives being considered?

These are examples of the types of questions that need to be raised in trying to understand the relationships between the problem under study and the larger system in which it exists. It might not be possible to answer such questions at this stage, but the analyst and decision-makers should be aware that they exist and try to answer them as the study progresses.

Summary and discussion

These then are the seven elements of a problem definition. We believe it is helpful if the analyst writes down the problem definition in a form that can be easily understood by the decision-makers. This written statement represents a type of contract between the people attempting to solve a problem and the people needing a solution. After reviewing this statement the decision-makers may wish to make changes or ask for certain points to be clarified. It is better to achieve agreement at this early stage in the total process than to waste a lot of time and money constructing a mathematical model and deriving a solution, only to find that the decision-makers do not agree with how the analyst has approached the problem and are, therefore, unwilling to implement the results.

Of course the analyst must be prepared to consider new information at any time in the solution process. We do not want to leave the impression that a problem definition is a static, unchangeable statement of how one views a given problem. The approach to solving a problem often changes with new information. However, to begin the process of problem-solving we should be able to write a definition of the problem based upon the best information that can be collected within the time available to collect it. And it should be something that all parties can agree is the basis for constructing the mathematical model that will be used to solve the problem.

Before taking up the topic of constructing mathematical models, the next phase of the process, it is worth returning briefly to the interaction between a problem's objective and constraints. Multi-objective problems are common and often we would like to judge alternative solutions by more than one criterion. Multiple criteria are usually considered by the analyst in making a recommendation and by the decision-makers in deciding which alternative solution to implement. However, the analyst is seldom able to incorporate more than one criterion in the objective of the mathematical model because models and solution methods are usually limited to treating only one objective at a time. We do not believe that this is a severe limitation on the use of quantitative methods for solving public sector problems and would like to show why.

Suppose the success of a public service is measured by the number of people served and how well they are served, but there is pressure on the department providing the service to cut the cost of the program. If the program were the subject of an operations research study, should the objective be to maximize the number of people served, optimize the way they are served, or minimize the cost of providing the service? Any one of these could be set as the objective, but this does not mean that the others are left out of the problem definition or the mathematical model. The other objectives can be incorporated as constraints and in this way they can play a very important role in determining the best solution to the problem.

Two recurring objectives in solving public sector problems are to improve the level of service and to minimize the cost of providing the service. Generally these two objectives are conflicting. As the level of service is improved, the cost of providing it also increases. However, it is possible to have as the objective the optimization of the level of service, with a constraint on the maximum amount of money available to provide the service. Alternatively, one could minimize the cost of providing the service with a constraint on the level of service that must be provided.

What gets set as the objective and what gets included as a constraint depends on several factors. For example, it might depend on how one wants the approach to a problem or its solution to be seen. It might be politically expedient to regard the level of service as the objective rather than a constraint on the problem. On the other hand, most decision-makers are very cost-conscious. As long as they and their constituents recognize that a certain level of service must be maintained, then it might be politcally expedient to call the cost the objective with a minimum level of service as the constraint.

The ambulance study presented in Chapter 2 can be used to illustrate some of the points raised in this discussion. In this study the standard of service was expressed in terms of response time. Ambulances were to arrive at the scene of an emergency within eight minutes of being notified for at least 50 percent of all calls and within twenty minutes for at least 95 percent of all calls. Meeting this response-time standard was clearly an important objective of the decision-makers who commissioned the ambulance study. But in defining the problem and constructing the mathematical model, this objective became a constraint, while the objective of the model was to find the minimum number of ambulances and their locations which satisfied this constraint. Other service objectives, such as maximizing a measure of the benefit that recipients of a service receive, or maximizing the number of recipients, can also be established through constraints. In some mathematical models there is no limit to the number of constraints that can be constructed and placed on the problem. It is generally true, however, that fewer alternative solutions will be found to be feasible the more constraints that are included in the model.

Suppose the objective in the ambulance study had been to minimize the average ambulance response time. To solve the problem this way it would have been necessary to put a limit on the amount of money available to provide emergency ambulance services, to keep the number of ambulances within reasonable financial limits. It is interesting to note that the study of short-term improvements in a bus system (Chapter 8) was the only study which explicitly built a financial constraint into the model. Here the problem was to find the best bus system and frequency of operation under the constraint that the public subsidy to operate the system would not be increased. In most other studies the objective was to minimize the cost of a system or some proxy for cost, with achieving a certain standard of service as one of the constraints in determining the best solution.

It is important that the analyst identify for himself or herself, for the public and for the decision-makers the criteria by which a solution will be selected, because this objective will be the basis for constructing the mathematical model and deriving a solution from it. The effort devoted to defining a problem properly should make the task of constructing the model easier and should make the model a better representation of the problem and the system in which it exists.

3 CONSTRUCT A MATHEMATICAL MODEL OF THE SYSTEM

A model is simply a representation of something. It is often used to gain a better understanding of the thing being represented, to test ideas, to teach, to test solutions to a problem, or to make decisions. Having defined the problem and analyzed the system in which it exists, it is now possible to construct a model or representation of that problem and system. In operations research this model will consist of mathematical (or economic or statistical) relationships based on the elements of the problem definition.

For purposes of this discussion we will classify models into two types: decision models and descriptive models. Decision models express the objective and effectiveness of the system under study in terms of a set of variables. At least one of these variables is subject to control. These controllable variables are called the decision variables of the problem and represent the alternative courses of action. By 'solving a decision model' is meant deriving from the model the value of the decision variable (or variables) which best satisfies the objective. In other words, decision models are used to find the best answer to the problem, the best alternative course of action. This assumes, naturally, that the decision model properly represents the system. Descriptive models are used to describe or represent part or all of the system under study. They may be used to obtain solutions to problems, but in a way different from decision models. We will have more to say about the distinction between these two types of mathematical models at the end of this section. First we give some examples of each type of model.

Up to now we have talked in general terms about mathematical models. It will be useful at this point to demonstrate a simple mathematical model, before going on to construct the model used in our invoice checking illustration. Consider the model

$$t = \frac{d}{s},$$

where t = time to make a trip (in hours),
d = distance to be traveled (in miles), and
s = speed of journey (in miles per hour).

This is a simple descriptive model that can be used to tell us how long it will take to make a trip, given the distance and speed of the journey. For example, if we plan to make a 200-mile trip and we expect to average 50 miles per hour, then the amount of time this trip will take is given by:

$$t = \frac{200 \text{ miles}}{50 \text{ miles per hour}} = 4 \text{ hours.}$$

This is not a decision model. There are no alternatives to consider, no decision variables, and there is no objective. This mathematical model merely describes the relationship between time, distance and speed.

Now we will construct two of the descriptive models and one of the decision models used in the study on checking invoices. The decision model is based on the problem definition given in the previous section. It will answer the question: 'which invoices should be checked for verification of delivery?' In order to construct this model we need to describe the system in terms of the number of invoices processed and their value.

The supplies department processed approximately 150,000 invoices in a twelve-month period during 1961/2. It is difficult to visualize, much less work with, such a large number of invoices. They have therefore been divided into groups according to the value of the goods they represent. The groups and the percentage of invoices in each group are shown in Figure 17.1. The bars in Figure 17.1 represent the percentage of the total number of invoices received during the twelve-month period that fall within each group. For example, 13.1 percent of all the invoices during this period were for values between $4 and $8, and 0.12 percent were between $2,048 and $4,096. By 'value of invoice' is meant the total value for all the items on an invoice.

Figure 17.1 is a descriptive model of the invoices received by the department. It represents the invoice-processing system in terms of the distribution of the value of invoices processed at any given time. Another way to represent this distribution is given by the descriptive model in Figure 17.2. This model shows the percentage of invoices (read off the vertical axis) that were greater than a stated value (read off the horizontal axis). For example, 97.5 percent of all the invoices received are expected to have a total value greater than $1, while

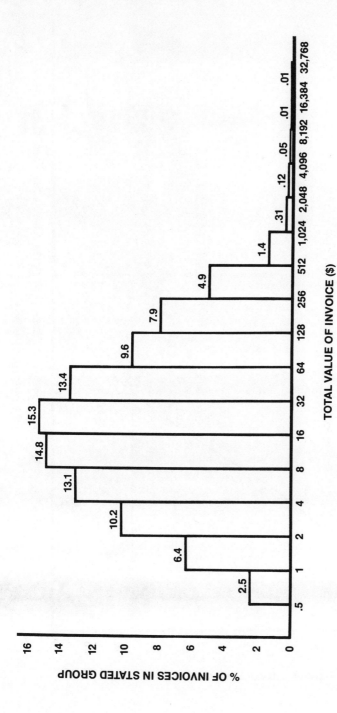

Figure 17.1   *Distribution of invoices received during 12 month period*

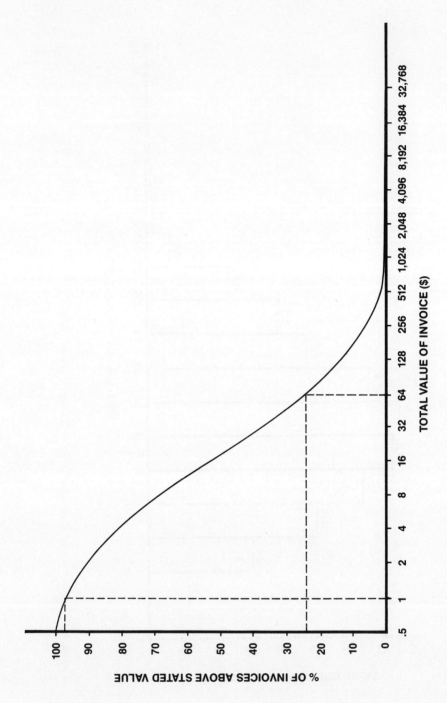

Figure 17.2   *Percentage of invoices greater than stated value*

approximately 24 percent are expected to have a total value greater than $64. We will use the information represented by the descriptive models of Figures 17.1 and 17.2 in constructing the decision model of this problem. This decision model will also be constructed on a graph. Then we will state the mathematical relationships shown by the graph.

Recall that our purpose is to decide which invoices should be verified for delivery of goods in order to minimize the expected cost of the system. Included in the cost of the system are two costs – the clerical cost of verifying delivery and the expected losses to the city resulting from not checking for the delivery of certain goods.

Under the invoice-checking system used at the time of the study, when an invoice arrived at the supplies department a clerical procedure was carried out to approve the invoice for payment by the city treasurer. No invoice was approved for payment unless it was verified that the correct quantity and type of goods shown on the invoice had been received by the customer department and that the goods were acceptable in terms of condition, quality and timing. This procedure, a 100 percent level of checking, is at one extreme of the set of alternative courses of action available for consideration as the solution to the problem. At the other extreme is the alternative of 0 percent level of checking. Under this alternative, an invoice would automatically be approved for payment when it arrived at the supplies department unless the department had received an advice note from the customer indicating some problem with the goods.

An analysis of the results of the current 100 percent level of checking identified nine distinct types of invoices that could result (see Chapter 13, Table 13.1), ranging from invoices for goods which had been delivered as ordered and in the correct quantity to invoices for goods which had not been ordered by the department. Based upon an analysis of the types of invoices identified by the existing procedure, it was estimated that if there were absolutely no checking for delivery a small number (0.047 percent) of all the invoices received would be for goods that were not dispatched or not delivered by a supplier, *and* the customer department which was to have received the goods would completely fail to report this fact *and* would accept without comment a charge from the supplies department for these goods which had not arrived. During the twelve-month period 1961/2 the supplies department received invoices amounting to $8,400,000. If there had been no verification of delivery (0 percent of checking) during this period the estimated maximum financial loss suffered by the city would have been $3,948 (0.047 percent of $8,400,000). Under the system of checking all invoices for delivery (100 percent level of checking), it is assumed all cases of nondelivery are caught and the city suffers no financial loss.

There are, however, a large number of other alternatives between a 0 percent and a 100 percent level of checking for delivery. For example, suppose only those invoices above a certain value, say above $128, were selected to be checked for delivery. From Figure 17.2 we see that this amounts to approximately 15 percent of all the invoices received in the twelve-month period. It is assumed that invoices for goods that

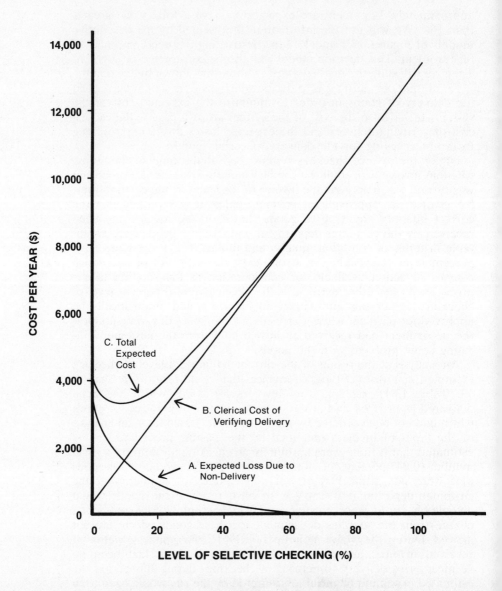

Figure 17.3   *Graphical representation of decision model*

were not delivered (and not reported as such) are as likely to occur for low-value invoices as for high-value ones; that is, goods that are not delivered are uniformly distributed among all the various values of invoices received between $0.50 and $32,768. Then a 15 percent level of selective checking would avoid losses amounting on average to:

$$\$260 \times 15\% \times 0.047\% \times 150,000 = \$2,750.$$

In this calculation $260 is the average value of all invoices greater than $128 in value, 15 percent is the proportion of all invoices greater than $128 in value (the ones checked for delivery), 0.047 percent is the proportion of losses that would occur as a result of nondelivery and 150,000 is the total annual number of invoices.

Thus if the supplies department were to perform a selective check of the highest-value 15 percent of all invoices received, that is, all invoices with a face value greater than $128, the city would avoid losses as a result of nondelivery amounting to $2,750 per year. Therefore the estimated annual financial loss experienced by operating at a 15 percent level of selective checking would be $1,198 ($3,948 at 0 percent level of checking minus $2,750 at a 15 percent level of checking). Similar calculations for a 7 percent level of selective checking (checking all invoices greater than $256 in value) and a 38 percent level of selective checking (invoices greater than $32) result in annual financial losses of approximately $2,000 and $400 respectively. The financial losses for a number of alternative levels of selective checking have been calculated. Points representing these losses for various levels of selective checking are plotted on the graph of Figure 17.3. The resulting curve that connects these points on the graph (curve A) gives the annual financial loss that the city should expect for any value of selective invoice checking between 0 percent ($3,948 loss) and 100 percent (no loss).

Recall that our objective is to minimize the total expected cost of the system. We have constructed a mathematical model, in graph form, to represent part of this total cost – the losses that are to be expected from checking only a selected number of invoices for delivery. We must now add to this model the clerical cost of checking. A study of the clerical activities of those staff responsible for checking invoices for delivery showed that 60 percent of their time was spent on this activity. Knowing the salaries of these staff it was possible to determine that the present 100 percent level of checking was costing the supplies department nearly $13,300 per year. If a selective checking system is installed, however, it will be necessary to verify the delivery of goods from a random sample of invoices with values below the checking level. This is important in order to maintain control over the system and it will be discussed in more detail later. Assuming that a 3 percent random sample will be satisfactory for control purposes, then at a 0 percent level of selective checking there would be a small cost of $400 (3 percent of $13,300) to carry out the verification of delivery on the 3 percent sample. It is assumed that the cost of a given level of checking is proportional to the costs found for 0 percent ($400) and 100 percent ($13,300). Thus the two points, $400 at 0 percent level of checking and

$13,300 at a 100 percent level, are connected by a straight line (line B) on Figure 17.3. This line represents the cost of selectively checking for the delivery of goods at any checking level.

The total expected annual cost of each level of selective checking (curve C, Figure 17.3) is found by summing the expected loss due to nondelivery (curve A) and the clerical cost of verifying delivery (line B). For example, at a 0 percent level of selective checking, the expected loss due to nondelivery is $3,948 and the clerical cost of verifying delivery is $400 (the cost of checking the 3 percent random sample). The total expected cost, therefore, is $4,348 ($3,948 + $400) at a 0 percent level of selective checking. At a 20 percent level of selective checking, the expected loss due to nondelivery is approximately $950 (read from curve A) and the clerical cost of verifying the delivery of 20 percent of the invoices (plus a 3 percent random sample) is approximately $3,000 (read from line B). Therefore the total expected cost of a system which selectively checks 20 percent of the invoices received is $3,950 ($950 + $3,000). Similar calculations are performed for a number of levels of selective checking, providing a set of points which, when connected, form curve C.

Curve C is a graphical representation of the mathematical model for the problem of deciding which invoices should be checked for verification of delivery. The other studies in this book represent a wide range of operations research models. Most are decision models, that is, mathematical models from which the alternative course of action which best satisfies the objective can be derived. Like this study, many of the others also use descriptive models to represent various aspects of the system being studied. In two cases, the study of bus operations (Chapter 8) and the design of a new vehicle maintenance facility (Chapter 14), descriptive models are used to test various solutions to the problem. These models provide measurements of how the system operates under a given alternative; for example, measures of service and cost for a given bus network and frequency of bus operation, or measures of vehicle availability and mechanic or space utilization for a given size repair shop. These descriptive models were used to analyze and compare a number of alternative solutions and thus provide the information on which the recommended solution was based.

For people not trained in constructing mathematical models it is a major step to transform the descriptive problem definition into a model. For this reason we have used in this chapter a problem which has a mathematical model that could be constructed graphically. Mathematical models in operations research are sometimes represented by a graph and, as is shown in the next section, the solution to a problem can be obtained by examining the graph. Graphical approaches to constructing a model and deriving a solution are perfectly acceptable. The reader should not be left with the impression that this is an inferior approach. On the other hand it is not always possible to use a graphical approach. Therefore, although it is certainly not needed in this case, we conclude this section with the mathematical representation of the decision model shown graphically in Figure 17.3. This is done to give the reader a more complete understanding of what is meant by a mathematical model and what can be involved in constructing one.

We begin by defining some symbols to be used in the model.

Let x = level of selective checking (%), and
y = total expected cost per year ($).

The symbol x stands for the decision variable in this problem. It can take on values between 0 percent and 100 percent, and we want to find the value of x that minimizes y, the total expected cost per year. To do this we need to find an equation which relates x and y, the relationship shown graphically by curve C in Figure 17.3. To construct this relationship it will be useful to define two more symbols.

Let y_c = total clerical cost per year ($), and
y_n = total expected loss per year due to nondelivery.

To find the mathematical relationship between x and y, we first find an equation which relates x and y_c and then one that relates x and y_n. When we have done this the equation relating x and y will follow directly, since

$$y = y_c + y_n. \tag{1}$$

The relationship between x and y_c is a straight line, shown graphically by line B in Figure 17.3. An examination of this line finds that it has a slope of 129 and a y–intercept of 400, that is, the line meets the y–axis at the point (0,400). Therefore:

$$y_c = 400 + 129x. \tag{2}$$

The relationship between x and y_n, shown graphically as curve A in Figure 17.3, is more complex. This curve appears to be exponential, which means that the general form of the relationship between x and y_n is

$$y_n = ke^{mx}$$

where k and m are constants that need to be determined. By examining the data used to form curve B, we find that this type of equation is a good representation of the relationship between x and y_n and that k = 3,945 and m = −0.06. Therefore:

$$y_n = 3945e^{-0.06x} \tag{3}$$

Substituting equations (2) and (3) into equation (1), we find that

$$y = 400 + 129x + 3945e^{-0.06x} \tag{4}$$

and this is the mathematical model for the invoice-checking problem. The next step is to derive a solution to this problem from the model constructed in this section.

4   DERIVE A SOLUTION FROM THE MODEL

Deriving a solution from a mathematical model means finding the answer to the problem statement that best satisfies the objective. This can involve complex mathematical manipulations and possibly the use of a high-speed computer to carry out numerous calculations. In some cases, however, deriving the solution is quite straightforward. This is the case with our invoice-checking illustration, where a simple examination of the graph which represents the model will yield the solution.

In this study the problem is to find which invoices should be checked for verification of delivery. The objective is to minimize the total expected cost of the system, where this cost includes the clerical cost of checking invoices and the expected losses that can result from not checking certain invoices before paying them. Total cost is measured in dollars per year and the mathematical model, represented by curve C in Figure 17.3, gives the relationship between the level of checking and the total cost of the system. An examination of this curve finds that its minimum occurs at the 10 percent level of checking. Therefore the solution to the problem is selectively to check 10 percent of all the invoices received – the 10 percent of all the invoices with the greatest value.

But this does not completely answer the question raised by the statement of the problem, because it does not tell us what the cutoff value is, the value above which all invoices should be checked in full. The answer to this question can easily be found from Figure 17.2. Drawing a horizontal line from 10 percent on the vertical axis of this figure to the curve, and then reading the number on the horizontal axis below the point of intersection, we find that 10 percent of all invoices have a value above $200. Therefore $200 is the decision rule, the solution derived from the model. For any invoice with a value equal to or greater than $200, a check should be made to determine whether the goods were received before the invoice is paid. If this rule is followed, and providing the rates of error do not change, the total cost of the system for checking delivery will be minimized.

To complete this illustration, we show how calculus would be used to derive the solution to this problem from the equation for total cost, equation (4), constructed at the end of the previous section. We want to find the value of x, the level of checking, which minimizes y, the total cost of checking for delivery. To do this we differentiate y with respect to x, set the result equal to 0, and solve for x.

$$y = 400 + 129x + 3945e^{-0.06x}$$

$$\frac{dy}{dx} = 129 - 0.06(3945)e^{-0.06x} = 0$$

$$w^{-0.06x} = 0.545 \tag{5}$$

Taking the natural logarithm of both sides of (5),

$$-0.06x = -0.067$$
$$x = 10.1\%.$$

The studies presented in this book use many different models and many different methods for deriving solutions from these models. These models and methods are not examined here because the reader would need to be given much more information about the details of the models and would need to know much more about operations research methods.

Having derived a solution from a mathematical model the analyst must ask if there are intangible factors which would alter this solution. This is the point at which the analyst and the decision-makers need to integrate the solution derived from the mathematical model with any intangible, subjective factors to produce a final recommendation and decision. A good illustration of how this can be done is given by the study to determine the best location of the bypass for a small town (Chapter 7).

Five alternative bypass routes were considered. Based on cost-benefit criteria, route 2 (*without* the extension) and route 3 were found to have benefits to road users that justified their cost of construction, with route 2 being preferable to route 3. Further analysis showed that route 3 was superior on the basis of a number of quantifiable environmental criteria, including noise on the bypass, severance of roads and footpaths and effects on farms. However, an analysis of the qualitative environmental impacts showed that route 2 (*with* the extension) and route 4 had the greatest potential for improving the environment in the town. Thus the routes that were the most benefit to road users were least beneficial to local residents; and those routes that were expected to remove the most congestion and noise from the town could not be justified in terms of user benefits.

In bringing these results together the analysts recommended that route 3 be built, but that an extension to remove more traffic from the town be evaluated when this route was in place. However, the qualitative factors had a stronger impact on the decision-makers, who finally approved a bypass which was a combination of route 3 and route 2 (*with* the extension). The final choice had many of the quantifiable environmental advantages of route 3 and the qualitative advantages of route 2 (*with* the extension), which removed more traffic and noise from the center of town.

5 TEST THE SOLUTION

There are a number of ways to test the solution derived from the mathematical model. We will examine three methods: implementing a solution; examining how changes in the assumptions or the data used to derive a solution change the solution; and using descriptive models to test and evaluate alternative solutions.

A solution can be tested by trying it out, that is, by implementing the solution. This is seldom done unless it is fairly certain that the solution is in any case going to be implemented, regardless of the results of the test. If it is uncertain that a solution will be implemented it can be very costly to try it out and then to find that the solution is a failure. It clearly makes no sense to build a $2 million refuse incinerator to determine whether incineration is a better way to dispose of refuse than pulverization.

Occasionally testing a solution will involve one or more demonstration projects, that is, trial implementations. This can be a useful approach when a solution is going to be implemented many times, say at a number of different local governments. Solutions to the problem of developing a national inter-library loan transportation system (Chapter 5) were tested in this way. Once it had been decided that a transportation system, if implemented, would be based on the existing regional library systems, pilot transportation schemes could be implemented in several of the nine regions on a trial basis.

The second method, testing how sensitive a solution is to changes in the assumptions and data used to build the model from which the solution was derived, is a much more common method than using a pilot study. The results of this type of test were given in four of the reports in this book, including the invoice-checking study. In determining the best level of selectively checking for the delivery of goods, it was found that 10 percent of all invoices should be checked. But this solution relied heavily on the estimate that 0.047 percent of all invoices received by the supplies department would be for goods that were not delivered and were not reported as such by the department that was supposed to have received the goods.

This estimate was, however, at best a crude one and it was decided to test how sensitive the solution was to changes in this estimate. The test found that if the 0.047 percent estimate of nondelivery was wrong by a factor of two, that is, was twice as great as assumed, then the solution would be selectively to check 20 percent of the highest-value invoices, rather than 10 percent. (It is just coincidence that doubling the estimate of percentage nondelivery doubled the amount of checking.) Furthermore, implementing the 10 percent solution, when in fact the best solution would be selectively to check 20 percent of the invoices, would result in a $400 error. That is, the total cost of the system would be $400 greater under the 10 percent solution than under the 20 percent one. It could be concluded, therefore, that the solution was not very sensitive to the crude estimate of the percentage of nondelivery.

What is the effect of such a test? For one thing, it helps an analyst determine how important it might be to improve some of the estimates of data used to construct a model. It can be very costly and time-consuming to obtain accurate estimates of certain data. To obtain a more accurate estimate of the 0.047 percent nondelivery figure used in the invoice-checking study it would have been necessary to perform an experiment to determine how often departments which did not receive goods subsequently accepted a charge for those goods from the supplies department. Performing a test to learn how sensitive the solution to a problem is to changes in particular data can help the analyst decide whether it is worth the expense to improve an estimate of the data, or whether a crude estimate is satisfactory.

Equally important is the impact that such a test can have on influencing decision-makers to implement the recommendations of a study. If decision-makers are uncertain about implementing the solution to a problem, for whatever reason, the natural tendency is to focus on the assumptions and data employed to obtain the solution. Showing that the solution is valid over the possible range of values for important data used to construct the model can help to remove this uncertainty and hence help to convince decision-makers of the validity of the solution.

Three other studies reported results of tests to determine how sensitive a solution was to changes in the data or assumptions used to derive it. In the ambulance study (Chapter 2) a number of tests were performed. After finding the minimum number of ambulances and their locations to satisfy the given response-time standard, tests were conducted to determine how far an ambulance could range from the ambulance station before the service fell below the required standard. This provided valuable information for locating standby ambulances to cover for a vehicle on an emergency call. The initial best solution derived during the ambulance study, which gave the number and locations of ambulances for the region as a whole, was also tested to see how well it provided coverage in isolated areas of the region and to determine the balance of service between the two former health districts which comprised the new region. As a result of these tests the number and locations of ambulances were increased in the final recommendations of the study.

A sensitivity analysis was also performed in the study to decide whether to construct a flood relief project (Chapter 9). The conclusion of the study was that the benefits of the project did not justify its cost. The purpose of the sensitivity analysis was to find the benefits that would need to result from the project in order to reverse this conclusion. Reduction of losses to property-owners and community services was the major benefit of the project and the analysis found that the losses of a major flood in 1969 would need to have been twenty times as high in order to justify the cost of the flood relief project.

Thirdly, a sensitivity analysis helped to select a strategy for a county's general plan for land development (Chapter 12). Five alternative strategies were ranked in terms of how well they achieved a set of objectives and in terms of the weights attached to the importance of each objective. A series of tests were then performed to learn how sensitive the ranking of the strategies was to a shift in its score in satisfying the objectives and a shift in the weights attached to the objectives. As a result of these tests it was found that a very large change in each of the individual weights and scores of the two worst strategies would be needed to give them an overall score equal to the best three strategies. Therefore, it was concluded that the county could drop from further consideration the two worst strategies and concentrate on a more thorough examination of the top strategies.

The last method to be discussed for testing solutions involves the use of descriptive models. Earlier we distinguished between decision models and descriptive models and we have shown in the case of the invoice-checking study how a decision model was used to obtain the best solution to a problem. Solutions can be derived from descriptive models as well, although not in the same way. Descriptive models are used to test solutions by describing how the system represented by the model behaves under a given solution. The output of such a test will be a measure of how well the solution satisfies one or more objectives. In this way a number of alternative solutions may be tested and compared in terms of the way they satisfy the criteria established for judging alternative solutions. Then the solution which best satisfies these criteria is selected as the solution to the problem. However, this solution can only be considered the best of the solutions tested, and there is usually no way of knowing whether it is the best possible solution to the problem.

Two studies illustrate the use of descriptive models to test alternative solutions. In both cases the models were computerized and describe very complex systems for which it is unlikely decision models could be constructed. In one study (Chapter 8) a model describing over fifty bus routes needed to be built. The model provided a very detailed representation of the bus system and was used to perform operational, financial and user benefit assessments of a number of alternative systems. The computer model described in Chapter 14 was used to simulate the operation of a large service facility for over 400 vehicles that had been planned but not yet built. Using the model, tests were performed to examine the utilization and availability of staff, vehicles and repair facilities under different plans for the size and staffing of the various repair shops.

6 DECISION AND IMPLEMENTATION

Eventually the study will be concluded and a set of recommendations will be made. At this stage public meetings are sometimes held to present and discuss the results of the study, as was the case in deciding where to place the bypass of a small town (Chapter 7). Often input from the public will already have been received during the course of the study; for example, through surveys of bus riders (Chapter 8), or questionnaires to obtain public opinion (Chapter 12). Now the decision-makers must review and weigh the recommendations of the study in light of their experience and judgment, expert opinion, public pressures and political influences and a host of other intangible factors that surround the problem. In some cases a decision can be reached quickly, in others the decision-making process can drag on for months or years.

A number of people played a role in making the decision to implement selective invoice checking. The supplies department was pleased with the results of the study and thought they should be implemented. The city treasurer, however, wanted to retain the current practice of checking all invoices in full. To resolve this difference of opinion the city council asked an independent local goverment financial auditing organization, the District Audit, to review the study's recommendations. The District Audit overwhelmingly supported selective checking. On this evidence the city council decided to implement the basic principles of the study's recommendations, although it was agreed to use a more conservative set of decision rules – a $150 (rather than $200) checking level and a 5 percent (rather than 3 percent) random sample.

Once a decision is made the process of implementing that decision begins. This stage of the problem-solving process can involve many things, including staff changes, the purchase of equipment, the construction of a new building, or the change of a procedure for doing a job or providing a service. Implementing selective invoice checking mainly involved changing some existing procedures, developing new ones and training staff to use the new procedures. The work of some people was reorganized and a few people were assigned new duties. One of the most important aspects of changing a procedure is to be certain that every person and every department that interacts with the procedure is informed about the change. In the case of implementing selective invoice checking the customer departments needed to know what information they now had to provide to the supplies department and which advice notes now needed to be returned. Taking care to inform everyone concerned about the new procedure helped to bring about a smooth implementation and avoid disruption of the other work carried out by the supplies department and the departments it served.

Changes in a process or procedure were also needed in implementing the final decisions of the ambulance study (Chapter 2), in setting up the pilot inter-library loan transportation system (Chapter 5) and in changing bus routes and the frequency of bus operations (Chapter 8).

Implementation often involves staff changes – reorganization of staff, the hiring of new staff who possess special skills not available within the organization, or the laying–off of staff. Care must be taken to keep staff informed about the possibility of changes. One solution is to involve them in any study which might result in changes affecting them. This was done in the local government reorganization study (Chapter 15), which concerned the physical relocation of staff from three local governments which were amalgamated into one government.

In a number of studies implementation involved purchasing equipment and constructing new facilities, for example, constructing refuse treatment plants, roads, a flood relief project, a civic center, a vehicle service and maintenance facility, and kitchens for the preparation of meals for elderly and handicapped persons. When an implementation is dependent upon large expenditures of money a considerable amount of planning must take place to search for funding, decide on the specifications of equipment or the design of a building and decide who will supply the equipment or undertake the construction. These processes can take a long time. The process of deciding whether to construct a flood relief project and the planning that went into implementing the decision took seven years from the time the report of the study (Chapter 9) was submitted until construction began.

In some of the studies presented in this book implementation was a major undertaking. Developing a new points scheme for the awarding of public housing (Chapter 4) was part of a larger project which included the development of a new information system. To implement the new points scheme it was necessary to interview over 30,000 applicants on a waiting list for housing, purchase computer terminals, develop computer software, enter data into the new computer system and inform the public how the new system for obtaining a house worked. This was a major effort that required the hiring of temporary staff and took a considerable time to accomplish.

Finally, a plan for evaluating the results of an implementation should be developed as part of the implementation process. We look at the evaluation stage in the next section.

7 EVALUATE RESULTS

As much as we would like to believe that a problem ends once a solution has been implemented, this is rarely the case. Solutions need to be monitored in order to provide information that can be fed back to the decision-makers for the purpose of evaluating the implemented solution. Such feedback serves to control and improve the solution over time, to change the solution as circumstances change and to identify new problems that could have a bearing on how well the new solution continues to perform. Continual monitoring and periodic evaluations of a solution can help avoid more serious problems in the future.

Monitoring is a continual process, such as the way a fuel gauge monitors the amount of gasoline remaining in the fuel tank of an automobile. Evaluation, on the other hand, is a periodic event that might happen once a year or once every several years. An evaluation often depends on the type of information that has been collected by monitoring the system. Therefore both the monitoring and the evaluation of a solution need to be well thought out and planned if the information that is collected is to be useful for improving the solution or for identifying problems. Methods for monitoring and evaluating a solution should be developed at the time the solution is implemented. But monitoring and evaluation systems are expensive to implement and for this reason many government programs have never been evaluated. From investigating the results of the studies presented in this book we found that in most cases a lot of information existed about the implementation of a study's recommendations; and in some cases this data had been used in a formal way to modify or improve the solution. The invoice-checking study services as an excellent example.

As a result of the invoice-checking study it was decided to check the delivery of goods for only those invoices with a total value of $150 or more. This amounted to approximately 13 percent of all the invoices received by the supplies department. A control device was needed, however, in order to protect the department against abuse of the system and to provide data for adjusting the level of checking should conditions change. Therefore it was decided also to check a random sample of 5 percent of all the other invoices. This random sample has proved to be a very effective means of monitoring the new checking system. It provides continual data on the risk of nondelivery, the distribution of nondelivery over the range of values for invoices, and a list of suppliers who might be likely to take advantage of a system which does not check all invoices in full.

The distribution of the number and value of invoices, shown in Figure 17.1, has changed over time as a result of inflation and changes in the types of goods purchased and the amount of purchasing. This distribution has been assessed periodically, and with the data on nondelivery obtained from the random sample and from the high-value invoices that are checked in full, it has been possible for the supplies department to evaluate regularly the selective invoice checking system and to make changes in the decision rules when necessary. The department has found that the best level of checking is still around 10 percent; that is, the relationship between the error rate and the cost of checking has remained such that checking only the top 10 percent of all invoices still minimizes the total expected cost of the system. However, it has been necessary to review the distribution of invoices periodically in order to maintain a 10 percent level of checking. By 1978 the cutoff point had reached $600, that is, approximately 10 percent of all invoices were now equal to or greater than $600 in value. The cutoff level has changed gradually between 1962, when it was originally set at $150, and the present. By 1970 it had reached $250 and in 1976 it was $450. The solution to the invoice-checking problem has needed to be changed as conditions have changed and the continued effectiveness of the solution has been assured by monitoring and evaluating the system.

In some of the other studies presented in this book evaluations have been planned or performed. Wanting to be assured that the response-time standards were in fact being met by the reassignment of ambulances recommended in the study presented in Chapter 2, the regional health authority commissioned a reexamination of the problem three years after implementing the recommendations of the original study. The new study found some evidence that the assignment of ambulances during the day shift fell slightly below the recommended response-time standards, while the coverage during evening and night just achieved the standards. The new study suggested that the health authority consider relocating one ambulance.

Often the full impact of a solution cannot be determined until some time after the solution is implemented. This is the situation in constructing the bypass around a small town (Chapter 7), where the highway department will not be able to assess the project until it has been in operation for at least two years. But plans for such an evaluation were well under way by the time the new roads were completed.

The solution to some problems is based on the forecast of data far into the future and the accuracy of such forecasts can have a strong bearing on how well the alternative course of action that is selected actually solves the problem. In such cases it is imperative that the implemented solution be periodically reassessed in light of actual experience. Such a reassessment was one of the recommendations resulting from the study presented in Chapter 10. After four of the five incinerators that had been planned for treating the refuse from the area had been built, it was found that the four plants had enough capacity to handle all the area's refuse and the site earmarked for the fifth incinerator could now be used for building a reclamation plant.

Our final example of evaluation makes use of the methods developed to solve a problem. In developing the new points scheme for ranking people on a waiting list for public-owned housing (Chapter 4), a mathematical model was built which found the allocation of points to needs factors which best matched the subjective assessments of housing officials. One of the advantages of developing and using such a model is that it provides a method for reevaluating the assignment of points as the needs factors change or their relative importance changes. The housing department now has a tool for easily reassessing the points scheme and plans to do so from time to time as conditions change.

Assessing results means more than determining whether the results were successful. It means establishing a system of monitoring and evaluating a solution in order to learn if the solution is continuing to perform the way it was designed to perform, to identify changes in parameters that could affect the solution and to identify new problems. It is important to realize that just because a good or an acceptable solution has been found this does not mean that the solution will necessarily remain the best solution for all time.

CONCLUSION

The purpose of this book has been to develop a general understanding and appreciation of some of the uses of operations research for solving public sector problems. We have tried to do this by presenting the final reports of twelve operations research studies and by describing what has taken place as a result of these studies. In Chapter 1 we set out a general process for problem-solving and in this chapter we have attempted to describe more fully and to illustrate that process by drawing on the studies in the previous chapters. We believe that decision makers should at least be aware of what is involved and at what points they should interact with the analyst, whether or not they have detailed understanding of the methodologies involved.

Finally, it is also important to recognize that the process presented here is only intended to represent the general or typical process that might be followed in solving a problem. Every problem is unique and the approach taken to solve every problem should also be unique.

Therefore in solving a given problem the process used or the order of performing the stages of the process could easily vary from what has been presented here.

We hope that the process illustrated in this chapter will be of help in furthering the understanding of operations research and its use in solving public sector problems and will help to reduce barriers to arriving at successful solutions.

Bibliography

REFERENCES

Ackoff, R. L. (1956), 'The development of operations research as a science', *Operations Research*, vol. 4, no. 3, pp. 265–95.

Anderson, L. G., and Settle, R. F. (1977), *Benefit-Cost Analysis: A Practical Guide* (Lexington, Mass.: Lexington Books).

Arthur D. Little, Inc. (1966), *Community Renewal Programming: A San Francisco Case Study* (New York: Praeger).

Arthur D. Little, Inc. (1968), *Cost-Effectiveness in Traffic Safety* (New York: Praeger).

Bailey, N. J. T., and Thompson, M. (eds) (1975), *Systems Aspects of Health Planning* (Amsterdam: North Holland).

Beardwood, J., Halton, J. H., and Hennersley, J. M. (1959), 'The shortest path through many points', *Proceedings of the Cambridge Philosophical Society*, vol. 55, pt 4, pp. 299–327.

Belford, P. C., and Ratcliff, H. D. (1972), 'A network-flow model for racially balancing schools', *Operations Research*, vol. 20, no. 3, pp. 619–28.

Brotherton, J., Gwynne, D., Renold, J., Thursfield, P., and Tomkinson, C. B. (1972), *Manchester's Old People*, Report No. C 120 (Reading, England: Local Government Operational Research Unit).

Brounstein, S. H., and Kamrass, M. (eds) (1976), *Operations Research in Law Enforcement, Justice, and Societal Security* (Lexington, Mass.: Lexington Books).

Byrd, J., Jr (1975), *Operations Research Models for Public Administration* (Lexington, Mass.: Lexington Books).

Carter, R. F. (1971), *Cost-Benefit Analysis of Towcester Flood Relief Scheme*, Report No. T 33 (Reading, England: Local Government Operational Research Unit).

Carter, R. F., and Wraith, R. E. (1971), *Evaluating Flood Relief in Towcester*, Report No. C 109 (Reading, England: Local Government Operational Research Unit).

Chadwick, G. (1978), *A Systems View of Planning*, 2nd ed. (Oxford: Pergamon).

City of Manchester Housing Department (1980), *Renting a Home* (February), p. 3.

Cooper, D. M., Rutherford, J., and Howell, R. G. (1974), *Office Reorganization in Medway*, Report No. C 178 (Reading, England: Local Government Operational Research Unit).

Daly, A. J., Last, A., Leak, S. E., Smith, P. J., Townsend, R., and Zachary, S. (1976), *Huddersfield Bus Study: Summary Report*, Report No. C 229 and *Huddersfield Bus Study*, Vols 1, 2 and 3, Report Nos. C 230, C 231 and C 232 (Reading, England: Local Government Operational Research Unit).

Daly, A. J., Leak, S. E., and Last, A. (1977), *Bus Operating Costs in Huddersfield*, Report No. T 71 (Reading, England: Local Government Operational Research Unit).

Daly, A. J., and Zachary, S. (1977), *Bus Passenger Waiting Times in Huddersfield*, Report No. T 67 (Reading, England: Local Government Operational Research Unit).

Edie, L. C. (1967), 'Vehicular traffic', in P. M. Morse and L. W. Bacon (eds), *Operations Research for Public Systems* (Cambridge, Mass.: MIT Press).

Faringdon Rural District Council (1973), 'A facelift for Faringdon', unofficial report, July.

Faulkner, G. J., and Miller, G. K. (1974), *Which By Pass for Faringdon?*, Report No. C 196 (Reading, England: Local Government Operational Research Unit).

Ferreira, J., Jr (1972), 'Driver accident models and their use in policy evaluation', in A. W. Drake, R. L. Keeney and P. M. Morse (eds) *Analysis of Public Systems* (Cambridge, Mass.: MIT Press), pp. 287–316.

Fishman, G. S. (1978), *Principles of Discrete Event Simulation* (New York: Wiley).

Forrester, J. W. (1969), *Urban Dynamics* (Cambridge, Mass.: MIT Press).

Fortune, May 7, 1979, p. 270.

Frost, M. J. (1971), *Values for Money: the Techniques of Cost Benefit Analysis* (London: Gower Press).

Gass, S. I. (1975), 'Models in law enforcement and criminal justice', in S. I. Gass and R. L. Sisson (eds), *A Guide to Models in Governmental Planning and Operations* (Potomac: Sauger Books), pp. 231–75.

Glasson, J. (1978), *An Introduction to Regional Planning: Concepts, Theory and Practice* (London: Hutchinson).

Green, J. A., Lister, N. S., and Whitworth, B. (1967), *Refuse Disposal in the Tyneside/Wearside Area*, Report No. C 14 (Reading, England: Local Government Operational Research Unit).

Groom, K. N. (1977), 'Planning emergency ambulance services', *Operational Research Quarterly*, vol. 28, no. 2, pp. 641–51.

Groom, K. N., Holloway, K. E., and Mann, W. R. (1975), *Planning Emergency Ambulance Cover in West Glamorgan*, Report No. 75/4 (Reading, England: National Health Service Operational Research Group).

Gross, D., and Harris, C. M. (1974), *Fundamentals of Queueing Theory* (New York: Wiley).

Grundy, F., and Reinke, W. A. (1973), *Health Practice Research and Formalized Managerial Methods* (Geneva: World Health Organization).

Halpert, H. P., Horvath, W. J., and Young, J. P. (1970), *An Administrator's Handbook on the Application of Operations Research to the Management of Mental Health Systems*, US Public Health Service Publication No. 2110 (Washington DC: Government Printing Office), p. v.

Harris, B. (1968), 'Quantitative models of urban development: their role in metropolitan decision-making', in H. S. Perloff and L. Wingo (eds), *Issues in Urban Economics* (Baltimore, Md: Johns Hopkins University Press), pp. 363–83, 406–12.

HMSO (1972), *Development and Compensation – Putting People First*, Cmnd 5114 (London: HMSO), pp. 1–2.

Horvath, W. J. (1967), 'Operations research in medical and hospital practice', in P. M. Morse and L. W. Bacon (eds), *Operations Research for Public Systems* (Cambridge, Mass.: MIT Press), pp. 127–57.

Houghton, A. G., and Nixon, M. (1976), *A National Transport System for Inter-Library Loans*, Report No. 5254 (Boston Spa, England: British Library).

Houghton, A. G., and Nixon, M. (1977), *A Pilot Transport Scheme for Inter-Library Loans in the North West*, Report No. C 256 (Reading, England: Local Government Operational Research Unit).

Houghton, A. G. (1978), *A Pilot Transport Scheme for Inter-Library Loans in London*, Report No. C 263 (Reading, England: Local Government Operational Research Unit).

Humphreys, H., & Sons (1970), 'Flood relief scheme' and 'Main drainage of

Towcester', consulting engineer's reports to Towcester Rural District Council.

Isard, W. (1975), *Introduction to Regional Science* (Englewood Cliffs, NJ: Prentice–Hall).

Jennings, J. B. (1972), 'Blood bank inventory control', in A. W. Drake, R. L. Keeney and P. M. Morse (eds), *Analysis for Public Systems* (Cambridge, Mass.: MIT Press), pp. 216–34.

Kraemer, K. L. (1973), *Policy Analysis in Local Government* (Washington, DC: International City Management Association).

Larson, R. C. (1972), *Urban Police Patrol Analysis* (Cambridge, Mass.: MIT Press).

Last, A., and Leak, S. E. (1976), 'TRANSEPT: a bus model', *Traffic Engineering and Control*, vol. 17, no. 1.

Laufer, A. C. (1979), *Operations Management*, 2nd edn. (Cincinnati, Ohio: South-western Publishing Co.).

LGORU (1973), *Better Plan Evaluation*, Report No. D 16 (Reading, England: Local Government Operational Research Unit).

Liebman, J. C. (1975), 'Models in solid waste management', in S. I. Gass and R. L. Sisson (eds), *A Guide to Models in Governmental Planning and Operations* (Potomac, Md: Sauger Books), pp. 139–64.

Little, J. D. C., Murty, K. G., Sweeney, D. W., and Karel, C. (1963), 'An algorithm for the traveling salesman problem', *Operations Research*, vol. 11, pp. 972–89.

Lowry, I. S. (1964), *A Model of Metropolis*, Memorandum RM-4035-RC (Santa Monica, Calif.: RAND).

Mackie, S. N. H. (1974), *Evaluation Tests for Northamptonshire*, Report No. C 200 (Reading, England: Local Government Operational Research Unit).

Marks, D. H. (1975), 'Models in water resources', in S. I. Gass and R. L. Sisson (eds), *A Guide to Models in Governmental Planning and Operations* (Potomac, Md: Sauger Books), pp. 103–37.

Martin, J. C. M. (1974), *Management Science and Urban Problems* (Westmead, England: Saxon House).

Mathie, R. C. (1978), *A Re-examination of Emergency Ambulance Cover in West Glamorgan*, Report No. 78/7 (Reading, England: National Health Service Operational Research Group).

Naylor, T. H., Balintfy, J. L., Burdick, D. S., and Chu, K. (1966), *Computer Simulation Techniques* (New York: Wiley).

Orcon Services, Cranfield Institute of Technology (1974), *Ambulance Service Performance Standards and Measurements*, report to DHSS.

Paelinck, J. H., and Nijkamp, P. (1975), *Operational Theory and Method in Regional Economics* (Westmead, England: Saxon House).

Palmer, B. Z. (1975), 'Models in planning and operating health services', in S. I. Gass and R. L. Sisson (eds), *A Guide to Models in Governmental Planning and Operations* (Potomac, Md: Sauger Books), pp. 347–74.

Pilgrim, B. (1971), *Simulation of the New Vehicle Workshop in the London Borough of Ealing*, Report No. C 112 (Reading, England: Local Government Operational Research Unit).

Powell, M. J. D. (1964), 'An efficient method for finding the minimum of a function of several variables without calculating derivatives', *Computer Journal*, vol. 7, no. 2.

Renold, J., and Wilson, R. (1976), *Developing a Housing Points Scheme*, Report No. C 226 (Reading, England: Local Government Operational Research Unit).

Roberts, K., and Gwynne, D. (1973), *Meals on Wheels in Worcestershire*,

Report No. C 134 (Reading, England: Local Government Operational Research Unit).

Sassone, P. G., and Schaffer, W. A. (1978), *Cost-Benefit Analysis: A Handbook* (New York: Academic Press).

Sheppard, H. L. (1976), 'Work and retirement', in R. H. Binstock and E. Shanas (eds), *Handbook of Aging and the Social Sciences* (New York: Van Nostrand Reinhold).

Singpurwalla, N. D. (1975), 'Models in air pollution', in S. I. Gass and R. L. Sisson (eds), *A Guide to Models in Governmental Planning and Operations* (Potomac, Md: Sauger Books), pp. 61–102.

Swanson, D. R., and Bookstein, A. (eds) (1972), *Operations Research: Implications for Libraries* (Chicago: University of Chicago Press).

Thrall, R. M., Heady, E., Schad, T., Schwartz, A. K., and Thompson, R. G. (eds) (1976), *Economic Modeling for Water Policy Evaluation* (Amsterdam: North Holland).

US Department of Commerce, Bureau of Census (1977), *Current Population Reports*, Series P-25, No. 704 (Washington, DC: Government Printing Office).

US Department of Commerce (1979), *The Statistical Abstract of the United States* (Washington, DC: Government Printing Office), pp. 313, 316, 325 and 474.

US Office of Management and Budget (1980), *The Budget of the US Government: Fiscal Year 1981* (Washington, DC: Government Printing Office), p. 46.

Walker, W. E., Chaiken, J. M., and Ignall, E. J. (eds) (1979), *Fire Department Deployment Analysis* (New York: North Holland).

Wall Street Journal, February 5, 1980, p. 3.

Ward, R. A. (1962), *The Checking of Invoices*, Report No. C 2 (Reading, England: Local Government Operational Research Unit).

Ward, R. A. (1964), *Operations Research in Local Government* (London: Allen & Unwin).

Ward, R. A. (1967), 'Operations research in local government', in P. M. Morse and L. W. Bacon (eds), *Operations Research for Public Systems* (Cambridge, Mass.: MIT Press).

Webb, K. W. Spielberg, F. L., and Loubal, P. S. (1975), 'Models in transportation', in S. I. Gass and R. I. Sisson (eds), *A Guide to Models in Governmental Planning and Operations* (Potomac, Md: Sauger Books), pp. 201–30.

Weiss, E. H. (1975), 'Models in educational planning and operations', in S. I. Gass and R. L. Sisson (eds), *A Guide to Models in Governmental Planning and Operations*, (Potomac, Md: Sauger Books), pp. 277-316.

Wilson, R. (1976), *Who Gets the House: A New Approach to Priorities and Points Schemes*, Report No. T 68 (Reading, England: Local Government Operational Research Unit).

Wolfe, J. N. (ed) (1973), *Cost-Benefit and Cost-Effectiveness: Studies and Analysis* (London: Allen & Unwin).

Wood, W. D., and Campbell, H. F. (1970), *Cost-Benefit Analysis and the Economics of Investment in Human Resources: An Annotated Bibliography* (Kingston, Ontario: Queens University Industrial Relations Centre).

SELECTED READINGS

Churchman, C. W. (1969), *The Systems Approach* (New York: Dell).

Hillier, F. S., and Lieberman, G. J. (1980), *Operations Research*, 3rd edn (San Francisco: Holden Day).

Quade, E. S. (1975), *Analysis for Public Decisions* (New York: Elsevier).

Wagner, H. M. (1975), *Principles of Operations Research*, 2nd ed. (Englewood Cliffs, NJ: Prentice-Hall).

White, M. J., Clayton, R., Myrtle, R., Siegel, G., and Rose, A. (1980), *Managing Public Systems: Analytic Techniques for Public Administration* (North Scituate, Mass.: Duxbury Press).

Index

Manchester
  housing department points scheme 50–60
Mann, W.R. 12, 15
manpower
  and ambulance services 14
  and office planning 243–4, 247, 249–51
  and vehicle maintenance 226–7, 232–3
mathematical models 5
  and qualitative factors 188
  and social welfare problems 94
  and solution finding 296–7
  and solution testing 297–300
  constructing 287–95
  of meals on wheels services 34, 36–44
  of refuse disposal 161, 163–4, 170–8, 186–7
mathematical programming, *see* linear programming; nonlinear programming; shortest path analysis; traveling salesman problem
meals on wheels
  costs 36–7, 39, 41–2, 44
  delivery of 33, 35
  goals 32, 38–42
  location of kitchens 38–40, 42–3
  mathematical model of 34, 36–44
  number of kitchens 33
  recipients 35
  staffing 33
  volume of 33, 35, 40–2
Medway Borough Council 242, 243, 244, 245, 251
medical conditions
  as housing need factor 57
Miller, G. 101, 102, 103
Ministry of Agriculture
  grants for flood relief 147
model building
  and problem solving process 3, 287–305
  graphical approach to 292, 294
  see also mathematical models
monitoring, *see* evaluation

needs
  and housing waiting lists 45, 47, 50–1, 52–60
  identifying 50
night time
  ambulance services 17, 23, 28
Nixon, M. 61
noise levels
  and road planning 106–8, 118–19
nonlinear programming 92–3, 186–7
Northamptonshire
  development of 194–205
  population 194, 195
Northamptonshire County Council 145, 146
North Regional Planning Committee 161

objectives
  and problem-solving 126–7, 267–9, 276–9, 285–7
office space
  and public convenience 255–6
  costs 256–7, 258–60
  needs 249
  planning 243–4, 245, 250–1, 256–61, 263
  reorganization 242, 246-7
  standards 249, 254
operations research
  and problem-solving 2–4, 94–6, 262, 268–9, 304–5
  definition 1–2
  organization of studies 6
operations research methods, *see* cost-benefit analysis; cost-effectiveness; mathematical programming; simulation technique
overcrowding
  as housing need factor 56–7
Oxfordshire County Council 102

participation
  of staff in planning 244
Pilgrim, B. 223, 225
pilot schemes
  in problem-solving process 62–5
plan evaluation matrix 264
planning 192, 263
  and use of operations research 268–9
  strategies in Northamptonshire 194–205, 262
points scheme
  for housing waiting lists 45, 46, 47–60
political influences
  on planning local authority buildings 243–4
pollution problems
  and operations research 188–9
population
  age distribution shifts 10
  and planning bus services 128–9
  of Medway 245, 260
  of Northamptonshire 194, 195
  of Towcester 145
  of West Glamorgan 15
postal services
  and inter-library lending systems 61, 67, 68, 89
Post Office Acts
  constraints of 68
problem
  constraints 280–3, 285–7
  definition 3, 275–87
  recognition 3, 273–4
  solution 3, 296–300
  statement 275–6
  see also problem-solving process
problem-solving process 3–4, 94–6, 262,